THIRD EDITION

THE SPEAKER'S PRIMER

Joseph M. Valenzano III

Melissa A. Broeckelman-Post

Stephen W. Braden

FOUNTAINHEAD
PRESS

Editorial Director: Christina Bruer

Developmental and Managing Editor: Katie Dickman

Senior Copy Editor: Lindsy Rice

Senior Designer: Ellie Moore

Designer: Kelly Jacobi

PREFACE

Language and the ability to communicate are things that make human beings unique. Our ability to connect with others and share our thoughts, ideas, interests, and specialties makes our lives richer and more special. That is why communication skills and the ability to speak publicly and deliver presentations are often key requirements in undergraduate education programs across the country. Learning how to communicate is an essential skill for any profession or vocation. We wrote this textbook with the goal of helping you, the reader, quickly learn the various components of effective oral communication.

Most handbooks on public speaking claim to have the same mission, so what makes this book any different? The answer is simple: context. This book still addresses all the nuts and bolts of crafting and delivering different types of presentations, just like other handbooks, but it also takes those principles and offers guidance for how to speak in particular professional arenas. For example, throughout the book you will find informational boxes where we address the importance and application of particular public speaking principles within the areas of business, health care, education, politics, and the STEM fields of science, technology, engineering, and mathematics.

Our book tries to not just introduce communication to students whose major area of study is not communication, but show them why it is essential to their long-term success in those fields. That is why when we cover informative speaking, we discuss it in terms of how to deliver complicated information to an audience of nonexperts. This is surely something doctors, teachers, and engineers do on a daily basis. We discuss persuasion as advocacy for a position and detail how to try and use persuasive principles to ethically appeal to others. Marketing and sales professionals, as well as politicians, do this on a daily basis. Regardless of which field you choose to launch your career, you will need to know how to speak well, and this book aims to help you understand how to do this in specific contexts.

Handbooks, however, are essentially quick guides, and so the chapters are designed to be short and to the point. You will not find many stories here—just tips, tricks, guidelines, and suggestions to help you become a successful speaker. To do this, you will notice the book has lots of tables, bullet points, and lists rather than extended narrative discussions. Key vocabulary is often highlighted to help you reference important terms and concepts. The book is also structured so that each chapter relates to and builds upon the previous ones.

In the beginning of the book, we address some basic concepts and issues, such as anxiety, ethics, culture, diversity, and civility in communication. We detail the important role listening plays in public speaking for both presenters and audience members. We then move on to preparation, where we discuss selecting a topic, audience analysis, and researching information. Once you gather information, it must be organized, and so we cover outlining and creating a strong speech structure through introductions, conclusions, and the body of the message next. We then address the different types of speeches you might be called upon to deliver (informative, persuasive, epideictic) while also addressing reasoning and how it relates to effective messages. We cover topics most connected to the actual speech itself, like delivery, presentation aids, language, and the importance of prior practice. Finally, we use up-to-date research to help explain group presentations and communication, as many people will eventually find themselves delivering talks in this format.

New to the third edition of the book is a complete chapter on civility in communication. Additionally, we have updated examples, including a new speaking outline in the outlining chapter and additional examples of professions in which certain public speaking skills are particularly useful.

We feel this book and our efforts fill a gap in the current textbook offerings for public speaking and oral communication. As schools move toward a more integrated general education curriculum, communication instruction has never been more important. We feel by creating a handbook that links basic principles of communication and public speaking to the varied disciplinary interests of our students, we will make communication courses appear more applicable to their educational experience. In short, students will see and read about why they should be in a public speaking course. We believe this book will help the future doctors, sales professionals, engineers, senators, teachers, industry professionals, and others in our classes become more ethical and more effective public speakers.

Joseph M. Valenzano III
Melissa A. Broeckelman-Post
Stephen W. Braden

CONTENTS

19 LANGUAGE 249

20 DELIVERY 261

UNDERSTANDING PUBLIC COMMUNICATION

Objectives

◊ Understand how communication works

◊ Differentiate between conversation and formal presentations

◊ Dispel myths about public speaking

The ability to use symbols, create meaning, and communicate ideas defines what it means to be human. To be sure, many different species communicate in their own way—dogs bark, snakes hiss, and some species of insects dance—but human beings are unique in our complex use of symbols to define our-selves and the world in which we live. Even more so, we influence people and move them to action through the creative and effective presentation of our ideas. Think about the different contexts in which we do this—contexts specific to the human world.

When we think of public speaking, the first context that comes to mind is politics. Public speaking is certainly an integral part of any democracy, and it remains one of the more commonly understood venues in which peo-ple deliver remarks to audiences. Debates, campaign events, presidential addresses, and a myriad of other situations provide politicians with oppor-tunities to speak to audiences. However, the political realm is not the only one in which public speaking skills are a necessity.

In the private sector, where companies seek to convince consumers to pur-chase their goods or services, representatives are often called upon to deliver presentations designed to facilitate sales. Corporate executives also address their employees and investors periodically to inform them about the state of the company's finances and what the goals are for the coming quarter or year. In business, these modes of interaction involving speech have been influenced greatly in recent years by the development of electronic media, such as Skype, Prezi, and even something as simple as conference calling. But the importance and utility of speech do not stop with politics and business—it even extends to our personal lives.

At some point in all our lives, we will attend a wedding and a funeral. We may also go to an anniversary celebration, awards ceremony, or some other function where we hear, and perhaps even deliver, speeches. Each of these situations requires us to know how to properly develop and deliver remarks to a specific audience in much the same way that political and business contexts demand we do. Quite simply, the use of symbols through speech is a central part of what it means to be human. In this handbook, we will help you learn how to create and convey effective presentations so that you can maximize your ability to deliver information, change minds, and influence audiences.

In this chapter, we provide a brief foundation of some important concepts related to understanding how the communication process works. This breakdown of the central components of communication is then followed by an explanation of how public speaking is different from casual conversation. Finally, we dispel some popular myths about public speaking so that you can move forward and learn how to deliver effective presentations.

COMMUNICATION MODELS

We use theories to explain most, if not all, human behaviors. The field of communication has several models that illustrate how communication functions between people. It is essential to understand how these models work because they inform the choices we make in preparing and performing a speech. In this section, we will cover three different models, each of which is a valid way of explaining communication in different contexts. First, we discuss the most basic model of the communication process, the linear model of communication. Then we explain the interactive model of communication, which complicates the linear model by introducing a few new variables to the communication process. Finally, we delve into the transactional model of communication, which is a bit more involved than the interactive model.

linear model of communication
theory that views communication as a one-way process in which a source conveys an encoded message through a channel to a receiver, who then decodes that message

Linear Model of Communication

The first model developed to explain the communication process was the linear model of communication (Figure 1.1), which is also known as the Shannon and Weaver model of communication or the action model of communication. This model views communication as something that one person does to another. In this model, communication flows in one direction only, much like a river. The idea is very basic and, at its most complicated, contains seven elements.

Figure 1.1 **Linear model of communication**

The first of these elements is the source, which in terms of public speaking is the speaker. The speaker is the person responsible for inventing the idea on which he or she intends to speak and crafting the message that conveys that idea to an audience. When the speaker converts the idea into words, he or she is encoding it. This encoding process is simply taking an abstract notion and giving it meaning through the application of symbols. The end result of the encoding process is a message, which is the content or idea the source initially wanted to provide to the audience. This message is then delivered through a channel, which in the case of public speaking is the voice. A person's voice is the channel through which a source's encoded message travels to an audience in a presentation.

So far this sounds fairly simple, and you may be wondering how it could get confusing or how a person's message could be misinterpreted. Well, even in that simple initial stage of encoding and delivery through the channel, speakers can make poor word choices that do not accurately reflect the meaning they wish to convey. The speaker may also use words the audience does not understand when encoding the message. These are two small ways this seemingly easy process can get confusing. Problems, however, are not limited to the source in the linear model, so let's take a look at how the linear model explains what happens after the message travels through the channel to its destination.

When a message is sent, it is also received, and the audience, also called the receiver, processes those symbols. The processing done by the receiver is called decoding, which essentially takes the symbols used to encode the message and draws meaning from them. This is much like what some kids do with decoder rings in cereal boxes. To understand the message, you need the

source
the person responsible for inventing the idea on which he or she intends to speak and crafting that idea to an audience

encoding
taking an abstract notion and providing it meaning

message
the content or idea that the source tries to convey to the audience

channel
the medium through which an encoded message is transmitted from a source to a receiver

receiver
the person or audience that a message is being transmitted to

decoding
the process of drawing meaning from the symbols that were used to encode a message

key to understand how it was encoded. In terms of public speaking, receivers need to understand the symbol system, or language, used by the speaker when sending the message.

As before, this may seem easy, but all of us have been in a situation where, as the receiver of a message, we did not exactly understand what was being said. This can occur in a classroom during a lecture, in a debate between two political candidates, and even in a casual conversation with a friend. We may be speaking the same language, but when we have different definitions of words we process them differently than the speaker might intend, resulting in confusion. What leads to the interruption or inaccurate decoding of a message sometimes comes not from a person's listening ability but from some other force.

noise
anything that can change the message after the source encodes and sends it

The other force that can impede the delivery and proper decoding of a message is called noise, and noise is the final component of the linear model of communication. Noise refers to anything that can change the message after the source encodes and sends it. There are a variety of different types of noise, some physical and some psychological, but all throw a wrench into the communication process. Table 1.1 shows the different types of noise speakers and audiences might encounter during a presentation.

Table 1.1

| TYPES OF NOISE ||
PHYSICAL NOISE	PSYCHOLOGICAL NOISE
• Other sounds	• Preoccupation with other thoughts
• Visual barriers	• Emotional reaction to the topic
• Poor volume and projection	• Prejudice or ill will toward the speaker
• Distractions in the room	• Unwillingness to listen
• Hunger, tiredness, and other bodily limitations	• Resistance to the message

The linear model seems to adequately explain a basic form of communication, but we all know that the process is more involved, because receivers are not simply sponges that absorb information provided by a source. So, although usable, this model provides an incomplete explanation of how communication functions between people. It was not long after the model was developed that it was rethought and extended to include a more active role for receivers. Next, we will go over the changes that were made in the more thorough interactive model of communication.

Interactive Model of Communication

The **interactive model of communication** (Figure 1.2) expands our understanding of the communication process by taking into account that messages flow back and forth from the receiver. Whereas the linear model of communication views the communication process as complete when the receiver decodes the sender's message, the interactive model does not; here we will see the sender and receiver are both responsible for encoding and decoding messages.

interactive model of communication
communication theory that views communication as a two-way process that includes feedback and the environment

The main way in which the interactive model is different from the linear model is in the concept of **feedback**. Feedback occurs after the receiver decodes the sender's message and is essentially the receiver's response to the message. This new message then flows linearly back to the sender, who becomes the receiver of the feedback to the original message.

feedback
the receiver's response to a message that is sent to the sender

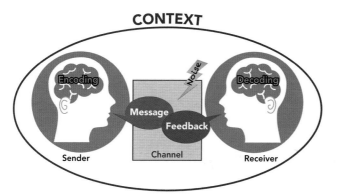

Figure 1.2 **Interactive model of communication**

When you say something to the receiver, the receiver processes your message and responds either verbally or nonverbally. You then receive that response, thus completing the communication process. The introduction of feedback creates a fuller picture of what happens when two or more people interact.

A second aspect added in the interactive model of communication is that of **environment**. The environment provides a deeper understanding of context than noise did in the linear model. In fact, noise is part of the environment, but not the whole thing. The environment is the context, which includes a plethora of different things that both help and hinder the communication process. See Table 1.2 for a few aspects of the environment that both senders and receivers should consider when encoding and decoding messages.

environment
the context in which the communication process takes place

Table 1.2

ENVIRONMENTAL ELEMENTS	
· Beliefs	· Physical setting
· Context	· Relationships
· History	· Values
· Participants	

Although it provides a better picture of how communication works, even the interactive model is not perfect. One of the major missing components in this model is the idea that receivers and senders do not wait to provide feedback. Next, we will look at perhaps the richest explanation of the communication process, the transactional model.

Transactional Model of Communication

transactional model of communication

theory that views communication as a constant process in which all parties simultaneously play the roles of sender and receiver

Although more illustrative of how the mechanics of the communication process works, the interactive model of communication did not take into account one very important aspect of how we communicate: the fact that both encoders and decoders send and receive messages simultaneously, and both parties use the same channel. The **transactional model of communication** (Figure 1.3) is a far more complete explanation of communication because it recognizes that communication is constant, and we play the roles of sender and receiver simultaneously in just about every interaction.

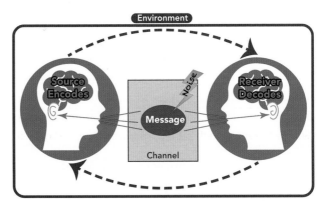

Figure 1.3 **Transactional model of communication**

This model is particularly useful when explaining the dynamic context of face-to-face communication, such as what occurs when we have a conversation or deliver a presentation to an audience. In both of these scenarios, the sender is also reacting in real time to how the audience is receiving the message. If the sender notices confused looks, perhaps he or she then asks a question to find out what needs to be clarified. This change in remarks is a direct result of feedback from the audience.

The transactional model of communication helps us understand that things never go as planned, and so we constantly adapt to feedback. This dynamic model, which explains how communication functions most accurately, reflects public speaking as a process. Now that we have a model for appreciating the complexity of the speech process, let's get a picture of how not all speech is the same by differentiating speech from casual conversation.

CONVERSATION VERSUS SPEECH

All speaking situations, and thus all forms of speech, are not equal, although there are similarities among contexts. Informal conversations and speech have several such overlaps but also some significant differences. When we understand some of these similarities and differences it can place public speaking in a new, less threatening light (see Table 1.3).

Table 1.3

SIMILARITIES AND DIFFERENCES IN CONVERSATION AND SPEECH	
SIMILARITIES	DIFFERENCES
• Audience-centered	• Language choices
• Attention to feedback	• Speeches require more organization
• Goal-driven	• Use of notes
• Logic is required	• No interruptions
• Stories for effect	• Delivery style
	• Physical arrangement

We all know how to talk to each other, and rarely does a day go by when we don't have a casual conversation with someone. Certain aspects of those interactions also color public speaking situations. First, both conversations and speeches are audience-centered. By this we mean that we pay attention to the audience when making choices regarding our speech. In conversations as well as speeches there are certain topics we address only with particular people or groups. We also pay attention to the feedback we receive from the receivers in both situations so we know how to respond. Both conversation and speech are activities centered upon the audience.

A third quality shared by conversation and speech is that both are goal-driven activities. We seek to accomplish something, whether it is conveying information or changing the audience's mind, whenever we have a casual conversation with someone or deliver more formal remarks. These goals differ with each event and interaction, but there is always something we want to achieve. A fourth area of overlap related to the achievement of goals is that, in both conversation and public speaking, we need to organize our thoughts logically in order for the receiver to understand what we are saying. Finally, in both situations, we want to tell stories to our audiences for maximum effect. In short, conversation and public speaking both seek the same outcome in an organized way that does not bore people. However, there are differences between the two communication practices.

One significant difference between the two relates to the language choices we make. Conversations tend to be colloquial and relaxed, while public speaking requires more formal language. For instance, in public speaking contexts speakers should not swear or use slang terms, but in conversations these things may very well happen.

There are a few other notable differences between public speaking and conversation. One of those pertains to the structure of the remarks. Although both conversations and speeches present information in a logical manner, speeches are more clearly organized and less prone to tangents than conversations, and note cards or outlines are often employed to help speakers stay on track. Additionally, whereas we all know people who interrupt a conversation, such interruptions are not the norm during formal presentations.

A final area of difference can be seen in delivery. Conversations often occur in very small, intimate settings that do not require people to raise their voices; however, when giving a speech you must make sure everyone in the audience can hear you. Physical delivery is also different in that when giving a speech we should avoid distracting mannerisms and verbal pauses, while these things often feature prominently in conversations. During a conversation, people are usually sitting or standing together so that every person can see the others' faces, but during a speech, the speaker usually stands at the front of the room facing a seated audience that is looking only at the speaker.

Now that we understand how communication works, and how public speaking is not all that different from conversation, let's cover some common misconceptions regarding public speaking that many people hold.

PUBLIC SPEAKING MYTHS

It is no secret that people communicate with varying degrees of skill. Some people are adept at interpersonal conversation, while some are more comfortable communicating in groups. When it comes to public speaking and formal presentations, some people naturally feel more comfortable, and even enjoy the experience, while others fear it more than they do death. While most people will feel a little bit of anxiety when asked to give a speech, with training and practice, anyone can deliver a competent speech. However, there are some myths that sometimes stand in the way of building speaking skills. In this section, we will cover those myths that keep people from developing their public speaking skills—and as the first myth indicates, public speaking is a skill, not a talent.

Public Speaking Is a Talent, Not a Skill　　　　　MYTH #1

Good speakers are made, not born, and they are made through hours of practice and preparation. Like any skill or complicated task, public speaking takes time to develop because of the many components involved. Thankfully, many ways exist to hone this skill and become a competent public speaker.

People can start improving their speaking skills by taking a public speaking course and reading and studying texts such as this one. These courses are available at colleges and universities around the country as well as more informally through organizations such as Toastmasters International. One course, though, is not a silver bullet and will simply provide you with the tools you need to improve. The real work comes when you practice with the tools provided to you.

Another way to develop your speaking skills is by watching and listening to good speakers. Many people learn well through modeling, and there is no shortage of good speakers or speeches for you to read and watch. This exposure to good practices will help spark ideas and provide samples upon which you can reflect as you work to improve your own speaking skills.

Finally, there is no substitute for preparation and experience. Taking as much time as necessary to develop your speech, practicing, and editing it will pay off. Additionally, the more speeches you deliver, the better you will be because you will become more comfortable with the context and more familiar with your own speech patterns. Don't shy away from chances to give presentations, but rather embrace them as opportunities to hone your skills.

MYTH #2   Speech Is Easy; We Do It All the Time

As we have shown, communicating is a natural human activity. As children, we begin trying to speak very early in life, and because we have been speaking for so long we think it is easy to do. But just because we do it all the time doesn't mean we do it correctly or as well as we could. We are all guilty of having said something at an inappropriate moment or of not being prepared to answer a question or deliver remarks. Presentations are not something that can be prepared the night before and then flawlessly delivered. They are, in fact, the opposite.

Choosing the right words to convey ideas to an audience takes thought, and thought takes time. It takes even more time to organize your thoughts into a coherent presentation, and so waiting until the last minute is simply not an option. Finally, we may be comfortable with speaking in conversation, but presentations to attentive audiences in a formal setting are an entirely different matter. This is why it takes time and practice to speak well. There is a big difference between speaking well and delivering a good, effective speech. Just because we have been doing something for a while does not mean that we do it well.

MYTH #3   There Is No "Right Way" to Deliver a Speech

Many people believe that there is no correct way to give a speech and that all ways of delivering a speech are equally acceptable and effective. If that were the case, we would not have great speeches or speakers, because we would all be equally good. There is a proper way to construct and deliver a speech, and to be a competent presenter you need to learn what is and is not effective.

To say there are "right" ways to deliver a speech does not mean there is only one way to approach a speech topic. There are untold ways in which a topic could be covered by a speaker; however, the principles of organization, delivery, language, and style apply to how the treatment of that topic is conveyed. In this book, we will show you these guiding principles for effective speech and illustrate that the idea that all speeches are equally good is simply not correct.

Summary

In this chapter we introduced you to some foundational ideas regarding communication and public speaking. We explained the three models of communication: linear, interactive, and transactional. We then showed how conversation and public speaking share certain similarities and differences. Finally, we dispelled a few myths people hold about public speaking. This overview of foundational concepts related to public speaking will help provide a clearer understanding of how to develop effective public presentations.

Key Terms

channel 3

decoding 3

encoding 3

environment 5

feedback 5

interactive model of
   communication 5

linear model of communication 2

message 3

noise 4

receiver 3

source 3

transactional model of
   communication 6

Activities

1   Consider the three models of communication. For each model, provide an example of a situation that best illustrates communication happening in a format that reflects that model.

2   Think about a recent conversation you had with another person. What types of noise distracted you and your partner during that conversation? How might you reduce or overcome some of those types of noise during your next conversation? How can you help reduce noise for your audience when you are giving a speech?

3   Re-examine the myths about public speaking on pages 9–10. Describe how these myths may have impacted you in the past when delivering a presentation.

SPEECH ANXIETY

Objectives

◊ Define communication apprehension

◊ Explain the physical effects of anxiety in speaking situations

◊ Suggest ways to manage communication apprehension

Many people have fears and anxieties about a variety of issues. Some people fear animals, others shiver at the thought of entering open spaces, some go rigid when they see spiders, and yet others are afraid of tight spaces. Fears are a part of being human, and either we must find a way to manage our fears, or they will manage us. In this chapter, we examine a common fear that grips people from all walks of life: the fear of delivering a speech. Most communication scholars label this anxiety *communication apprehension*. There has been a plethora of research and testing done in the communication discipline over the last forty years, and coping methods of varying degrees of success have been developed to help alleviate the anxiety produced by the mere prospect of public speaking.

We have many anxieties, and some of these manifest as a **phobia**, or "a persistent, irrational fear of a specific object, activity, or situation that leads to a compelling desire to avoid."[1] Phobias are more than discomfort or anxiety; they are an intense activation of the base instinct to avoid a threat. For instance, those with arachnophobia, the fear of spiders, will run at the sight of a spider or leap onto a couch just to avoid contact with the small creature. Phobias are, in many instances, irrational responses to something that should not be perceived as a significant threat.

phobia
a persistent, irrational fear of a specific object, activity, or situation that leads to a compelling desire to avoid

There are a great many phobias. These phobias impact our lives, often in negative ways. They may prevent us from doing things we want to do, sometimes including advancing our own careers, because a fear makes us incapable of completing a task. In this respect, it is not hard to imagine how a fear of public speaking, or communication apprehension, can impede our ability to get a promotion, complete a sale, or excel in a classroom. In this chapter, we

---

1. Dictionary.com, s.v. "phobia," accessed January 31, 2012, http://dictionary.reference.com/browse/phobia; Corinne O'Keefe Osborn, "Common and Unique Fears Explained," Healthline, updated January 3, 2019, https://www.healthline.com/health/list-of-phobias.

will focus on apprehension in a public speaking situation. We will provide an overview of communication apprehension, go over the physical effects induced by this condition, and finally present some ways in which you can cope with anxiety in public speaking situations.

Ten Most Common Phobias

◊   acrophobia: fear of heights

◊   aerophobia: fear of flying

◊   arachnophobia: fear of spiders

◊   astraphobia: fear of thunder and lightning

◊   autophobia: fear of being alone

◊   claustrophobia: fear of confined or crowded spaces

◊   hemophobia: fear of blood

◊   hydrophobia: fear of water

◊   ophidiophobia: fear of snakes

◊   zoophobia: fear of animals

https://www.healthline.com/health/list-of-phobias

COMMUNICATION APPREHENSION

communication apprehension
the fear or anxiety associated with real or anticipated communication with another or others

Anxiety caused by the prospect of public speaking is often referred to as **communication apprehension**. Communication apprehension is defined as "the fear or anxiety associated with real or anticipated communication with another or others."[2] This is a broader definition than simply calling it a "fear of public speaking" for two reasons. First, communication apprehension is not specific to public speaking; rather, it can manifest in a variety of different speaking contexts, including one-on-one interactions. Second, "fear" is an absolute term, whereas apprehension is best understood on a linear scale (see Figure 2.1): On one end, we are completely comfortable communicating with others, and on the other, we are always reluctant and fearful to communicate with others. Most people fall somewhere in the middle of the continuum and experience some communication apprehension in some communication contexts.

---

2. James C. McCroskey, "Oral Communication Apprehension: A Summary of Recent Theory and Research," *Human Communication Research* 4, no. 1 (September 1977): 78–96.

There have been numerous studies regarding communication apprehension and its effects on people. Those who experience higher degrees of communication apprehension are less satisfied with their ability to express themselves and are not as assertive in interactions with others.[3] One would think that, as a result of this, those with high communication apprehension would begin working on presentations in advance, but the opposite is actually typically true. People with high communication apprehension often procrastinate because they do not believe they will succeed.[4] This is an example of the self-fulfilling prophecy, which is a process in which your expectations about yourself, another person, or an entity eventually lead to you, the other person, or the entity behaving in ways that confirm your expectations.

self-fulfilling prophecy
a process in which your expectations about yourself, another person, or an entity eventually lead to you, the other person, or the entity behaving in ways that confirm your expectations

The self-fulfilling prophecy can be negative or positive. If you convince yourself that you will fail a calculus examination, then with that mindset, you likely will. However, convincing yourself that you will do well in an upcoming soccer game, although certainly not a guarantee, will enhance your chances of success. These preconceived notions have a powerful effect on people, and later we will suggest some ways to help ensure that you have a positive vision of delivering your speech.

One important step in understanding your level of communication apprehension is identifying to what degree you are anxious about interacting with others. Professor James McCroskey developed a survey instrument that helps individuals measure their level of communication apprehension in a variety of contexts. The PRCA-24, the latest version of this scale, can be very helpful in identifying your own degree of communication apprehension. You can get a copy of the PRCA-24 online and calculate your score at http://www.jamescmccroskey.com/measures/prca24.htm. Another measure, the Personal Report of Public Speaking Anxiety, measures the anxiety that you feel specifically during public speaking situations, and can be found online at http://www.jamescmccroskey.com/measures/prpsa.htm.

apprehensive

comfortable

Figure 2.1
Communication apprehension

Learning about yourself is just one step in managing communication apprehension; you must also understand what the fear physically does to you. Many people believe they know the answer to this, but what we are about to tell you may surprise you and help you find ways to overcome your fear.

---

3. Joe Ayres and Brian L. Heuett, "The Relationship between Visual Imagery and Public Speaking Apprehension," *Communication Reports* 10, no. 1 (1997): 87–94.

4. Ralph R. Behnke and Chris R. Sawyer, "Public Speaking Procrastination as a Correlate of Public Speaking Communication Apprehension and Self-Perceived Public Speaking Competence," *Communication Research Reports* 16, no. 1 (1999): 40–47.

PHYSICAL EFFECTS OF COMMUNICATION APPREHENSION

Anxieties begin in the brain with thoughts and perceptions about things around us that we believe threaten us. Once they emerge in our thoughts, anxieties then physically manifest themselves, and to some people this is more distressing than the mental duress. In fact, the physical dimensions of anxiety are what we naturally focus on when we feel fear or trepidation toward some external stimulus.

Suppose you are batting in a fast-pitch softball game with two outs in the bottom of the ninth inning; the bases are loaded, and your team is down by three runs. You go to the batter's box, your stomach is churning, you are perspiring, and there are butterflies in your stomach. You are aware of all these physiological feelings, but how much do the fans in the stands actually see? The answer is that they see very little, and often none, of your anxiety—even the physical effects. The same principle is true of giving a speech to a live audience. You may have the same feelings as the batter, but the audience is likely to notice very few, if any, of the physical symptoms of your anxiety.

Rise in Blood Pressure

To further illustrate the invisibility of anxiety, let's take a look at some of the common physical reactions that occur when we are anxious or stressed. One physical effect of anxiety is a rise in blood pressure. This is not necessarily a bad thing, as it can give you energy, nor is it anything an audience will notice and correctly attribute to fear on your part. Higher blood pressure in these situations sends signals to the brain that it needs to pay heightened attention to your surroundings. Blood pressure is also something that is internal, and thus not likely to be noticed by people around you, though it can cause your face to flush red.

Shortness of Breath

In addition to higher blood pressure, some people also experience shortness of breath when they are anxious, and in speaking situations this can negatively affect the delivery of the speech. Speakers sometimes speak too quickly, fail to project their voice enough, or do not have enough vocal variation when they are experiencing shortness of breath.

Galvanic Skin Tightening and Sweat

A third physical effect of stress and anxiety is called galvanic skin tightening. Your skin, like any organ, responds to stimuli and stress. Specifically, your skin tightens when you are anxious, nervous, or stressed. Obviously we do not even feel this happening, so it stands to reason that the audience cannot see it either. Interestingly enough, this particular response to anxiety is used as an indicator of deception on lie detector tests and is virtually impossible to fake. The tightening of the skin also causes a fourth symptom of anxiety, perspiration.

Visibility of Communication Apprehension

Most of the time, your audience will not notice these four symptoms of anxiety, even if they feel really significant and seem like they must be obvious from your perspective as the speaker. Even if your audience can see some of these symptoms, however, they are likely to recognize that these are symptoms that most people (including your audience members) experience to some extent while giving a speech or might even attribute them to other causes, such as a warm or crowded room, a cold, allergies, or extra heat from the sun or spotlights.

There is no doubt that stress and anxiety, particularly in public speaking settings, can elicit physical reactions from each of us, from heightened blood pressure to perspiration. There is also no doubt that audiences do not automatically correlate the physical responses to the anxiety we may be feeling—that is, unless we tell them the two are related! The more you focus on your physical responses, the more likely you are to experience even more anxiety. It is far better to just let the body do what it does and not focus on it. After all, if you pay attention to your physical response to anxiety, your audience will do so as well.

So, we now know that everyone experiences communication apprehension to some degree or another and that our bodies react to the stress produced by anxiety in these situations in ways that are virtually invisible to the audience. Both of these facts should provide some comfort when you prepare a presentation, but there is more we can do to manage our anxiety than simply understanding the situation. In the final section of this chapter, we will go over a few things to assist you with managing both the mental and physical manifestations of anxiety.

Personal Report of Communication Apprehension

This instrument is composed of 24 statements concerning feelings about communicating with others. Please indicate the degree to which each statement applies to you by marking whether you: Strongly Disagree = 1; Disagree = 2; are Neutral = 3; Agree = 4; Strongly Agree = 5

____ 1.   I dislike participating in group discussions.
____ 2.   Generally, I am comfortable while participating in group discussions.
____ 3.   I am tense and nervous while participating in group discussions.
____ 4.   I like to get involved in group discussions.
____ 5.   Engaging in a group discussion with new people makes me tense and nervous.
____ 6.   I am calm and relaxed while participating in group discussions.
____ 7.   Generally, I am nervous when I have to participate in a meeting.
____ 8.   Usually, I am comfortable when I have to participate in a meeting.
____ 9.   I am very calm and relaxed when I am called upon to express an opinion at a meeting.
____ 10. I am afraid to express myself at meetings.
____ 11. Communicating at meetings usually makes me uncomfortable.
____ 12. I am very relaxed when answering questions at a meeting.
____ 13. While participating in a conversation with a new acquaintance, I feel very nervous.
____ 14. I have no fear of speaking up in conversations.
____ 15. Ordinarily I am very tense and nervous in conversations.
____ 16. Ordinarily I am very calm and relaxed in conversations.
____ 17. While conversing with a new acquaintance, I feel very relaxed.
____ 18. I'm afraid to speak up in conversations.
____ 19. I have no fear of giving a speech.
____ 20. Certain parts of my body feel very tense and rigid while giving a speech.
____ 21. I feel relaxed while giving a speech.
____ 22. My thoughts become confused and jumbled when I am giving a speech.
____ 23. I face the prospect of giving a speech with confidence.
____ 24. While giving a speech, I get so nervous I forget facts I really know.

Scoring:
Group Discussion: 18 – (scores for items 2, 4, & 6) + (scores for items 1,3, & 5)
Meetings: 18 – (scores for items 8, 9, & 12) + (scores for items 7, 10, & 11)
Interpersonal: 18 – (scores for items 14, 16, & 17) + (scores for items 13, 15, & 18)
Public Speaking: 18 – (scores for items 19, 21, & 23) + (scores for items 20, 22, & 24)

Group Discussion Score: ____   **Interpersonal Score:**   ____

Meetings Score: ____   **Public Speaking Score:**   ____

To obtain your total score for the PRCA, simply add your sub-scores together. Scores can range from 24–120. Scores below 51 represent people who have very low CA. Scores between 51 and 80 represent people with average CA. Scores above 80 represent people who have high levels of trait CA. To see entire report, go to: http://www.jamescmccroskey.com/measures/prca24.htm.

COMBATING COMMUNICATION APPREHENSION

Our bodies' reactions to stress may be outside our direct control, but there are several ways we can mitigate the potential damage that anxiety can cause. In this section we will provide several simple tips for preparing a presentation that will help reduce communication anxiety.

Practice, Practice, and Practice

We mentioned earlier that people with high communication apprehension are more likely to procrastinate preparing a speech, despite the fact that they should be spending more time getting ready so they can overcome their fear. So it stands to reason that the first suggestion we have for coping with communication anxiety is to practice your presentation as much as possible for as long as you can.

At first, practice giving the speech alone so that you become more comfortable with what you plan to say. Once you have a final version of your speech prepared and you have practiced it alone, add a mirror to the practice equation. Practicing in front of a mirror can increase your comfort and allow you to see what you look like when delivering the speech. Practicing in front of a mirror is not enough, though, as it does not accurately simulate the situation in which you will be presenting. So, after taking advantage of the mirror, add some actual people to create an audience. Make sure these are people you know and with whom you are comfortable, such as friends and family. Ask them for honest feedback, and make some adjustments. This practice regimen helps simulate the experience of delivering your remarks to an actual audience, but there is something else to try to simulate when practicing. We will cover practice regimens more extensively in Chapter 21.

In addition to an audience, whenever possible you should try to have a few practice sessions in the environment within which you will be speaking. If it's a boardroom, then practice at a dining room or kitchen table; if it's a large conference room, see if you can get access to it in advance; if it's a classroom, try to go when there is not a class occupying the space. It is as important to become comfortable and to practice within the environment in which you will speak as it is to simulate the audience to whom you will speak. Practicing with both of these things in mind will help alleviate some apprehension about delivering your talk.

Communication Apprehension

Sarah was not looking forward to taking a public speaking class. She remembered the time that she had to give a speech in her history class and was afraid she would have to relive that speech all over again. On that day, Sarah had been so anxious about giving her speech that she waited until the day before to prepare, didn't sleep at all, and did not even eat breakfast before she went to class. Throughout the morning she couldn't concentrate on anything except the fear of standing up in front of the class to speak. By the time Sarah got to her history class she was sweating, having trouble breathing, and worrying that she would forget everything. While she was speaking, Sarah kept tripping over her words, forgot several things she wanted to say, and could feel her face flushing as she struggled to get back on track.

This time, Sarah decided to do things a little differently. As soon as her instructor handed out the first speech assignment, she began doing research and creating an outline, even though she knew she would not need to give her speech for a couple more weeks. She practiced her speech in a mirror several times and then asked several of her friends to listen and provide feedback as she practiced a few more times. Each time she practiced her speech, Sarah could feel her fear subsiding, and she became more and more confident. The night before her speech, Sarah felt ready to give her speech, so she went to bed early, and before she fell asleep she spent some time visualizing herself giving her speech successfully. The next morning, Sarah still felt a few butterflies in her stomach and could feel her palms sweating, but she tried to keep her focus on her speech and on her audience. Though she still made a few mistakes, Sarah could see her audience nodding in support, and when her speech was over she felt like she had done a great job and was even starting to look forward to the next speech assignment.

Employ Relaxation Techniques

Practicing remarks in advance is the best suggestion we can offer, but often-times you will not be afforded much notice before giving a presentation, thus limiting the amount you can feasibly practice. Such short-term presentations only serve to heighten our apprehension about public speaking, so they require more immediate methods for reducing stress and tension. One such method is to learn to use relaxation techniques before presentations. This is very useful in situations in which you have little time to prepare and practice but can also be helpful when you have had time to practice.

There are a variety of relaxation techniques that can help calm nerves, lower blood pressure, and help you focus before giving a talk. Some require a little more time than others, but all are helpful in a pinch. Simply taking a few minutes to stretch your back, shoulders, and legs will help unleash some pent-up tension in your muscles and allow you to feel and look more comfortable in front of an audience. Remember, public speaking is a physical activity in much the same way jogging and weightlifting are, so it stands to reason that we should prepare for giving speeches in a way similar to how we prepare for workouts.

For some people with high communication apprehension, it might also be beneficial to engage in more structured and consistent stretching exercises. In these instances, joining a yoga or pilates class might help train you in more varied methods of relaxation and stretching. It also might provide the opportunity for you to go to a class before or even after a presentation to help reduce tension and relax.

A third relaxation technique is deep breathing, and of all the relaxation techniques we have discussed, this one takes the least amount of time. There is a lot to be said for closing your eyes and taking a few deep breaths before beginning a presentation. This helps improve the flow of oxygen in your blood, reduces blood pressure, and focuses your thoughts. There are various forms of deep breathing exercises in which you can engage, and all are helpful in reducing anxiety before speaking situations.

Breathing Exercises

4-7-8 Breathing

This exercise also uses belly breathing to help you relax. You can do this exercise either sitting or lying down.

1   To start, put one hand on your belly and the other on your chest.

2   Take a deep, slow breath from your belly and silently count to four as you breathe in.

3   Hold your breath and silently count from one to seven.

4   Breathe out completely as you silently count from one to eight. Try to get all the air out of your lungs by the time you reach eight.

5   Repeat several times or until you feel calm.

Breath Counting

Sit in a comfortable position with your spine straight and head inclined slightly forward. Gently close your eyes and take a few deep breaths. Then let the breath come naturally without trying to influence it. Ideally it will be quiet and slow, but depth and rhythm may vary.

1   To begin the exercise, count to one as you exhale.

2   The next time you exhale, count to two. Repeat until you're counting to five.

3   Then begin a new cycle, counting to one on the next exhalation.

Never count higher than five, and count only when you exhale. You will know your attention has wandered when you find yourself up to eight, twelve, or even nineteen. Try to do ten minutes of this form of meditation.

Finally, it is imperative that when speaking you feel your best, and so you should always get a good night's sleep before your presentation and make sure you are not hungry. When it comes to sleep, you may feel the need to stay up late the night before a talk to practice as much as you can, but if this keeps you from being well rested the next day, the efforts will be counterproductive. In terms of food, be careful not to be hungry when you talk but also not to be so full that you want to take a nap. Before you speak, have a nutritious meal that includes a healthy balance of complex carbohydrates, proteins, and fats that will be digested slowly, and try to avoid simple carbohydrates and refined sugars that will give you a burst of energy followed by a crash as your blood sugar levels spike and then fall quickly. You should also avoid eating heavy meals that might make you drowsy (see Table 2.1).

Table 2.1

WHAT SHOULD I EAT BEFORE I GIVE MY SPEECH?		
MEAL	**POOR CHOICE**	**BETTER CHOICE**
Breakfast	• Sugary cereal and white toast with jam • Pancakes or waffles with maple syrup	• Oatmeal with fruit, nuts, and a glass of milk • Scrambled eggs and whole wheat toast
Lunch	• Fettuccini alfredo • Large burger and fries	• Grilled chicken with steamed vegetables and brown rice • Turkey, Swiss, lettuce, and tomato sandwich on whole grain bread

WHAT SHOULD I EAT BEFORE I GIVE MY SPEECH?		
MEAL	POOR CHOICE	BETTER CHOICE
Snack	• Cookies or candy bar • Potato chips and energy drink	• Fruit and yogurt • String cheese and whole wheat crackers

Visualize Success

Those with high communication apprehension envision giving a speech as a torturous experience, and they see all the possible ways they can fail or make mistakes. Like the self-fulfilling prophecy, visualizing failure often leads to that result, thus perpetuating the cycle of communication apprehension. No amount of practice or relaxation techniques can change the way we envision the speaking experience, so this third way to reduce anxiety aims to combat the negative mental picture we might have of delivering a presentation.

The best time to visualize success is following a practice session; however, it works just about any time you want to do it. After you have practiced your speech a few times and feel more comfortable with it, get in a relaxed position on your bed, the sofa, or a recliner. One thing that is required is for you to be alone, with no distraction. Visualization requires concentration, and so it is important that you do not listen to music, watch television, email, text, or use Facebook or Twitter when trying to do this. Close your eyes and see yourself giving the speech from beginning to end. Visualize your confidence, pride, and good delivery. Concentrate on visualizing what you have control over instead of focusing on audience reactions. Focusing on audience reactions might lead to a letdown if the visualized responses do not occur when you deliver the speech. Visualizing success can work, just like the self-fulfilling prophecy.

Dialogue With the Audience

One of the scariest aspects of public speaking is that you are speaking to an audience of many people, all of whom are focused on you. One way to reduce the anxiety this situation creates is to change the way we understand the public speaking context. Instead of viewing it as a presentation to a large group, treat it like multiple simultaneous dialogues or conversations. That is to say, instead of presenting to a class of thirty, you are holding thirty conversations at the same time. We all have conversations daily, and so this may help you reduce the anxiety that a group of people may induce.

This dialogic approach can be extended as well if you want to create actual give-and-take with the audience. This can work, especially if the audience is small and well mannered. Before letting audience members join in the discussion, make sure you have a strong grasp of the makeup of your audience and their feelings toward you and the ideas you plan to advocate. One final word of caution regarding dialoguing with an audience: If someone asks a question to which you do not know the answer, be honest and tell the audience you do not know, but that you appreciate the question and will find out and get back to them if you can.

Systematic Desensitization

systematic desensitization
the process whereby a person is slowly introduced to a fear such that each time he or she overcomes the fear the intensity is decreased

Each of the suggestions we have made thus far pertains to specific speech situations, and although they are applicable every time you deliver a speech, in isolation they can have little impact on your overall apprehension toward public speaking. This is where the approach called systematic desensitization comes in. Systematic desensitization is the process by which a person is slowly introduced to a fear, and each time he or she overcomes the fear the intensity decreases. So, in the case of a fear of heights, a person might go to the second floor of a building until he or she is comfortable there, then the third, and so on. This gradually desensitizes a person to the cause of their anxiety.

This approach can be applied to help overcome a fear of public speaking. First deliver a speech to one person until you are comfortable, then add a person you do not know, and soon you will be speaking to larger and larger groups. This slow immersion can only happen over a long period of time, but it is tremendously effective at assisting people in overcoming their fear. It can also be applied to practice sessions before a single speech to help speakers slowly get used to the audience they will soon encounter. Ultimately, managing our communication apprehension involves a combination of each of these strategies but also requires persistent, consistent, and dedicated practice.

Summary

In this chapter we defined speech anxiety, which is more broadly labeled communication apprehension. We then covered the physical effects of speech anxiety and explained that, although we might believe we know what causes it, the audience does not necessarily know. Finally, we provided several ways to help manage communication apprehension but emphasized that practice and repeated public speaking experiences were key to managing apprehension.

Key Terms

communication apprehension 14

phobia 13

self-fulfilling prophecy 15

systematic desensitization 24

Activities

1   Think about the last presentation you gave. Which symptoms of communication apprehension did you experience?

2   Public speaking anxiety is the type of communication apprehension experienced specifically while giving a speech. While still thinking about your last speech, go to http://www.jamescmccroskey.com/measures/prpsa.htm and complete the Personal Report of Public Speaking Anxiety. Calculate your score. Do you have high, moderate, or low public speaking anxiety?

3   Once you reflect on your speaking anxiety after completing the Personal Report of Public Speaking Anxiety, consider ways that you can cope with any kind of speaking anxiety you might experience. Make a list of which ways of coping make the most sense for you and describe how you will employ those mechanisms as you prepare for your next speech.

SPEAKING AND ETHICS

Objectives

◊ Understand the importance of ethical speech

◊ Recognize the ethical responsibilities of a speaker

◊ Appreciate the ethical obligations of audience members

Communication, and speech in particular, is a very powerful tool. It can be used to enhance the public good, or it can be wielded in a way that manipulates and harms people. Like any tool, the operators involved need to understand how to apply the device to achieve the maximum benefits from it. Instruction manuals are easy to identify for things like drills, Blu-ray Disc players, and even cars, but for good speech there is no such manual. Instead, good speakers follow good ethical principles, and those principles constitute the "instruction manual" for speech-making.

In this chapter, we will broadly define ethics and discuss why speech must be governed by sound ethical principles. We will then lay out the basic ethical responsibilities of speakers and audiences, both of whom play a role in speech-making and meaning construction. Before we explain why ethics are important to the practice of speech, however, we must provide you with a definition of ethics. **Ethics** involve morals and the specific moral choices to be made by a person. It is, for all intents and purposes, a way for people to make good, sound choices for themselves and their communities. Since we build communities through communication with others, ethical speech is at the core of a healthy community, and we must be careful about what we say and how we interact with others.

ethics
morals and the specific moral choices to be made by a person

PUBLIC MESSAGES CANNOT BE TAKEN BACK

Once we say something, we cannot take it back. In that way it is much like shooting a bullet from a gun, because you cannot "un-say" the words, just as you can't "un-fire" a gun. Think of an interpersonal situation in which a couple is dating and one partner is angry with the other. In a moment of frustration, one shouts out, "I hate you!" to the other person. The sender of that message may begin to regret the words and apologize, noting that anger and emotional pain caused the outburst. The offended party can accept the apology and forgive the person, but the words were said and an apology in this situation can't fully undo the damage. Words matter because they leave an indelible mark on a relationship.

We all know words can inflict significant damage in an interpersonal relationship, but they can do even more damage in a public speaking setting. Even though public speaking may seem like a less intimate setting, saying something unethical or offensive can be more damaging than in an interpersonal setting. Whereas much of interpersonal communication is spontaneous, public speaking is more planned and formal, so the audience often attributes careful thought to the speaker in a public speaking setting. That is to say, they believe you say what you mean. Of course, in interpersonal settings, especially those with people who know you, such a slip can be explained away as just that—a "slip." In speeches, it is harder to say you "slipped" when you had time to prepare your comments.

The damage done when we say something unethical or offensive is not just done to the listener. Yes, the audience may take offense, walk out, and suffer discomfort after hearing your comments, but you also are harmed when this happens. Your credibility as a speaker takes the brunt of this damage, and you may not be invited to speak again, depending upon what you said. Knowing that communication is irreversible, and thus permanent, as well as acknowledging the lasting impact our words have on ourselves and others is an important step toward becoming an ethical speaker.

Our words also let the audience into our minds, allowing them to see how we see the world. Our word choices reflect our impressions of our environment and carry with them significant meaning for ourselves and others. The words we use reveal what we feel about everything from the audience to our political views and reflect our personal values and beliefs. In this way, our messages to audiences in public speaking settings impact how the audience sees us and will have an impact on the effectiveness of our messages. If the audience does not understand or agree with our worldview, it can increase the challenges we face in a public speaking setting.

In today's mediated environment, this is especially crucial. Many people upload commentaries, speeches, presentations, and even casual blogs to the internet via YouTube and other online websites. We may not think that what we say will hurt anyone, because there is no one in front of us when we videotape these comments and post them. The truth is that once we send our videos into the digital world, they can reach many people, even those we don't know. For that reason alone, it is especially crucial that we pay careful attention to our words and what we say; once we send them into cyberspace, they will never disappear and may go viral.

ETHICAL RESPONSIBILITIES OF SPEAKERS

As the originator of a message in a public speaking situation, the speaker is bound by several ethical responsibilities. These obligations begin at the start of the speech-making process, then progress through the research stage, and culminate with the delivery of the presentation itself. It is important to be attuned to the moral issues that arise throughout the development of your remarks, because doing so will help you keep the best interests of your audience in mind. In this section, we briefly cover the ethical responsibilities of speakers from the planning of a presentation, to researching the topic, all the way through the delivery of the speech.

The Ethics of Choosing a Topic

In many instances, speakers know the broad topic on which they will present, but even in these instances it is important to maintain a focus on ethics when narrowing the topic. This means that speakers must choose topics and messages they firmly believe are in the best interests of their audience. Choosing self-serving messages or crafting topics in a way that is designed to manipulate an audience is a perversion of a speaker's responsibilities. As the creator of the message, you own what you say and so you should take care to keep others in mind when you decide what you will say. Remember, words cannot be taken back.

When choosing or narrowing the topic of a presentation, we often find ourselves balancing various ethical responsibilities that sometimes compete with one another. Upon entering the workforce, we have a duty to ourselves to do the best we possibly can, a duty to our families to provide for them by keeping our jobs, a duty to the audience and the greater public to seek the common good, and a duty to our employers to achieve results. It is not hard to envision a situation in which these duties conflict and present us with an ethical dilemma. When it comes to message construction and meaning-making through speeches and statements, how do we maintain our ethical principles when the situation is not so clear? This is the hard work we must do before we even decide what to say to someone, but once we know what we will say and how we will balance our ethical obligations, our requirement to do what is right does not stop.

Personal Duties for Balancing Ethical Responsibilities When Choosing a Topic

◊   A duty to ourselves to do the best we possibly can

◊   A duty to our families to provide for them by keeping our jobs

◊   A duty to the audience and the greater public to seek the common good

◊   A duty to our employers to achieve results

The Ethics of Research

The ethical requirements of speech-making are not restricted to keeping the audience in mind when we choose a topic; they also come into play in research and speech development. In almost every instance in which you will be called upon to deliver a speech, you will need to incorporate some degree of evidence that you researched. In a business meeting, it could entail explaining sales figures; in a design presentation, it could be the history of the site upon which you plan to build; and in a class, it will most likely be scholarly research on a topic. In each instance, however, you must keep the interests of the audience in mind, properly evaluate the evidence you choose to cite, and properly attribute the sources of that information.

Thanks to technology, we have vast amounts of information at our fingertips. This is both good and bad—good because we can easily conduct research from our desks, but potentially hazardous because the internet is rife with biased and fabricated information. For that reason, it is essential we know how to properly evaluate information we find before we decide to use it in a presentation or report. As researchers, we need to discern the true from the false and facts from opinions. Facts are bits of information that can be verified and substantiated. They can be qualitative, as in historical events or testimony, or quantitative, as in polling results and the outcomes of scientific experiments. Opinions, on the other hand, vary from person to person and from group to group and are not as reliable as facts because they are often biased. Identifying the differences between opinions and facts will help you enhance your credibility. That credibility can be greatly diminished if the audience realizes you are citing a biased source.

When evaluating a source, there are several questions you should ask yourself to help determine whether the source can be trusted.

1 **Will this person benefit from getting me to believe that this information is true?** A source who is being paid as a spokesperson for a company and who is trying to sell you something or trying to win your vote is biased. Sometimes biased sources are accurate, but they are often misleading, and as an ethical communicator, you have a responsibility to do additional research and find a more credible source.

2 **Is this person an expert in this area or in a position to know this information?** Individuals who have special training and experience related to the information they are sharing are more reliable sources than those who do not. For example, a cardiologist is a better source than an auto mechanic for information on how to keep your heart healthy, but an auto mechanic is a better source than your family doctor for learning how to change the oil in your car.

3 **Are the claims made by this source substantiated by other credible sources?** If you have a single source that makes a claim, but find ten other reliable sources that say the opposite is true, it is likely that the ten sources that agree are accurate. For example, if you find one source that says you can lose weight by eating three pizzas every day, but find many other sources that say you must limit your calories and exercise in order to lose weight, it is probably not true that eating large quantities of pizza will help you lose weight.

4 **Is this source recent enough to be relevant?** If you are speaking about a current topic, you should use the most recent sources you can find. For example, an article written twenty years ago is not a good source for learning about the most energy-efficient cars available today. However, if you are giving a speech about an important figure in the Civil War, a source that is twenty years old might be acceptable.

Biased sources and opinions are not the only pitfalls of which researchers must be aware, and their use is not even the most grievous mistake a speaker can make. Plagiarism is perhaps the greatest offense a speaker can commit because it takes advantage of both the audience and the actual source of the information. When speakers plagiarize, they steal the intellectual achievements of another person and present them as their own, thus deceiving the

plagiarism
taking the intellectual achievements of another person and presenting them as one's own

audience into believing the speakers were responsible for more than they actually were. Like many crimes, plagiarism comes in many forms, so let's take a moment and describe what these various forms look like.

global plagiarism
taking an entire piece of work and saying that it is your own

The first type of plagiarism is global plagiarism, which is taking an entire piece of work and saying it is your own. Suppose a roommate gave a speech in a class different from your class and you took that speech and put your name on it. That would be an example of global plagiarism. Many consider it the worst kind of academic dishonesty. In these cases, speakers do no original work, but act as if they did. They have robbed the source of the credit deserved for creating the speech and tricked the audience into believing they themselves are a reliable source of information.

incremental plagiarism
using part of someone else's work and not citing it as a source

The second type of plagiarism is incremental plagiarism, which involves using part of someone else's work and not citing it as a source. An example of incremental plagiarism would be copying a few sentences from someone else's speech or paper and putting them directly into your speech without citing the source or using quotation marks. Despite the fact that in this case the work is not stolen in its entirety, it is clearly still an incident of dishonesty. This type of plagiarism is a bit more common than global plagiarism, but it is just as unethical because of the way it treats the source and the audience.

patchwork plagiarism
taking ideas from more than one piece of work and putting them together into a new piece of work, and then presenting them as original work without giving due credit to the sources

The last type of plagiarism we will address is patchwork plagiarism. Patchwork plagiarism takes ideas from more than one piece of work and presents them as original work without giving due credit to the sources. This is perhaps the most common form of plagiarism, but just because more people do it does not make it right. It is deceitful and unethical in that it still robs others of the credit they deserve for work they conducted, and it falsely inflates the credibility of the speaker.

patchworking
taking original source material and changing a few words in it, but not enough to consider it a paraphrase, all the while not citing the original source material

Patchworking is a process that closely resembles patchwork plagiarism. When writers or researchers employ patchworking, they take original sentences or work from another source, changing a few words in it and not citing the source. The changes are minimal and do not really change the idea presented in the original source; without any attribution to the source material, this remains plagiarism. It is sometimes evidence of a poor attempt at paraphrasing, but may also be a deliberate attempt to deceive an audience. In both instances, however, it is an unethical practice and speakers and writers need to avoid it.

As we have mentioned when discussing each of these types of plagiarism, it is important to cite sources in your written work. It is also essential that when speaking we verbally attribute those sources, because failure to do so also constitutes plagiarism. Having the sources in your outline or manuscript is not enough; you must mention them to your audience as well.

When delivering a speech, you must note where the work came from by mentioning the author or publication in which you found the information. Ideally, your verbal citation should include as many of the following four pieces of information as possible for your source: (1) the name of the publication, (2) the date the source was published, (3) the author of the work and/ or name of the person who is providing the information used in the source, and (4) the credentials of the source. It is best to cite your source first and then give the information, not the other way around. Citing the source after sharing the information is awkward and can hurt the flow of your speech, but citing the source before sharing the information can heighten audience attention and help the audience sense the importance of the information you are sharing. For example, in a speech you might cite your source by saying, "According to the February 10, 2012, issue of *Time*, Dr. Gary Landreth, a scientist at Case Western Reserve University, has discovered that a drug called bexarotene can reverse Alzheimer's disease in mice."

Thus far we have discussed the ethical requirements of a speaker when choosing and researching a speech topic. There is one more area in which speakers have an ethical requirement, and that is when they actually deliver the speech. In the next section, we will provide some general guidelines for ethical speech delivery.

The Ethics of Language and Delivery

Even if you prepare a topic with the best interests of the audience in mind and research the topic appropriately and thoroughly, there are still ethical pitfalls of which you must be aware when you actually deliver the speech. These ethical responsibilities primarily involve the language you choose to use when describing ideas, people, or things to an audience. Let's look at some general guidelines that will help you make good choices regarding the language and delivery of your presentations.

Maintain Composure. Every time we speak to someone, whether individually or in group settings, we must pay the person the same respect we hope he or she will give us. Sometimes our audience agrees with us, which makes conversation and discussion easier in many ways. Other times, some or even all of an audience will disagree with what we are saying, but that doesn't allow us to suspend civility and respect for them. In fact, it makes it even more important to be respectful and civil. There are also times when an audience will be neutral toward you and your topic, but respect is important in these instances as well.

Regardless of how the audience feels toward you or your topic, always show them respect. Knowingly insulting or offending an audience, even a single audience member, will get you nowhere. You may not like a particular person or his or her position, but purposely injecting unneeded negativity into the situation will damage your credibility and destroy any chance of conveying your message successfully. Sometimes it is hard to maintain your composure if someone is heckling or being rude when you are speaking, but even in these instances you should keep a moderate tone of voice. People always respond to your tone before your message, so staying moderate and calm will help diffuse the situation and enhance your credibility because you will be seen as reasonable.

Beyond keeping a moderate tone, you also owe it to yourself and your audience to be polite and professional. Losing your patience or temper will eliminate any chance of reaching an audience, and you could even lose the respect of those people who support you. This does not mean you cannot call the hecklers out on their behavior, but you must do so in a civil way. This involves first describing their behavior and then asking them to hold their comments and concerns until after you have finished speaking. Unfortunately, there are occasions when this technique does not work, but you still cannot allow yourself to get agitated and focus on the heckler. This is not what the rest of the audience came for, and you should not give one person more attention than everyone else in the room. Explaining this may also help the situation. Additionally, members of the audience may come to your aid if you appear reasonable in dealing with the heckler.

Describe People With Respect. As speakers, we often like to use colorful language to describe ideas, places, and even people. We must be careful, however, in choosing how we describe others so we don't risk offending our audience by not treating others as people. When we use images of animals or objects to refer to people in a negative way, we are dehumanizing the people—that is, making them appear to be less than human. This insults and demeans people by depriving them of being the very thing that they are: human beings.

Using dehumanizing language to describe people is very tempting when we do not agree with them or if we are in conflict with them over something. In fact, such a technique is very common in presidential war rhetoric. It makes it more likely that other people will see the person being dehumanized as an animal and not a person, thus making it less likely that the target audience will respect the person. In war, such imagery actually makes it easier for people to engage in violent behaviors against an enemy they do not view as being human.

Furthermore, it is important to use gender-inclusive language when describing roles so you are not using language to inadvertently exclude a particular group. The titles of many professional roles have changed to reflect the inclusion of both men and women in those professions, and as a speaker you should respect others by using inclusive language. Table 3.1 provides several examples of gender-inclusive language.

Table 3.1

GENDER INCLUSIVE LANGUAGE	
INAPPROPRIATE	APPROPRIATE
Policeman	Police officer
Mailman	Mail carrier
Stewardess	Flight attendant
Mankind	Humankind

Language, as we will discuss later, is a very powerful tool. Being an ethical speaker requires you to respect your audience's humanity even when you do not agree with them. Such respect will help foster a more effective dialogue over differences, instead of a combat rooted in insults.

Carefully Consider Profanity. Profanity is a common part of everyday language. We see it in movies, hear it on television, laugh at it when it is used by comedians, and even use it to describe everyday situations and frustrations. Despite its common usage, you should think very carefully before making an intentional rhetorical decision about whether to use profanity in your presentation. Evaluate your audience; while some audiences might be amused at a well-placed curse word, others may find the use of profanity offensive and unprofessional. Curse words can be used to convey powerful emotions, which in some situations might deepen the impact of a particular moment in your speech, but in others can damage your credibility and leave an impression that you do not respect the audience or that you do not have the linguistic sophistication to choose more meaningful language.

Balance Simplicity and Complexity. Acting ethically when delivering a speech also requires that you make an honest attempt to speak to your audience on their level. What this means is that you take care not to oversimplify or overcomplicate things for your audience. To ensure you understand what your audience knows about a subject or concept, you should review any audience analysis data available. This will enable you to approach topics with a clearer idea of what the audience knows and what they do not.

If you walk into a speech expecting that your audience knows nothing about the subject on which you are speaking, then you run a high risk of insulting their intelligence and losing their attention during the presentation. For example, if an engineer delivers remarks to a group of mechanics on the model for a new engine design and begins with a detailed description of why cars need engines, the speaker will have lost the audience and will likely be perceived as condescending. On the other hand, if you expect your audience to know things they do not know, it will result in negative audience perceptions as well. Take the case of the engineer and change the audience to a group of middle school students. If the engineer uses technical terms that middle schoolers do not know, then he will lose the audience, and they will also see the engineer as arrogant and ineffective. For this reason, knowing your audience and making an attempt to meet them on their intellectual level is essential for ethical speaking. No one likes to be made to feel unintelligent.

Balance Emotion and Logic. Oftentimes when we feel passionate about an issue or idea, we inject that enthusiasm into our speech. Additionally, we try and "push" people to agree with us by using emotional stories. These elements of an appeal definitely have their place, but capitalizing on emotion to move an audience denies them the opportunity to sift and weigh the evidence for themselves and come to their own decisions on the matter. As speakers, we need to respect the ability of our audience to make an informed decision for themselves and not fear that they might disagree with our position. To that end, we must balance emotion with logic, for emotional appeals can be very influential when speaking to an audience.

Emotions are a powerful force in our lives, and some of the strongest emotions are negative. Consider anger, rage, jealousy, hatred, and envy. These are powerful forces that have been manipulated by speakers time and again throughout history to get audiences to act in ways they normally would not if they were also provided accurate evidence. Look no further than the case of Adolf Hitler, whose words capitalized on a downtrodden German populace by igniting anger in them toward a specific group of people. This resulted in one of the most inhumane periods in human history: the Holocaust.

The power of emotions does not solely lie in negative feelings; positive emotions can also be powerful. Some of these are love, pride, joy, and gratitude. Think of commercials calling on you to donate to Doctors Without Borders, a charity that finances medical assistance in impoverished countries. The appeal focuses on activating your love, or even sympathy, for the plight of other humans in order to get you to donate to their cause. This is a positive emotion you feel, and an equally positive cause, but creating an appeal based on emotion alone denies the audience the opportunity to properly evaluate the organization and its mission.

Although humans are emotional beings and emotions can be used successfully, especially in a persuasive speech, relying upon them alone constitutes unethical behavior. If people make decisions based primarily on emotion, then they might make decisions that lack logic and reasoning. Audiences make better decisions, and speakers make better cases for their argument, when emotions are tied to logic. So, when developing your speech, incorporate appeals to emotions in tandem with the logic and evidence you use.

Up until now, we have focused our attention on the ethical requirements of speakers, but they are not the only ones with such obligations. In the next section, we discuss the ethical dimensions of being a good audience member.

ETHICS AS AN AUDIENCE MEMBER

Even though the spotlight remains on a speaker during a presentation, there are still ethical responsibilities to which audience members are beholden. Too often in today's smartphone-dominated world audience, members do things such as send text messages, check emails, or even do work during someone else's presentation. These types of behaviors are not innocuous and innocent; rather, they are rude and unethical. Speakers put a lot of work into their presentations, and audience members have the responsibility to listen attentively and respectfully.

Listening as an Audience Member

One of the most important ethical obligations of audience members is to listen to the speaker. Listening is more complicated than people realize. Often we confuse it with **hearing**, which is the physiological process of capturing sound conducted by ears to the brain. **Listening**, however, as defined by the International Listening Association, is "an information processing task carried out in a social, interactive, or communicative environment."[1] More succinctly, listening is the process of receiving and interpreting spoken or nonverbal messages. Listening, therefore, is communicative, while hearing is physiological. Hearing is something our bodies do, while listening is a skill we can develop and improve. There are four primary listening purposes that we can engage in.

The first reason we engage in listening is for appreciation. When we **listen for appreciation**, our goal is to enjoy something on which we focus our attention. The most common examples of this type of listening are listening to music while driving or working out, listening to dialogue in a movie or television show, listening to a comedian on the radio, and listening to a story told by a friend. There is not a high degree of cognitive effort when we listen for appreciation. The goal here is to have fun with what you are listening to, and not to necessarily understand the motives behind what is said or to disagree with what the other party may be proposing.

The second reason we listen is to comprehend or understand something. When we **listen for comprehension**, we want to understand something we do not know so that we can learn something new. We engage in listening for comprehension when we take a class and listen to a lecture, go through orientation with a new employer, and even when we meet someone new and they share information about themselves. This type of listening requires more mental effort than appreciative listening, and the goal is not necessarily enjoyment, but rather, understanding.

The third reason we listen is to show support in a relationship. When we **listen to show support**, we are listening to someone else because we want the other person to feel like they are valued and that we care about what they have to say. The goal in this type of listening is to develop or maintain a relationship and to demonstrate how much we care about the other person. When we listen as someone tells us about their day, share in a friend's good

---

hearing
the physiological process of capturing sound conducted by ears to the brain

listening
the process of receiving and interpreting spoken and/or nonverbal messages

listening for appreciation
listening for enjoyment; it is not high in cognitive commitment

listening for comprehension
listening to understand and learn something new; requires a significant degree of mental effort

listening to show support
listening to someone in order to make them feel valued and to show that we care about what they have to say

---

1. International Listening Association, *Priorities of Listening Research: Four Interrelated Initiatives*, 2008, http://www.listen.org/Resources/Documents/White_Paper_PrioritiesResearch.pdf, 9.

news, or lend a sympathetic ear to someone who needs to vent about a tough situation, we are listening to show support for that relationship.

The fourth, and final, purpose listening serves is criticism, but not in the form of negative attacks on someone else. **Critical listening** is when we evaluate a message and assess whether or not we agree with what is said. When we listen critically, we also are open to the fact that we may disagree with a part or even all of a message, yet we take in everything offered by the other side before making our judgment. To do this requires the largest degree of cognitive effort of the three listening purposes. We may listen critically to a political speech, a proposal for weekend plans by friends, and sometimes to lectures on controversial topics or materials.

critical listening
when we evaluate a message and assess whether or not we agree with what is said; requires the most cognitive effort of any listening purpose

Regardless of what our goal is with listening, we use listening in one of two different ways. The first is **active listening**, which occurs when we pay a high degree of attention to a message. We process, store, and potentially evaluate the content of the message to come to conclusions or an understanding about what was said. We also usually show that we are listening by using eye contact and facial expressions to respond to the message, and perhaps even leaning in or nodding. We use active listening at times for each of the four purposes we just explained.

active listening
when we pay a high degree of attention to a message; we process, store, and potentially evaluate the content of the message to come to conclusions or an understanding about what was said

We might be watching a murder mystery or someone may be telling us a very engaging story about a trip he or she just took, and we pay those messages a great deal of attention because we want to understand or evaluate what is being relayed to us. That would constitute active listening for appreciation. Active listening for comprehension or criticism would involve paying attention so you completely understand what is said and can either integrate it into your own body of knowledge (comprehension) or determine whether you agree with what was proposed or not (criticism).

The second way we might listen is passively. **Passive listening** occurs when we do not engage the topic in any noticeable way and just try to absorb what is said. When we listen passively, we do not engage in much evaluation, nor do we question our own understanding of what is said. Most listening for appreciation is passive listening, but you can also see examples of people who are passively listening for comprehension or criticism when you look around a classroom and see people who do not participate or ask questions about the content. Passive listening can be risky because you elevate the chances of daydreaming and losing your ability to follow the speaker.

passive listening
occurs when we do not engage the topic in any noticeable way and just try to absorb what is said

Regardless of which listening purpose we try to achieve and whether we do so actively or passively, we do not always listen the way we want, and sometimes we fail to listen at all. In the next part of this chapter we will unpack several different behaviors people may think are listening, but really are not.

Other Responsibilities for Audience Members

Keep an Open Mind. Audience members should always approach a speech or presentation as an opportunity to learn something new. If you do this and keep an open mind to what the speaker is saying, you are giving the speaker the respect that their work and effort deserve. There might be ideas in the speech with which you disagree, but there might also be ideas in the speech with which you agree. Being ethical and responsible audience members means that we should give the speaker the benefit of the doubt and hold our own biases in check so we can concentrate on the message. It is entirely possible that the speaker might change our opinion on something, but even if we do not ultimately change our opinion, we have allowed the speaker the opportunity to present ideas to us. It is, after all, what we would want if the situation were reversed.

Do Not Heckle. Too often we see people attending political meetings who interrupt speakers and yell at them in the middle of their presentations. Just because we disagree with speakers does not give us the right to attack them and interrupt their remarks. Heckling is particularly nasty when the interrupter tries to demean the speaker. The end result of heckling is an uncomfortable environment for everyone else, and hecklers actually call negative attention to themselves. A heckler's disruptions can upset and throw off the speaker, and heckling can upset and interfere with the message reception of the other audience members. Just as you have ethical responsibilities to the speaker, you have ethical responsibilities to your fellow audience members. If the speaker or the message upsets you so much that you feel warranted to engage in heckling, you should remove yourself from the environment and let the event continue instead of disturbing it for everyone else. Hecklers often wrongly assume that everyone else in the audience agrees with them, and they have thus prejudged not only the speaker, but also their fellow audience members.

Pay Attention. It is true that we will find some speakers and their topics boring, but our lack of interest doesn't mean we can do something else during the presentation. We might think speakers can't see us holding our cell phones, searching the internet, or sending a text, but they almost always notice, and it distracts them. Such behavior tells speakers that you think they are boring and unimportant and can damage the speaker's confidence in an already challenging situation.

There are nonverbal behaviors that audience members engage in that distract the speaker and the audience. For example, putting your head down on your desk, slouching in your seat, and closing your eyes are all disrespectful to a speaker. A speaker could infer a lot of different things from these behaviors, such as laziness, indifference, and even contempt. That said, these nonverbal behaviors are not the worst things an audience member can do; the worst is when members of the audience start talking to each other during a presentation. It is a simple rule not to engage in side conversations when someone else is speaking.

In your public speaking class, you have the ethical obligation to pay attention to all speakers, just as you would want your classmates to do when you're speaking. Giving a speech is hard for many people, as we covered in the last chapter, and your attention can actually give them support and strength while they are speaking and can improve their performance. No one likes to be ignored or mocked when they are speaking, so we should all be respectful audience members when someone is delivering remarks.

Summary

In this chapter, we discussed the concept of ethics and how it applies to public speaking. We explained that messages cannot be retrieved once spoken, and we covered the ethical responsibilities of a speaker throughout the speech preparation and delivery process. Finally, we covered the ethical obligations of audience members. Ethics are important in all walks of life and are certainly an important element in the communication process.

Key Terms

active listening 39

critical listening 39

ethics 27

global plagiarism 32

hearing 38

incremental plagiarism 32

listening 38

listening for appreciation 38

listening for comprehension 38

listening to show support 38

passive listening 39

patchwork plagiarism 32

patchworking 32

plagiarism 31

Activities

1   For each of the four purposes of listening, identify a couple of situations not already included in the book in which you should use each type of listening.

2   Find a newspaper article or academic research article. Write a one-paragraph summary of the article that uses appropriate paraphrasing rather than patchwork plagiarism.

3   Identify three words or phrases (not the ones already identified in the book) that might exclude members of your audience. What are some more inclusive words or phrases you can use instead?

4   Find three examples of what you consider to be unethical behavior by a speaker or an audience member. Explain why they are unethical.

CIVILITY

Objectives

◊ Define the core components of civility and its relationship to communication

◊ Identify foundational civil behaviors that can increase communication effectiveness

◊ Discuss civility in action in a variety of different contexts

At some point in all our lives we all have, or will be, subjected to the rude, nasty, and impolite comments or behaviors of others. Incivility takes many forms, from the "horrible boss" to the lazy colleague, from vandalism to making physical threats, from belittling others to interrupting someone when they are speaking, from giving someone the silent treatment to talking over them, and the list goes on and on. Even though most people believe that incivility is unethical, wrong, and inappropriate, people fail to realize it comes with tangible costs from the damage it does to the receiver.

The *Harvard Business Review* conducted a survey in 2013 and discovered that incivility results in significant unforeseen expenses to the organization; those expenses come from the way people internalize such actions. They found that of those who been treated uncivilly in the workplace:

◊ 48% decreased their work effort

◊ 47% intentionally decreased the time spent at work

◊ 38% intentionally decreased the quality of their work

◊ 80% lost significant time worrying over the uncivil incident

◊ 63% lost time avoiding the perpetrator of the offense

◊ 66% reported their productivity declined

◊ 78% reported that their loyalty to the organization declined

Of all who responded to the survey, a quarter of those even said they took out their frustrations on customers.[1]

---

1. Christine Porath and Christine Pearson, "The Price of Incivility," *Harvard Business Review*, January/February, 2013, https://hbr.org/2013/01/the-price-of-incivility.

These facts are staggering and should serve as further evidence as to why civility is an effective and ethical part of our communication repertoire.

In this chapter we will discuss the concept of civility, specifically as it pertains to our speaking choices. First, we will define the core components of civility and illustrate that the concept is not what many people seem to think it is. We will then describe the foundational behaviors of civility. Finally, we will describe what civility looks like in action in a variety of contexts.

DEFINING CIVILITY

Many people today confuse the notion of civility with a form of fakery, where people hide their own feelings about something or someone to avoid conflict. Others view civility and politeness as a form of weakness that invites bullying and leads to sacrificing personal positions, goals, and feelings for no good reason. These misconceptions make the idea of civil behavior appear useless and ineffective in society. Instead of viewing civility in a negative light, it is useful to conceive of it in relation to "civilization" and "being civilized." In these contexts, civility does not mean fakery. Rather, it means the ability to have lasting, stable, and peaceful interactions with others. In this part of the chapter, we explore some of the components that serve as the foundation of civility. Understand that each of these is a component of civility, but on their own, the components are not synonymous with civility.

Politeness

polite
showing consideration for others in accordance with social decorum

It is understandable that civility is often confused with politeness because politeness is a component of civility; however, the two are not the same. The term polite refers to showing consideration for others in accordance with social decorum. Politeness may be best understood in contrast to rudeness, which is acting in a way that violates social decency or demonstrates a lack of social skills and appreciation for others. On the one hand, people who are deemed "polite" have made some effort to consider other people and how they feel. On the other hand, we sometimes view politeness in others not as a nicety, but as a tool to manipulate and deceive us or as a condescending form of communication.

Politeness can mask our own feelings, but being civil requires us to assert our feelings in a respectful manner. A civil person is honest, but not in a way that offends the other party. Civil politeness requires that we be polite not by sparing others the truth, but by making both them and us feel good about our deeds and actions through an honest and respectful delivery of information. For instance, there should not be a need to issue a polite lie, because it comes across as disingenuous and simply plays upon the perception most people have today when someone is "just being polite." Rather, polite civility issues the truth in a way that does not intentionally hurt anyone involved. This is, as you can imagine, a challenging task to accomplish. Politeness, though, is only one part of the civility equation.

Good Manners

The second component of civility might remind you of children because they are constantly reminded to say "please" and "thank you" as elements of good manners. **Good manners** refer to behaviors that societies deem appropriate and positive ways of interacting with others. As you can imagine, when understood this way, good manners are not restricted to children, nor are they as simple as just saying "please" and "thank you." In fact, we have even gone so far as a society to police certain types of manners to ensure they are practiced.[2]

good manners behaviors that societies deem as appropriate and positive ways of interacting with others

Some good manners are laid out in rules, while others are born more out of social expectations. In terms of rules, consider when we go to the movies or a play and we are asked to silence cell phones before the start of the show because the noise of a phone ringing, holding a conversation, or texting during a show distracts others from enjoying it. There are other good manners people should practice simply because they demonstrate an appreciation for other people, such as the following:

◊   Be on time for meetings and appointments.

◊   Don't gloat when you win or sulk when you lose.

◊   Don't talk with your mouth full.

◊   Patiently wait in line.

◊   Don't ask intimate or sensitive questions—even if you ask permission first.

◊   Don't make rude or sarcastic comments that devalue the work or character of others.

Such behaviors are core elements of civility and represent practicing politeness, especially in American culture. They also easily apply to public speaking. If you are speaking, be on time and stay within the time you are given

---

2. For examples of the codification of manners in society, see the *Miss Manners* website, which can be found at http://www.missmanners.com/.

to speak—especially if others will be speaking after you. Do not use a speech to gloat, ask insensitive questions, make rude comments, or attack another's character. Civility is, however, even more than being genuinely polite and practicing good manners.

Courtesy

courtesy
a show of consideration for and attention to others

A third component of civility is **courtesy**, which refers to showing consideration for and attention to others. We often refer to courtesy as common because we believe that everyone exhibits these basic behaviors. Common courtesies include actions such as holding a door open for the next person to come through, standing up to greet someone when he or she enters your room or office, and acknowledging drivers who allow you into traffic in front of them. These are small gestures in a day that cost nothing, but generate good feelings by letting others know we pay attention to and value them. In a speaking situation, courtesy can be waiting for someone to finish speaking before leaving or speaking yourself, and perhaps even clapping at the end of a presentation, even if you disagreed with the presenter. At their heart, common courtesies involve an understanding of one's surroundings and respect for others, which brings us to our next component of civility.

Respect for Others

respect
an acknowledgment of the inherent humanity and dignity of other people

Civility requires that we be polite, practice good manners, and extend courtesy to others because it is fundamentally about respecting other people. By **respect** we mean to say an acknowledgement of the inherent humanity and dignity of other people. Respect does not require deference to others, but rather an acknowledgement of them, and an attempt to understand how they may feel about a statement, action, or event. We belittle others when we ignore them or behave as though their thoughts, feelings, and opinions do not matter. When such things are done to us, we become upset and feel as though we do not belong. Referring to people by their proper names and titles, and learning how to correctly pronounce their names before speaking are all basic ways we can show respect to others when we deliver remarks.

Respect can be shown in different ways. It can mean we place individuals or their opinions in high esteem and value them more than others because of an existing relationship or some type of expertise they bring to the table. It can also mean an appreciation for an honor or the position a person holds. At a minimum, however, we should display empathy toward everyone as individuals and acknowledge their feelings and thoughts. Doing so will encourage reciprocity, which means the other person would hopefully return that respect in their interactions with you. This is the road to creating a culture of civility, and is also the road to creating a positive environment in which to speak. There is, however, one more dimension of civility we must discuss.

Assertiveness

After detailing the first four elements of civility, it may seem as though civility largely asks us to suppress our own ideas and thoughts in deference to others, but nothing could be further from the truth. It may seem easier to simply try to please others by allowing them to state their positions while we keep ours to ourselves, but such actions actually do not demonstrate a respect for ourselves or others. Civility demands honesty and the ability to clearly and confidently state our positions, as well as respectfully listen to those of others. In fact, one of the hardest actions to assert is also the first word many children learn: the ability to say "no."

As Pier Massimo Forni, a professor at Johns Hopkins University who taught and wrote about civility, notes, "'No' to others is nothing but a 'yes' to ourselves," and by saying "no" we aren't "taking something that belongs to others; we are simply keeping something that is rightfully ours."[3] When people ask something of us, we are not required to give it, nor are we required to explain why to them, though we may feel it right and necessary to do so in some situations. The ability to say "no" to others and "yes" to ourselves is a key element of civility. We may believe that saying "no" will injure, or perhaps even destroy, our relationship with the other person, but if we do not protect our own interests and time, we might be doing that anyway.[4] In freely giving our time, treasure, and talents to others, even when we do not want to do so, we may create an imbalanced relationship with the other person. Being assertive simply means we respect ourselves just as much as we respect others. Without this final piece, civility is nothing more than sacrificing oneself to the interests of the other.

To that end, we define **civility** as the use of tact when dealing with others—a genuine and reciprocal expression of respect for ourselves and others through our actions and statements. Now that we have explained the characteristics of civility, we turn our attention to how we practice civility.

civility
the use of tact when dealing with others; a genuine and reciprocal expression of respect for ourselves and others through actions and statements

---

3. Pier Massimo Forni, *Choosing Civility: The Twenty-Five Rules of Considerate Conduct* (New York: St. Martin's Press, 2002).

4. Forni, *Choosing Civility*, 2002.

FOUNDATIONAL CIVIL BEHAVIORS

We have already covered the five core components of civility and how civility relates to the presentation of ourselves to others. We now move to a discussion of three foundational behaviors that all civil communication has in common: mutual respect, listening, and disagreeing without being disagreeable.

Mutual Respect

A civil culture depends on its members valuing mutual respect. We all must begin believing in the best that people can be and the goodness of their intentions, and show respect for their values, experiences, and expertise in the same way we wish them to do for us. Mutual respect is not driven by our achievements, positions, or titles, but rather by our inherent humanity and value as human beings. All people bring something to the table from which we might learn, and we must respect that for them to respect what we have to offer. Without genuine mutual respect, we cannot have a civil society.

This is not to say that everyone must behave this way for it to work; in fact, that is not the case even today. It is, however, an invitation to begin the effort of making society more civil by respecting those with whom we come into contact. Think about other people and their potential reactions when crafting your speeches, pay attention to their reactions when they hear what you have to say, and show appreciation to them for listening to you. This applies to audience members as well; when acting in that capacity, pay attention to your reactions and show mutual respect while listening and asking questions.

Listening

To be civil, we must listen to what the other party is saying, giving them our undivided attention. We may believe we can multitask and pay attention to multiple items at once, but this is a myth. In his book *Brain Rules*, John Medina explains that it is actually physically impossible for our brains to focus on two things at once, which makes paying attention to more than one person impractical and uncivil.[5] Genuine listening is the manifestation of respecting other people and being present with them.

Listening also entails the ability to come to an understanding of what the other person is saying. This may require you to ask clarifying questions,

---

5. John Medina, *Brain Rules: 12 Principles for Surviving and Thriving at Work, Home and School* (Seattle: Pear Press, 2008).

paraphrase messages, or otherwise check perceptions when the time is appropriate to do so. Remember that making sure you understand the other person is a hallmark of genuine listening. It does not mean that you agree with the other person, just that you understand what is being said.

Disagree Without Being Disagreeable

Civility requires us to express ourselves and assert our positions. This does not limit itself to moments of agreement. We also must be able to express ourselves when we disagree. Unfortunately, people tend to view agreement and disagreement as the only two options available, when in fact they are not absolutes. More often than not, we find ourselves wanting to agree with parts of a person's argument while disagreeing with other aspects of it.

To express such complicated positions in which we both agree and disagree at the same time calls for specific and delicate skills. In order to do this, it is important to first stress areas of agreement with the other party. This establishes a more comfortable climate for the interaction and enables both parties to see the exchange in a positive and constructive light. When focusing on areas of agreement, be as detailed as you would be with those things with which you disagree. Then, after expressing agreement, detail those points with which you disagree and explain why.

The explanation is important because it shows you listened to the other party but have information of your own to offer to the discussion. In more tense situations, it may also be necessary to conclude with a statement reinforcing that just because you disagree with all or parts of the other person's argument, it does not mean you do not like or appreciate that person. The position is not the person, and agreement and disagreement are not "all or nothing" propositions.

Now that we have reviewed the foundational civil behaviors (which are also listed in Table 4.1), next, we will briefly explore the practice of civility today.

Table 4.1

SUGGESTED BEHAVIORS FOR A CIVIL INTERACTION
· Describe instead of evaluate.
· Focus on the problem, not on controlling the outcome.
· Acknowledge the feelings of others.
· Be provisional instead of certain.
· Control your facial expressions.
· Do not interrupt others when they are speaking.
· Do not disparage others when they are not present.
· When disagreeing, describe both the points with which you disagree and agree.

CONTEMPORARY CONTEXTS FOR CIVILITY

In this section of the chapter we briefly discuss four settings in which we can apply civil communication to improve understanding and general wellness in our social relationships. We begin with those in your own immediate context: the classroom.

Civility in the Classroom and on Campus

Learning for every student in a classroom depends upon a civil atmosphere, and the responsibility for creating this environment falls on both instructors and students. This is why some faculty choose to engage students in creating a "code of conduct" in their classes, complete with agreed-upon consequences for violations. In public speaking courses, this often takes the form of expectations such as not working on assignments for another class when you should be listening to a peer's speech, waiting outside the room until a speech is finished before coming in, and staying silent during a speech by a classmate, just to name a few. Faculty, on the other hand, may pledge to allow students time to begin their speech so they can get comfortable in front of the classroom, help keep question-and-answer sessions running smoothly, and provide prompt and specific feedback for student performances.

Students also bear a significant portion of the responsibility for creating a civil classroom climate. Students should not argue with instructors for the sake of arguing, nor equate instructor experience and knowledge with opinion. Students should also begin emails and visits to the office with cordial introductions and conclude them with genuine notes of gratitude. They also should treat one another with respect and listen to peers when they offer questions and commentary, and rather than judge peers for their ideas, engage with them to understand the thinking behind the statements their peers make. Finally, students should follow course rules and policies as outlined in the syllabus, particularly those regarding laptop and cell phone use. Searching the internet or texting a friend during class is rude to both one's instructor and classmates. Simple behaviors such as these, when followed by both instructors and students, create a classroom environment that is more conducive to learning.

Civility in Interpersonal Relationships

We maintain multiple relationships in our lives. These include those with friends, family, coworkers, and even the barista at your local coffee shop. At home, you probably behave with respect toward your parents, siblings, and significant others, but conflicts still arise. With your friends you also practice a degree of civility, but sometimes you may say something to which they might take offense. Generally, people are accepting of genuine apologies, but these apologies are also simultaneously very difficult for us to issue. We do not like admitting when we are wrong, and even when we do admit it, we often qualify the apology with some explanation. If you are going to apologize, do so earnestly and without a qualification. This civil practice can go a long way toward maintaining healthy relationships with those closest to you.

Civility, however, also extends to those you encounter elsewhere, but with whom you may not be close. Salespeople, hotel front desk agents, and even the person who makes your morning coffee all deserve the same type of respect and civility you accord to family and friends. Sometimes, simply having a brief conversation in which you ask about a person's day or just say "good morning" can go a long way toward showing appreciation for that other person. It is also important to recognize that people in these roles have lives with which you are unfamiliar, and they are "real people" too. So, if someone in one of these roles says something or behaves in a way that frustrates or upsets you, concentrate your disapproval on the behavior or statement and not the person. If you do this, you will more likely come to a quicker and more acceptable resolution, while not unnecessarily upsetting or ruining someone else's day.

Civility in Business

To conduct business effectively requires civil conduct by people in various positions. These behaviors can be as simple as respecting the time of others by not being late to scheduled meetings or calling well in advance to reschedule them if necessary. It also includes things such as knocking before entering offices, not taking calls or checking text messages in the middle of meetings, and learning the names of those present at a meeting. Business relationships occur between two or more people, and the emphasis should be on the fact that they are people first. People are very quick to change providers or go with a different company if they feel they are treated as numbers instead of valued clients.

In an increasingly global environment, successful business relationships also require that people learn and value the cultural backgrounds of all parties. This means adhering to cultural expectations of host countries, but also understanding how other people interact. In some Asian cultures, for example, direct discussion of business only comes after a lengthy socialization process so all involved get to know each other. In fact, people often make business deals with others with whom they feel the most comfortable, not necessarily those who submit the best offer. It is important to know that up-front, blunt communication may not always be the best route to go.

Civility and Social Media

People today increasingly use social media to stay in touch with friends and family, conduct business, and promote themselves and their products. Snapchat, Instagram, Twitter, and the business-oriented LinkedIn are just a few of the social media tools employed to accomplish these tasks. Even though these resources do not allow for face-to-face communication, they do not reduce or eliminate the need for civil communication. Civility is more than just behaving well when others are in front of you; it is a lifestyle where we always genuinely think about how what we say and do can affect other people.

To this end, it is instructive to think before posting status updates to Facebook, issuing a tweet about how you feel regarding an event or issue, or even uploading your resume to LinkedIn. Remember that you need not share everything on social media sites, and that what you choose to share is now on the internet forever, for everyone.[6] The internet is like plastic—it never goes away—so you should make sure that what you post will be acceptable later, as well as now. Take care when issuing comments to others as well, and even if you disagree, do so with respect and make sure it is the position, and not the person, with which you disagree.

And yet, just because you may feel a certain way and can post it through social media does not necessarily mean you should. Additionally, we communicate more and more through email, but that medium is not always used in a way that promotes civil correspondence between people. Email is an extraordinary tool for communication, but it is also rife with potential pitfalls. Table 4.2 provides some guidelines for email and social media use that will help ensure you use them to maximum effect while also remaining civil in the tone of what you write.

Table 4.2

SOME THINGS TO CONSIDER WHEN WRITING AN EMAIL
IN GENERAL
• Use email to request or provide succinct pieces of objective information.
• Avoid discussing sensitive issues through email.
• Use email to publicly praise, but not to blame employees.
• Use email to share insights, not to instigate confrontation.
• Judiciously use the "blind carbon copy" function.
AS SENDER
• Give emails a clear and direct subject heading.
• Get to the point.
• Avoid hedgers and qualifiers as phrases.
• If asking a question, be sure to ask the question (don't issue evaluation).
• Specify who should respond.
• Be clear about when you need a response.
• Provide relevant context.
• Limit email to one message, one topic.
• Provide brief summary when sending an "FYI" or forward email.
• Don't use sarcasm.

---

6. Meredith Fineman, "What We Post Online Is Forever, and We Need a Reminder," *Inc.*, November 24, 2014, https://www.inc.com/meredith-fineman/what-we-post-online-is-forever-and-we-need-a-reminder.html.

SOME THINGS TO CONSIDER WHEN WRITING AN EMAIL
AS RECEIVER
• Don't make assumptions about sender's emotional state.
• Don't escalate by sending an emotionally charged response (sleep on it; perhaps don't reply by email).
• Don't respond right away.
• Be careful quoting emails out of context in a reply.

Summary

In this chapter we have covered the concept of civility. We have defined it as something that contains certain core components, such as politeness, good manners, courteousness, respect for others, and assertiveness. We detailed some specific behaviors that help us practice civility and described how those behaviors should and could manifest in specific everyday scenarios in which we find ourselves.

Key Terms

civility 47

courtesy 46

good manners 45

polite 44

respect 46

Activities

1 Using some of the suggested behaviors for civil interaction from the chapter, as well as the foundational behaviors of civil interaction, develop a code of conduct for students and instructors in a classroom environment. Then develop one for the workplace. Are there any differences? What are the differences, and why do you think they exist?

2 Just as the norms of civility in Western civilization have changed throughout history, so too are they different between cultures. What are some cultural differences in expectations for civil behavior?

3 Civility can sometimes be used to silence others from speaking, such as telling someone who is disagreeing with you that they are "not being civil." How does this application differ from the use of civility in this chapter? Does this make civility bad? Why, or why not?

SPEAKING IN YOUR CAREER

Objectives

◊ Introduce students to the relationship between speech and context

◊ Explain some general contextual factors that can influence a presentation

◊ Discuss speech in different academic and professional contexts

What is the most important skill for career success? Surveys of employers across a wide range of industries show that oral communication is the most sought-after skill, followed closely by critical thinking and analytic reasoning, ethical judgment and decision-making, and the ability to work effectively on teams.[1] The findings are echoed by numerous other employer surveys.[2] Even Google, one of the companies that historically focused on hiring specifically for engineering talent, did an intensive analysis of all hiring, firing, and promotion data since the company was founded, and discovered that communication skills were among the most important skills that predicted success as an engineering manager and as a member of an engineering team.[3] Another even more recent study sought to identify the most important foundational skills in the digital economy, and again, communication was identified as one of the most important skills, regardless of industry, and was also noted as being critically important for moving up into management roles in the digital economy.[4] Even though

---

1. Hart Research Associates, *Fulfilling the American Dream: Liberal Education and the Future of Work*, July 2018, https://www.aacu.org/sites/default/files/files/LEAP/2018EmployerResearchReport.pdf.

2. Francesca Levy and Christopher Cannon, "The Bloomberg Job Skills Report 2016: What Recruiters Want," *Bloomberg*, February 9, 2016, https://www.bloomberg.com/graphics/2016-job-skills-report/; "Job Outlook 2016: The Attributes Employers Want to See on New College Graduates' Resumes," NACE Center for Career Development and Talent Acquisition, National Association of Colleges and Employers, updated 2016, http://www.naceweb.org/career-development/trends-and-predictions/job-outlook-2016-attributes-employers-want-to-see-on-new-college-graduates-resumes/ .

3. Valerie Strauss, "The Surprising Thing Google Learned About its Employees—and What it Means for Today's Students," *Washington Post*, December 20, 2017, https://www.washingtonpost.com/news/answer-sheet/wp/2017/12/20/the-surprising-thing-google-learned-about-its-employees-and-what-it-means-for-todays-students/.

4. Burning Glass Technologies and Business-Higher Education Forum, *The New Foundational Skills of the Digital Economy: Developing the Professionals of the Future*, 2018, https://www.burning-glass.com/wp-content/uploads/New_Foundational_Skills.pdf?fbclid=IwAR0OMRKPNLXPxwimhhsAotaI3dng8myAZy2R9koj4hReQM3y0OxJeoEZ9-M.

communication skills—including public speaking, listening, interpersonal skills, teamwork, intercultural communication skills, and more—are often referred to as "soft skills," they are critical to your success in any career and are now being referred to by many as "essential" or "fundamental skills."[5]

Communication does not take place in a vacuum. In fact, understanding messages requires an appreciation of the situation in which the message is conveyed. In the United States, people communicate very directly with each other, often trying to "say what they mean." This is not the case in other cultures where people will be more indirect, requiring audience members to examine situational cues and information to infer the meaning in a statement. Whether a message is direct or indirect, however, we are still called upon to examine and appreciate context when developing and interpreting messages.

In addition to cultural differences, specific fields and professions have certain expectations regarding how messages should be communicated. Regardless of whether you want to pursue a career in teaching, politics, engineering, business, health, or something else, knowing how to present your ideas to an audience is essential. In this chapter we will first discuss the concept of context and some of its common aspects—regardless of your chosen career field—to which you need to pay attention when constructing and delivering messages. Then we will discuss five popular professional contexts in which you may find yourself: politics, education, the STEM fields (science, technology, engineering, and mathematics), business, and health. In each of these contexts, the process of developing and delivering messages holds different expectations and challenges. To better appreciate these challenges, though, let's begin with a discussion of some general characteristics of contexts.

CONTEXTUAL FACTORS

Regardless of your profession, there are some typical contextual factors that exist in virtually any public speaking situation. These elements of the speaking environment include the external environment, the speaking format, and general audience characteristics. In this section of the chapter, we will briefly discuss each of these before delving into more specific issues pertaining to particular careers.

---

5. Carmine Gallo, "Public Speaking Is No Longer a 'Soft' Skill. It's Your Key to Success in Any Field," *Inc.*, January 4, 2019, https://www.inc.com/carmine-gallo/public-speaking-is-no-longer-a-soft-skill-its-your-key-to-success-in-any-field.html.

External Environment

It's easy to imagine a variety of speaking situations. You could be called upon to deliver remarks outdoors, or in a large or small room. As the speaker, it is important to pay attention to the environment in which you will speak, because each environment carries with it certain advantages and challenges.

One speaking environment is outdoors. Despite the fact that we think most presentations take place inside a boardroom or conference hall, there are still plenty of opportunities to speak outdoors, so it is important to understand the environmental issues related to this speaking situation. Many weddings and festivals have moments when key participants are called upon to make brief remarks, and these situations have some challenges not present when speaking in an enclosed space such as a meeting room.

When speaking outdoors, there are more competing noises that can overshadow your remarks. Airplanes, cars, and the wind can create an environment that requires you to speak loudly or find a microphone. When a speech takes place outside, audience members may also come and go more freely because of the open nature of the space, creating more distractions. Finally, outdoor presentations are often controlled by weather, so speakers must be prepared to move indoors if the weather changes.

When speaking indoors, there are two different environments in which you may find yourself: a large room or a small room. You could have a large or small audience, but let's assume for the sake of the discussion that there is an adequate-sized audience in either environment. There are significant challenges to both situations, so let's discuss the large-room environment first.

In a large room, you will not know everyone in the audience, and so the first obstacle is identifying with such a large group. Typically, you must make an effort to verbally identify with the audience early in your speech by mentioning one or two members of the audience whom you do know or the underlying purpose that brought the group together. Another environmental factor you will need to consider is how the size of the room will affect the audibility of your voice. Make sure that everyone in the audience hears you, and whenever possible, try to get to the room early to see if there are microphones available.

Smaller rooms with smaller audiences do not usually require microphones, although they might be available. That said, smaller rooms are more intimate, and people tend to pay closer attention to the speaker. With that in mind, you can make your presentation more dialogic and conversational in smaller venues by asking questions, soliciting verbal feedback, and even conversing with specific people for brief moments. That said, environmental factors are not the only contextual factors that speakers in every situation must confront.

The Speaking Format

Thanks to technology, there are now, broadly speaking, two different formats for presentations: in-person and mediated. Both of these have different variations, but for our purposes we will consider these in broad terms. When we speak of in-person formats, we simply mean the traditional format of a presenter and a live audience that are in the same place at the same time. Mediated formats are those that allow a speaker to speak to an audience from an entirely different location, possibly even at a different time. Each of these contains aspects for which speakers must specifically plan.

The in-person format is one with which many people are familiar. In these situations, there is often a raised platform from which speakers or presenters deliver their remarks. On the platform there is sometimes a lectern, or stand, behind which the speaker positions themselves to present the speech. This layout is common in large venues, but it is increasingly appearing in small-room formats as well. This setup places the audience directly in front of the speaker, often at a lower level than the presenter. Sometimes this format is used in a room that has stadium-style seating, where the rows of seats for the audience gradually rise like those in an arena. This allows for each audience member to have a good view of the presenter, regardless of where he or she sits.

In today's fast-paced environment, it is not always feasible for speakers and presenters to meet their audiences in person. Thankfully, there are numerous technologies that allow people to speak to an audience from a distance. Satellite feeds on news programs make it possible to talk with an audience in a different location, as do more readily available programs such as Skype and FaceTime. Web-based programs such as YouTube and Vimeo also allow taped video presentations to be sent to people across the globe, making it even easier for people to deliver presentations to audiences at more convenient times without the hassle of traveling.

When it comes to these mediated formats, however, the expectations of the audience drastically increase, especially for presentations that are prerecorded. Since you can record and rerecord until the presentation is delivered the way you believe it should be, audiences expect more pristine delivery. This requires speakers to prepare and practice the speech more often, because if they do not, they will be doing numerous retakes of their video remarks. This format also either reduces or greatly eliminates the chance for audience feedback, which means you have no chance to change or adapt mid-presentation. This is a challenge. If you tell a joke that falls flat or report data that is confusing to the audience, you have no ability to recover or to clarify the information. Thus, knowing the format in which you'll be speaking is essential for creating effective presentations and is also a common concern, regardless of your profession.

General Audience Characteristics

In a later chapter we will discuss audience analysis techniques, so for the moment, when speaking about common contextual issues confronted by speakers in almost every scenario, we will simply say that audiences are a constant challenge to speakers. Some audiences are large, some small; some audiences agree with you, some are neutral toward your ideas, and others oppose your position; some audiences know a lot about your topic, others know very little but want to know more; some audiences are compelled to be present, while others willingly and voluntarily come to hear your remarks. All of these audience-related potentialities, and others we will explore in greater depth later, exist in every speaking situation and therefore are important contextual factors to which every speaker must pay attention.

Ultimately, the more you know about the audience, as well as the speaking format and the environment, the more prepared you will be when delivering your presentation. In the following section of this chapter, we will break down five popular professional fields in which speeches take place and briefly explain how each of these three contextual factors manifests itself in those fields.

SPEAKING IN DIFFERENT FIELDS AND PROFESSIONS

Many students, once they have decided on a field, believe that there are few, if any, situations in which they will be required to deliver a presentation. However, this is not the case, since professionals in all fields engage in delivering presentations to others. Employers list communication skills among the most important skills they look for in new hires and they would like to see them emphasized more in colleges and universities.[6] In politics, candidates

---

6. Hart Research Associates, *Fulfilling the American Dream,* https://www.aacu.org/sites/default/files/files/LEAP/2018EmployerResearchReport.pdf.

deliver speeches to gain votes, advisors deliver remarks to staff members on a campaign, and even engaged citizens may prepare remarks for local PTA or Knights of Columbus meetings. Teachers need to prepare effective presentations almost every day so their lessons are coherent and lead to student achievement. Engineers, scientists, and mathematicians need to be able to explain their projects, findings, and recommendations to people unfamiliar with their field. In business, whether in accounting, marketing, or sales, individuals must be able to think on their feet, prepare reports of data for unfamiliar groups, and persuade clients to purchase products. Doctors, nurses, dentists, and other health professionals educate patients about their medical conditions and sometimes give public presentations about health care. Clearly, regardless of the field, it is essential for career success that students learn how to prepare and deliver competent and effective presentations.

Politics and Speech

The public is most familiar with speech in the political realm, so much of what we will say here should not come as much of a surprise. Speech for those involved in politics can take many forms and occur in almost all of the contexts we laid out earlier. As a result, political speakers need to be well-versed in speaking in these different situations.

We have all seen political speeches in a variety of different settings. Perhaps a mayor has spoken during a festival or celebration outdoors. Presidents often give addresses in the Rose Garden or outdoors at commemorative events. Politicians also give speeches inside to large audiences of people, such as during the State of the Union address or a political debate. Finally, small rooms are often employed as venues for local clubs and organizations, or even town hall meetings with city councils or school orientations for parents. The external environments for political speeches are as varied as the topics and positions taken by the speakers.

In terms of the speaking format, again we find great variety for political messages. These occur in person with microphones and elevated platforms, as well as in mediated scenarios in which remarks are taped and delivered on the Web so audience members can watch at their leisure. One wrinkle in both of these settings is the intense desire on the part of the speaker to create an intimate relationship with the audience. When delivering remarks live, this is often done by moving from behind the lectern and speaking from among the audience. In mediated and taped presentations, the focus is on the head of the speaker to create the impression that he or she is having a conversation with one lone viewer.

Audiences also vary a great deal for political speakers, especially during a campaign. Sometimes, such as at rallies, the audience is predisposed to agree with the speaker and thus will be more supportive. At other times, often during town hall meetings, for example, some audience members may be hostile to the speaker's ideas and the situation and topic must then be carefully managed. Audiences can also be both small and large for political speakers, and often you never really know what to expect. The great variance in political speech-making contexts makes it ever more important to learn how to create an effective presentation by understanding the context in which you are speaking.

Speaking for Educators

Political speeches receive most of our attention, but the one profession that may deliver the most presentations every year is that of an educator, be it a teacher or professor. Just think about how many times you went to school and listened to a lecture or participated in a lesson during which you took notes and learned something new. Nearly every class taught contains an informative speech, though the format might be a little bit different than the speeches that you will give in class. Some classes also involve persuasive speaking, workshops, and debates, and each of these types of instruction requires attention to organization and delivery, just as are required for any other type of public speaking event.

Public speaking in an educational context is largely restricted to an indoor environment. Sure, there are a few exceptions to this, but the overwhelming majority of lessons taught by teachers and professors occur inside a classroom. These classrooms vary in size, especially at the college level. In elementary and high school, we often have classes that do not contain more than thirty or so students with one teacher. In those rooms, instructors do not need to use a microphone and can move about the class, get to know their students as an audience, and be more conversational in their delivery. This size may change in college, when students might register for a large lecture course with hundreds of students. In these situations, microphones may be used and the instructor is less likely to be able to move around the room.

The speaking format in the educational field has traditionally been in-person and in a physical classroom, but thanks to technology, even that has begun to change in recent years. Today, it is not uncommon for students to enroll in hybrid courses that meet online part of the time and in the classroom for part of the time, or to enroll in online classes in which students and instructors might never meet in the same physical location. In some of these classes, students might view prerecorded lectures online and participate in activities and discussions in a virtual environment. The prerecorded lectures present all of the same challenges we mentioned earlier for mediated presentations and, additionally, have to be revisited each term to update their content. In other online classes, students and teachers might hold class using videoconferencing technology that allows everyone in the class to interact at the same time from many different locations. Online instruction is not an easy endeavor for either the instructor or the student, but it does present a wider context in which educators need to be proficient in presentation creation and delivery.

Audiences for teachers and professors are also unique. Unlike in most other professions, students are a teacher's typical audience, and the messages teachers create are not usually designed to persuade the audience. Rather, this profession is especially dependent on delivering information to an audience in an unbiased manner, and so informative speaking tends to be its focus. This heightens speakers' concerns about what their audience knows before deciding what to put in a lesson. Should the students be expected to know what was in the book? If so, this drastically changes what information a professor includes in a lecture. It also reduces the speaker's need to worry about whether an audience agrees or disagrees with what is presented because the content is not meant to convince, but rather, to inform.

Speaking in the STEM Fields

STEM stands for Science, Technology, Engineering and Mathematics, and these fields are typically understood as applied fields of study. In these fields, people apply math and science knowledge to invent, design, create, or build things to solve practical problems, but, more often than not, people in these fields must share their ideas with others who do the work of implementing the plans. Because of this, it is especially important that students in STEM fields learn to deliver effective presentations. Moreover, the work done by people in these fields affects others in very tangible ways, such as in the design of the buildings and roads where we live and work, the medical advances that might save our lives, the computer technologies that are increasingly important in allowing us to work and communicate with others, and the generation and delivery of electricity to our homes. In these fields, ideas must be explained to others in a way that makes sense—particularly since there is sometimes very little room for error.

In terms of the environments in which people in these careers speak, presentations by scientists and engineers often involve speaking to small groups indoors. Sometimes, scientists and engineers give presentations for a larger audience at a conference, such as when Tim Cook announces the development of new Apple products or when Mark Zuckerberg testified in front of Congress. However, most presentations in STEM fields are given for much smaller audiences, such as when a team of engineers presents a proposal to potential investors, scientists share their research findings with other scientists in smaller conference sessions, or developers present their plans to the various team members who will be responsible for the actual work of creating the final product. Thus, it is especially important for people in the STEM fields to understand how to speak in smaller, more intimate environments.

When it comes to the speaking format, the focus is usually on the traditional face-to-face format in smaller settings, but there is an increasing emphasis on knowing how to deliver remarks remotely and online. Smaller settings require more ease and finesse, so those in STEM fields must appear comfortable in these settings. In remote presentations delivered online during a WebEx or videoconference session, remarks must also appear polished and often must effectively incorporate visual aids because the material being conveyed is complicated. The expectations of a polished performance are even higher for prerecorded presentations that can be accessed at any time.

Audiences for STEM professionals often include colleagues and others in the STEM fields, but it is also just as common to find situations in which scientists and engineers must explain complicated projects and complex ideas to groups of people not familiar with their technical areas of expertise. This can include providing project details to government officials, business professionals, and future investors. Sometimes, scientists and engineers try to craft persuasive arguments for their projects, but more often their responsibility is restricted to helping an audience understand complex processes and projects. This makes it important for STEM professionals to understand language and how it can be used to help uninformed audiences understand what can seem to be inaccessible technical jargon. We will provide greater elaboration about language as a skill later in the book.

Speaking in Business Settings

Around the country, faculty in colleges of business and employers hiring their graduates almost always cite public speaking and oral communication as skills they want in university students—and with good reason. The ability to speak effectively, clearly, and coherently is as necessary in business as it is in politics, the field we began this section discussing. Whether it is in accounting, marketing, or sales, the business field is saturated with situations requiring professionals to deliver remarks to an audience.

Business professionals most often find themselves in small conference room settings, but every once in a while, they will also need to speak outdoors or even in large conference halls. Think about the chief executive officer who is asked to speak at the company picnic or the chief financial officer who provides details on the performance of the company to an annual meeting of investors. Those situations aside, smaller units of the company often meet when someone delivers a report or recommendation for improvement relevant to the people in that room, and salespeople must frequently prepare remarks to persuade a potential client to purchase the product they are selling. Business settings do vary, but for many, the smaller room remains the most common context in which business presentations take place.

Perhaps more than those in the other fields we have discussed, business professionals find themselves meeting with potential clients and delivering pitches in a mediated environment. Computer technologies such as WebEx, GoToMeeting, Adobe Connect, and Zoom make it possible for individuals to hold videoconferences during which they can share one computer screen with all attendees, such as when a PowerPoint presentation is used, or to hold videoconferences using webcams, similar to a Skype videoconference, with a large group of people. It is increasingly common for members of the same division or team to be located in different areas of the country or for sales teams to work with clients who are located far away. By giving presentations and holding meetings virtually, businesses can connect with more clients in more locations, reduce travel costs associated with on-location meetings, and reduce the need for and expense of office space, since employees can often work from home. For this reason, it is essential for business professionals to learn how to craft, deliver, and respond to presentations in mediated settings.

Audiences also vary for business professionals, depending upon their occupation. Accountants, for example, often deliver financial information internally to colleagues who have only a passing understanding of financial information. Salespersons, on the other hand, attempt to persuade external parties to buy products or services. Members of the management team may do both of these tasks as well as attempt to inspire their staffs to excel and hit their targets. All of these contexts require very different understandings of context and audience but are essential for a business to thrive and survive. It is no surprise that faculty and employers all want students to learn the skills we are teaching you in this book.

Speaking in Health Care Settings

Health professionals speak in a variety of contexts, and effective communication is now seen as so important that the Accreditation Council for Graduate Medical Education (ACGME) has announced that interpersonal and communication skills will be one of six competencies that will be measured and reported in order for a program to remain accredited.[7] Why do those responsible for overseeing medical education think that communication skills are so important? The ability to communicate effectively with other members of the medical team and with patients is crucial for ensuring effective health care.

Health care professionals speak in a variety of contexts, but it is most common to speak to a small group in an intimate situation. Health professionals, including doctors, nurses, dentists, physical therapists, and others, must be able to speak effectively with other members of a health care team. Whether it's sharing a plan before doing a procedure, sharing information about patients when changing shifts, or discussing a diagnosis and trying to decide which treatment is the best course of action, health professionals must be able to speak effectively so that they can share information accurately and quickly in order to ensure the best possible medical care and prevent mistakes. Equally important, health professionals must have strong communication skills to speak with patients. Every conversation with a patient requires the same skills as a more formal presentation: health professionals must adjust their language to the audience and the situation, organize information clearly, use visual aids to enhance comprehension of the material, use informative speaking strategies to teach about health conditions and explain treatments, and use persuasive speaking skills to persuade others to follow care instructions.

---

7. Thomas J. Nasca, Ingrid Philibert, Timothy Brigham, and Timothy C. Flynn, "The Next GME Accreditation System—Rationale and Benefits." *New England Journal of Medicine Special Reports* 366, no. 11 (March 2012): 1051–56, https://doi.org/10.1056/NEJMsr1200117.

However, it is important to note that health professionals also give presentations to much larger audiences from time to time. Health professionals might teach community first aid and birthing classes, give presentations to students at a local school, give presentations at conferences, or even give expert testimony in a trial. In these situations, it is likely that the health professional will be standing in front of a seated audience and, in larger venues, might need to use a microphone and visual aids.

Summary

In this chapter, we began to shift our attention from some basic communication principles toward an application of those principles in specific professions. We began by explaining the three aspects of context that are common regardless of your career path. We then explored how each of those three characteristics manifest themselves within the public speaking settings of five different professional and academic fields: politics, education, STEM, business, and health care. As we move through the remainder of the book, we return to these three aspects of context to illustrate practical applications and scenarios in which speech played a role for people in these fields.

Activities

1   Think about a possible situation in which you will need to give a speech in the future. What are some contextual factors that you will need to consider and adapt to in that situation?

2   What are three ways that you will use public speaking in your future career?

3   What are some of the biggest communication challenges you will likely face in your future career?

CULTURE AND DIVERSITY

Objectives

◊ Learn how culture and diversity impact communication with others

◊ Understand how specific categories of cultural backgrounds create diverse audiences

◊ Enhance communication with diverse groups of people in a variety of situations

We live in an increasingly global society, and understanding how this impacts your communication with others is incredibly important. Now, more than ever, speakers encounter diverse audiences, work with a variety of different colleagues, and live in communities with people who are different than them in some ways. Appreciating the backgrounds and the experiences of others helps us become more effective communicators because we become sensitive and respectful toward others when we speak, making it more likely that they will listen to what we have to say.

In this chapter, we explain how culture and diversity impact our communication with others. First, we define culture and unpack the different dimensions of it. We then provide some detail on specific categories of backgrounds that create and influence the diverse audiences we encounter when we communicate in almost any context. Finally, we offer some concrete suggestions for enhancing your ability to interact successfully with diverse groups of people in a variety of situations.

UNDERSTANDING CULTURE

According to the *Oxford English Dictionary*, **culture** is "the distinctive ideas, customs, social behavior, products, or way of life of a particular nation, society, people, or period."[1] Geert Hofstede, one of the first social psychologists

culture
the collective programming of the mind distinguishing the members of one group or category of people from another

---

1. *Oxford English Dictionary online*, s.v. "culture," http://www.oxforddictionaries.com/us/definition/american_english/culture.

to study culture, defines culture as "the collective programming of the mind distinguishing the members of one group or category of people from another. The 'category' can refer to nations, regions within or across nations, ethnicities, religions, occupations, organizations, or the genders."[2] No matter which definition you prefer, culture is a complicated and powerful component of human development and life. It influences our self-concept, our priorities, our personalities, and the ways we communicate with one another.

co-cultures
a variety of smaller, specific cultures that intersect in our lives

Culture, however, is not so simple as to say a person belongs in, or is affected by, only one culture; the fact is, we belong to and are impacted by a variety of smaller, specific cultures that intersect in our lives. These smaller groups, called co-cultures, exist within and alongside larger cultural groups, allowing individuals to simultaneously belong to several cultures and co-cultures.

Let's look at an example to illustrate how cultures work and collide in our lives. Darius grew up in a Russian-American family and is a practicing Roman Catholic. Darius happens to be quite proud of his ethnic heritage, and also makes sure he goes to Mass every Sunday. That said, he does not speak Russian, nor does he agree with all the Church's teachings. Nevertheless, many of the customs and beliefs of both groups inform Darius's perspective on the world around him. Many of his friends in the neighborhood he lives in are Russian, and he belongs to the Knights of Columbus as well, but none of his Russian neighborhood friends are affiliated with that organization. Darius belongs to both cultures, which constitute co-cultures within the larger American or Western culture.

One type of culture that is particularly influential is national culture. The specific traditions of a national culture vary greatly between countries, but their national cultures can all be understood through six consistent dimensions. Hofstede identified the following six dimensions that help us understand differences in national cultures:

◊ **High vs. Low Power Distance:** Cultures with high power distance have high levels of inequality in power distribution in organizations, families, and other institutions; cultures with low power distance, on the other hand, have less inequality. This is best understood through where power lies in social structures. For example, democratic countries typically have low power distance because everyone has an equal share in decisions, while high power distance is best

---

2. Geert Hofstede and Gert Jan Hofstede, "Culture," Geert Hofstede 2013, http://www.geerthofstede.nl/.

characterized by monarchies and dictatorships where only a few have access to power and others are removed from decision-making.

◊ **High vs. Low Uncertainty Avoidance:** Cultures with high uncertainty avoidance have a low tolerance for ambiguity and minimize the possibility of uncomfortable, unstructured situations by enforcing strict rules, safety measures, and a belief in absolute truth. Cultures with low uncertainty avoidance have fewer rules, take risks, and are more tolerant of change.

◊ **Individualism vs. Collectivism:** Individualistic societies have loose ties between individuals and expect each person to look out for him/herself and their immediate family. Collectivist cultures have strong ties between individuals and strong communal bonds, and members of those cultures often live in extended families that are deeply loyal to the group.

◊ **Masculinity vs. Femininity:** Masculinity and femininity refer to the distribution of emotional roles between the genders and the difference in the values of men and women. In masculine cultures, men are typically highly assertive and competitive, and women are somewhat assertive and competitive. In feminine cultures, men and women are both much more modest and caring.

◊ **Long-Term vs. Short-Term Orientation:** Cultures with long-term orientation are pragmatic and focus on future rewards, with an emphasis on saving, persistence, and adaptation. Cultures with short-term orientation focus on the present and past and emphasize national pride, tradition, social obligations, and saving "face" in the here and now.

◊ **Indulgence vs. Restraint:** Indulgent cultures freely allow gratification of desires that allow individuals to enjoy life and have fun. Restrained cultures have strict social norms and discourage acting simply out of want.

It is easy to see how different nations and countries can differ along these spectrums. It is important to note, though, that Hofstede felt that these dimensions fell along a continuum, and do not exist as simply "either-or." For example, a culture is not either collectivistic or individualistic, but falls somewhere in between each on a spectrum.

In addition to the six dimensions of culture identified by Hofstede, Edward T. Hall explains that most national cultures can also be identified by how much importance is placed on nonverbal cues.[3] In **low-context cultures**, such as

low-context culture
culture where meaning is derived mostly from the language used in an interaction, and very little emphasis is placed on the nonverbal communication, environment, and situation

---

3. Edward T. Hall, *Beyond Culture* (New York: Doubleday, 1976).

high-context culture
culture where meaning is derived from the nonverbal expressions, environment, and situation in which the communication is taking place, and less emphasis is placed on the words

the United States and Germany, meaning is derived mostly from the language used in an interaction, and very little emphasis is placed on the nonverbal communication, environment, and situation. In **high-context cultures**, such as Korea and Saudi Arabia, a great deal of meaning is derived from the nonverbal expressions, environment, and situation in which the communication is taking place, and less emphasis is placed on the words.

These seven different dimensions of culture allow us to begin to understand the complexity of different cultures. This understanding can enhance our ability to interact with people by helping us see how they might differ from us in terms of values along these continuums. Next we will explore some different cultural categories in addition to nationality, beginning with race and ethnicity.

RACE AND ETHNICITY

race
a set of physical characteristics shared by a group of people, such as skin color, body type, facial structure, and hair color

A common cultural marker happens to also be a demographic category we find on college and job applications, census data, and other types of reports. **Race** refers to a set of physical characteristics shared by a group of people, such as skin color, body type, facial structure, and hair color. These physical characteristics are genetically inherited and reflect adaptations to the geographic region in which someone's ancestors previously lived. However, there is no biological difference between races in other characteristics, such as intelligence, athleticism, or other abilities. Due in large part to the fact that these characteristics developed in particular groups in specific regions, those groups created a culture themselves because of the fact that they lived within close proximity. The common physical characteristics helped individuals identify with each other and eventually form communities together.

ethnicity
a group of people who identify with each other based on a common experience, which might include geographic or national origin, ancestry, history, cultural and social norms, religion, race, language, ideology, food, dress, or other factors

Another cultural marker that developed due to the close proximity of people is ethnicity, but ethnicity should not be confused with race. **Ethnicity** refers to a group of people who identify with each other based on a common experience, which might include geographic or national origin, ancestry, history, cultural and social norms, religion, race, language, ideology, food, dress, or other factors. Ethnicity can sometimes (but not always) be related to national heritage. At times, violent conflicts and disputes evolve out of differences in ethnic heritage and values between two or more groups. The results of these conflicts can sometimes create new national boundaries, such as when the former Yugoslavia split into the nations that exist today. At other times, several ethnic groups might co-exist in the same nation. In fact, Tufts professor

Colin Woodard argues that the United States is really made up of eleven nations, each of which has a different history, ancestry, and set of deep-seated attitudes.[4]

A recent example of ethnic tension can be seen in the Crimean region of the Ukraine, where Russian-speaking citizens of Ukraine sought support from the Russian Federation when the political situation in the country became unstable. Ukrainian nationals in Crimea disagreed with this approach and an international crisis—which has yet to be resolved—ensued.

Ethnic heritage can also be a source of reinforcement for individual identity through cultural celebrations. Twice a year in some major American cities, Italian Americans celebrate the Feast of San Gennaro, a food festival central to their culture. A number of cities also have areas designated as Little Italy, Little China, and so on where people who share that ethnic heritage settled. These areas offer a great opportunity to explore some of the ethnic differences between people in fun, interesting, and if you like food, tasty ways.

SEX, GENDER, AND SEXUAL ORIENTATION

Another set of significant cultural categories refers to one's physical, psychological, and romantic definitions of their identity. To properly appreciate how these aspects of a person's self-concept relate to culture, we must first differentiate between the ways we define our sexuality. According to the American Psychological Association, **sex** refers to one's biological classification as male, female, or intersex (having both male and female physical characteristics) based on one's reproductive organs and chromosomes.[5] Sex is an objective way of identifying the group to which a person belongs based on biology. Often, job applications and college applications ask for this information, but are prohibited from using it to make job hiring decisions.

sex
one's biological classification as male, female, or intersex (having both male and female physical characteristics) based on one's reproductive organs and chromosomes

Sex is also often incorrectly used as a synonym for gender, and the two are actually quite different. **Gender** is a social construction that includes all of the beliefs, attitudes, actions, and roles associated with being masculine or feminine. One's biological sex does inform one's gender identity, but gender is more than a simple reflection of physical characteristics. Gender includes one's psychological sense of self as being male or female, regardless of their physical biology. Gender also includes the societal expectations for

gender
a social construction that includes all of the beliefs, attitudes, actions, and roles associated with being masculine or feminine

4. Colin Woodard, "Up in Arms," *Tufts Magazine*, Fall 2013, http:// www.tufts.edu/alumni/magazine/fall2013/features/up-in-arms.html.

5. American Psychological Association, "Practice Guidelines for LGB Clients," accessed 2014, https://www.apa.org/pi/lgbt/resources/guidelines.

behaviors, attitudes, and roles filled by feminine- or masculine-minded individuals. It is important to note that these expectations vary by the larger culture in which one exists. Where biology defines our sex, psychology creates our gender identity. If a person's gender identity matches the sex characteristics with which they were born, they are considered cisgender, and would likely categorize themselves as male or female. If a person's gender identity is different than the sex characteristics with which they were born, they are considered transgender, and would likely categorize themselves as trans male or trans female. Someone who does not consider themselves to be male or female in gender might identify themselves as gender queer or gender nonconforming.

sexual orientation
refers to the sex and gender to whom a person is romantically and sexually attracted to

In addition to the physical and psychological aspects of our sexuality, there is an emotional and romantic dimension as well. A person's sexual orientation refers to the sex and gender to whom a person is romantically and sexually attracted. Sexual orientation includes many categories along a continuum. The three most common categories are: heterosexual (attracted to members of the opposite sex), gay or lesbian (attracted to members of the same sex), and bisexual (attracted to members of both sexes). The declaration and enactment of sexual orientation is both an intensely personal decision and, for some people, a public declaration of belonging to a group.

This public declaration of belonging to a group presents us with an example of how sexual orientation can be construed as a culture. Many cities across the globe hold Gay Pride Parades which, in effect, are public celebrations of LGBTQ culture. These parades reinforce ties between individuals who identify with this culture and help serve to promote their beliefs, attitudes, and values.

AGE

We do not often think of age as a cultural marker, but it definitely operates as one in any society. While none of us will be the same age for the rest of our lives, age is not a permanent characteristic; a person's age may tell you something about their life experiences, as well as some possible attitudes and beliefs they may hold. Let's look at a few examples of different generational cultures in the United States:[6]

◊ **The GI Generation:** Also sometimes referred to as the Greatest Generation, this is the generation that fought during World War II.

---

6. Neil Howe and William Strauss, *Millennials Rising: The Next Great Generation* (New York: Vintage, 2000).

◊ **The Silent Generation:** This generation was too young to fight in World War II, but came into adulthood during the rise of the middle class and the relatively prosperous time that followed.

◊ **The Baby Boomers:** The children of the GI generation; they grew up with Woodstock and the Vietnam War. People in this generation tended to focus on careers and set high expectations for their children.

◊ **Generation X:** Born between the mid-1960s and 1980, many Gen Xers were "latchkey kids" and came from families with high rates of divorce. People of this generation often value self-reliance and maintaining a work-life balance.

◊ **The Millennials:** Born between 1982 and 2004, millenials grew up in an increasingly electronic and online world. This generation is the most ethnically diverse and is most tolerant of difference, but also has the largest amount of student loan debt of any generation.

The generation that each person lives in shapes their experiences, expectations, and attitudes toward others. Not everyone from a specific generation acts and believes the same way, but people always identify with the times in which they grew up. As these different generational groupings illustrate, age as a cultural group is not as simple as labeling someone "old" and "young," or "elderly" and "middle-aged." Those labels are defined purely by a number and fail to recognize the importance of the experiences each person lives through and how those experiences inform a person's generational culture.

PHYSICAL AND COGNITIVE DIVERSITY

Age, ethnicity, race, and sexuality are not the only ways in which we are different. In fact, unless you have an identical twin, you are probably the only person who looks exactly like you, acts like you, and thinks like you. When you consider that there are now over seven billion people on earth, there is inevitably a great deal of physical diversity among humans. However, our differences go beyond appearances to include abilities. Some people have especially high levels of specific physical abilities (for instance, Usain Bolt holds world records in both the 100- and 200-meter dashes), while others have different levels of specific physical abilities (for example, Helen Keller could not see or hear). These differences make us no better or worse than someone else, but rather, add to the richness of the human experience.

At some point, most, if not all, of us will experience some type of physical or cognitive impairment. Some of these are permanent, while others are temporary; some are due to genetics, others still an illness or accident. For example, some people are born blind, while others may develop blindness due to macular degeneration or an accident. Furthermore, other people may temporarily lose their sight after surgery as well. This is important to note because not all people with the same impairment are the same, they just may simply share a limitation or different level of ability. Above all, it is important to note that these differences do not define the person, but rather are a part of them, just as are their age, ethnicity, and race.

Likewise, there is great diversity in our cognitive abilities and preferences. There is a broad range in IQ, learning styles and preferences, interests, memory, and experiences among people. Many cognitive challenges—such as dyslexia, ADHD, Alzheimer's, or memory loss—are not immediately apparent when we meet someone. Like the physical impairments we discussed a moment ago, some people live with these challenges for their entire life, while others might experience them for a shorter period of time. For example, medication or a concussion can temporarily impact a person's short-term memory, while the effects of Alzheimer's are permanent.

IDEOLOGICAL DIVERSITY

ideology
a set of ideas, beliefs, and ideals that form our worldview and provide a basis for action

Thus far, we have primarily focused on physical differences between people, but the diversity of thought is just as important. Often the debate over this emerges in politics, where people hold different ideas on policy and effective governance. These views are the result of a commitment to an ideology, or set of ideas, beliefs, and ideals that form our worldview and provide a basis for action. Ideology forms the basis for political beliefs and is heavily influenced by both the family and society in which we grow up. As Colin Woodard showed when defining the eleven nations of the US, there is a great deal of ideological diversity even within the United States, and that ideological diversity expands even more when we consider the entire globe.[7] Not every country has, or even wants, a democracy. That said, let's focus a bit on ideological diversity in the United States specifically.

We often think of the United States as practicing a two-party system, and for all practical purposes this is true, but to believe the two parties contain groups that completely agree or share worldviews would be foolish. The

---

7. Woodard, "Up in Arms," http:// www.tufts.edu/alumni/magazine/fall2013/ features/up-in-arms.html.

Democratic Party, for example, consists of people who care about different issues in varying degrees, and this sometimes manifests in intra-party squabbles. Some Democrats care about limiting government spending (they are sometimes called Blue Dog Democrats), while others are more concerned with civil rights and social issues. They do not act in unison on every issue. The same can be said for Republicans, who consist of some libertarians who believe in a very small government, others who care about advancing social issues from a religious perspective, and others still who want to lower taxes and promote business. The fact of the matter is the two parties merely cloud the vast political and ideological diversity that exists in the United States. To use "liberal vs. conservative" dichotomies to describe people and groups does not come close to acknowledging the variety of thought on public issues that exists in the United States.

RELIGIOUS DIVERSITY

One final area of difference that both creates its own cultural norms and also enhances diversity in the United States and around the world is religion. There are numerous faiths practiced in the United States.

Despite the prevalence of the Abrahamic faiths (Judaism, Christianity, and Islam), each contributes to the fabric of our culture in their own way. In 2009, the US Census Bureau issued a statistical breakdown of the religious affiliations of people in the United States. In it they found a tremendous amount of diversity, including within Christian faiths. For instance, the report lumped thirty different denominations of Christianity under one group; each of these faiths has different religious perspectives, practices, and beliefs. The report also included a note to the growing number of Muslim, Wiccan, Buddhist, and nonreligious persons in the US.[8]

The growth of nonreligious and unaffiliated but spiritual people requires some discussion. It is a mistake to assume the beliefs of someone based on their specific affiliation, just as it is unwise to assume someone has no faith or belief in morality/spirituality because they are unaffiliated with a religious group. Many people still hold these beliefs privately, and should not be discounted or counted simply based on the religious groups with which they identify. Understanding and appreciating these differences, while not

---

8. U.S. Census Bureau, "Table 75. Self-Described Religious Identification of Adult Population: 1990 to 2008," *Statistical Abstract of the United States: 2011,* https://www2.census.gov/library/publications/2010/compendia/statab/130ed/tables/11s0075.pdf.

necessarily agreeing with them, is essential for developing a respectful community in which to live.

Religious groups also play important roles in local, state, and national communities. They often do good work on behalf of the communities in which their members live and help promote charitable endeavors across the world. Churches, synagogues, mosques, and temples also practice their own cultures by providing members with opportunities to connect with each other and share stories and experiences. These efforts build their religious culture, but also help to contribute to the larger communal culture.

SOCIOECONOMIC STATUS

socioeconomic status
a person's relative position in society, usually measured as a combination of their education, income, and occupation

Another way in which the experiences of individuals differ is socioeconomic status, or the experiences that accompany someone's access to economic resources. Socioeconomic status is usually measured as a combination of someone's education, income, and occupation.[9] What each person considers to be a "normal" part of life, the careers we choose, our expectations, the types of support we might or might not receive from family members, what we believe is attainable, what we eat, where we shop, the type of entertainment we tend to seek out, the types of exercise we select (if any), how we expect to be treated by others, what we think of as expensive or inexpensive, and more are influenced by our own socioeconomic status and the socioeconomic status of the family in which we were raised.

COMMUNICATION, CULTURE, DIVERSITY, AND DIALOGUE

As a speaker and listener, it is important to understand, acknowledge, and appreciate the many dimensions that impact each person's identity and contribute to diverse human experiences and cultural differences that coexist in our society. The differences in language, experiences, values, beliefs, and perspectives can enrich our lives in many ways, but also first requires communication grounded in the purpose of understanding others. It requires us to be perceptive of both the context in which we find ourselves and the way that context might be different for someone else.

---

9. "Socioeconomic Status," American Psychological Association, accessed 2016, http://www.apa.org/topics/socioeconomic-status/.

So far, this chapter has focused primarily on describing some of the differences experienced by groups of individuals to help us build a greater understanding of others and to help to provide a shared language for identifying and describing those differences. However, we must go beyond simply understanding that differences exist and work toward understanding one another, respecting each person's dignity and individual experience, and communicating effectively in ways that help us see beyond our differences. In this final section, we provide several tips to help enhance your ability to use communication to understand and respect differences between people, and then discuss the concept and practice of dialogue as a vehicle to promote understanding.

◊ **Don't try to define others based on a single demographic characteristic.** While it is helpful to understand the ways that various demographic and personal characteristics might influence a person's experience and ways of communicating, we should recognize that a single characteristic does not make up someone's entire experience. Each person's perspective is shaped by a complex combination of experiences, including, but certainly not limited to, each of the dimensions discussed in this chapter. Those unique combinations help each of us see the world a little bit differently.

◊ **Use appropriate terminology that is respectful of differences.** Much of this chapter was descriptive and helped to provide terminology that is generally considered appropriate and respectful when describing specific differences, but is certainly not comprehensive in doing so. When you are speaking with or describing others, use the most respectful language possible. If someone shares terminology that they prefer to describe specific characteristics of themselves, use their preferred terminology. Language is constantly evolving to reflect our changing world and experiences, and this includes the language that we use to describe aspects of our identity.

◊ **Make the message accessible.** As a speaker, it is important to consider the range of abilities in your audience and to adapt your presentation where possible to help the entire audience understand what you are saying. For instance, you might need to add captions to film clips, avoid combining red and green on slides so that those with colorblindness can read your text, and include signposts and transitions that make it easy for your audience to follow along if their attention wavers for a few moments. Using microphones, handouts, and other assistive methods may help people better follow your message, regardless of any limitations or challenges they may have.

◊ **Don't highlight differences in others.** Though you might think that acknowledging the different abilities or backgrounds of others during a speech makes you seem like you understand them or are trying to help them, highlighting those differences is often unwelcome. It calls others out in front of the audience and specifically heightens the differences that might have been intended to remain private. Whenever possible, if you need to make accommodations during your speech to make your message accessible to meet the needs of specific individuals, do so in a way that makes the accommodation for the entire audience without drawing unnecessary attention to any one person or group so that you do not unintentionally segregate your audience.

◊ **Avoid "-ist" language.** This is the type of language that demeans, ignores, inappropriately calls attention to, or disrespects members of a separate culture or group. This includes ageist, racist, and sexist language that does not respect the humanity of other people. This type of language depicts the other group as a passive object and not an active subject, thus making them seem less than the group of the person making the statement.

dialogue
speaking in a way that encourages others to listen, and listening in a way that encourages others to speak

In addition to these tips, a commitment to ethical communication is central to respecting diversity. This ethical commitment is made real through the practice of **dialogue**, or speaking in a way that encourages others to listen and listening in a way that encourages others to speak.[10] In addition, dialogue is communication where the goal of both the speaker and the listener is to understand, not necessarily agree with, the other. Dialogue is key to respecting diversity because it encourages us to understand, though not always agree with, the experiences, perspectives, practices, and beliefs of others.

Dialogue is not easy and requires a variety of different skills. First, it involves listening with an open mind and not pre-judging other individuals based on incomplete information or stereotypes. To do this, we must also engage in the dialogue through asking clarifying questions to make sure we understand what the other person is saying before making a decision regarding their statements. These questions should not come in the form of interruptions, but rather after individuals are done speaking. Dialogue also asks us to respect the inherent humanity of the other person in the interaction, and not devalue them or their experiences because they may be different. In

10. Em Griffin, *A First Look at Communication Theory*, 8th ed. (New York: McGraw-Hill, 2011).

short, avoid being ethnocentric, or believing your group's perspective is the only correct one and thus judging others based on their conformity to your way of doing things.

Dialogue allows us to appreciate cultural differences in a respectful way, thus keeping those aspects of diversity that improve our lives and communities. As you can see, communication is the core of a robust, vibrant, and interesting community that values diversity in appearance, action, and thought.

ethnocentric
believing your group's perspective is the only correct one and thus judging others based on their conformity to your way of doing things

Summary

In this chapter, we discussed the relationship between culture, communication, and diversity. We first explained the theoretical underpinnings of culture and explored the various dimensions all national cultures share to some extent. We then discussed several categories of difference that are their own cultural groups and contribute to a diverse society. We also offered some suggestions for how to effectively engage in understanding and appreciating difference through communication, specifically by practicing dialogue.

Key Terms

co-cultures 68

culture 67

dialogue 78

ethnicity 70

ethnocentric 79

gender 71

high-context culture 70

ideology 74

low-context culture 69

race 70

sex 71

sexual orientation 72

socioeconomic status 76

Activities

1 What are some of the cultures and co-cultures that you identify with? How have these cultures and co-cultures impacted your everyday experiences?

2 Which national culture most strongly influences you and your family? Identify where you think that culture fits into each of the seven dimensions of culture. (For instance, it is a high or low power distance culture?) How does this culture influence the way that you interact with others?

3   Watch this video on privilege: https://www.youtube.com/watch?v=
hD5f8GuNuGQ. How would you define privilege? In what ways have
you experienced privilege (or the lack thereof) in your life? How do
your experiences help you to understand visible and invisible types
of diversity.

TOPIC SELECTION

Objectives

◊ Identify appropriate speech topics

◊ Help develop appropriately narrowed topics

◊ Determine specific purpose for speeches

The first and perhaps most important task in the speech-making process is to select your topic. In some situations this can be difficult, and in others it is easy because the topic has already been provided. Determining what to speak about is also called the process of **invention** because it involves the creation of not only your topic but also what you plan to say about it. Topic selection is a creative process that allows you to identify what you want your audience to understand by sharing with them how you understand the topic.

invention
the creation of a topic and how it will be addressed

In this chapter, we will provide guidelines to help you develop your speech topics. This process begins broadly, with establishing the general purpose of your speech. Once this is clearly laid out, you will begin to narrow that purpose to a specific topic. When you have a more concrete topic, you will then narrow your purpose even further by stating what it is you want to specifically say about that topic. Let's begin by discussing how we figure out the general purpose of a speech.

GENERAL PURPOSE STATEMENTS

Every speech begins with a general idea. This general idea covers what you want to do with your presentation. Do you want to inform an audience? Persuade them? Perhaps celebrate some accomplishment? Each of these is a very broad and general purpose, but it helps you begin to identify what you might say in your speech. For that reason, it is important to start by clearly writing your general purpose statement.

A **general purpose statement** is brief, usually only a few short words. It describes the type or category of speech you will prepare and deliver. There are three types of general purpose statements: those for informative speeches, persuasive speeches, and commemorative speeches. As you

general purpose statement
a brief statement representing what you aim to do with the speech; there are three types

develop your speech, this general purpose can help guide what you choose to say and how you deliver it to the audience.

An informative speech gives the audience information but does not try to convince an audience to do or believe something. Think about instructors' lectures as speeches with the general purpose "to inform." In fact, the general purpose statement for any informative speech begins with "to inform," "to describe," or "to demonstrate." Notice how these general purposes would be helpful if you found yourself veering off and making a case for the audience to agree with something, rather than staying true to informing, describing, or demonstrating something.

A persuasive speech has a much different general purpose than an informative speech. Persuasive speeches are intended to change or to reinforce the audience's attitudes, actions, beliefs, or values. These speeches might try to convince the audience to take a particular position on an issue or to induce the audience to take a course of action. Clearly, the general purpose moves beyond informing, describing, and demonstrating. A persuasive speech's general purpose statement is "to persuade" or "to convince." Again, as with an informative speech's general purpose statement, these can help you stay on track when writing the body of your speech.

A commemorative speech is generally a speech of celebration, honoring someone, or presenting or accepting an award, such as a wedding toast or a funeral eulogy. Here the purpose is not to simply describe something, as in an informative speech, nor is it to try to convince someone of something, as in a persuasive speech. The general purpose of a commemorative speech is "to honor," "to commemorate," or "to celebrate." Each of these phrases gives a different tone to the speech than that of a persuasive or informative speech.

After you decide on the general purpose, you should choose and begin to narrow your topic. This next step is crucial because topics that are too broad will lack substance. For example, an informative speech on the Olympics is extremely broad and could include any number of items. A speech that encapsulates all aspects of the Olympics would take weeks to deliver, and even then it is unlikely that all of it would be covered. There have been books and documentaries about one specific Olympic event, just one sport, or even just one athlete. So, with that in mind and with your general purpose clear, it is time to begin focusing your topic.

CHOOSING YOUR TOPIC

Once you know what your general purpose is, the next step is to choose something more concrete upon which to speak. Topics can be chosen in a variety of different ways, depending upon your situation. In many cases, the occasion will determine your topic. At other times you might be asked to speak about something on which you have knowledge or experience. In still other cases, you might decide you want to speak about something that piques your curiosity; sometimes you want to learn about something new and share it with your audience. This last situation may be the case in most classrooms, but when you are speaking as part of your career, you often do not get this opportunity.

In many professional situations in business the occasion will dictate your topic. For instance, salesmen try to sell particular products, thus limiting their ability to create a topic from their own interests. CEOs will provide input on the company to stockholders and employees, again dictated by the situation in which they find themselves. Accountants need to prepare updates on financial information for presentations to colleagues. In each instance, the meeting situation dictates the topic to the speaker.

Despite the overwhelming influence of meeting types on selecting a topic, there are times when you might be called upon to speak based on your knowledge or expertise. For example, people who possess expert knowledge in science and engineering are often asked to explain those concepts to an audience with general knowledge. Think about doctors and medical researchers who try to explain cancer, heart disease, and other health risks to patients and advocacy groups, or engineers who need to describe structural changes to bridges and buildings. Experts from medical fields are sometimes called upon as expert witnesses in court cases. In each of these scenarios people from STEM and health care professions give presentations in which their topics flow from their area of expertise.

There are also times when your topic is something that interests you, but it is not very familiar to you. When this happens you teach yourself about your topic through your research, and then you teach it to the audience. This opportunity is rare in the professional world but very common in the classroom, where you are encouraged to explore ideas and topics that you are curious about. In education, instructors sometimes develop seminars and courses designed around ideas they want to study. These chances, though rare, are something you should take advantage of because they give you the opportunity to expand your knowledge.

Whichever of these approaches you choose for selecting a topic, it is imperative for you to narrow that topic to something that can be reasonably explored and covered in the amount of time you have for the presentation. In the next section of this chapter, we will discuss how to narrow a topic to a focus that fits your time.

NARROWING THE TOPIC

The amount of time you may have to narrow your topic will vary, but in most instances, classes allow more time than the professional world for generating presentations and so give you more time to narrow your topic. Classroom settings mirror professional situations when it comes time for speeches; there are time constraints, and your professor will likely give you minimum and maximum time limits for your speech. Many professors will penalize your grade for violating the time target, much like going over the time limit will result in a negative experience in the professional world. This is why it is important to develop skills for quickly narrowing the topic of your speech. One of the most common methods for doing so is to brainstorm (Figure 7.1).

brainstorm
to create a list of possible topics and keep adding to this list as you think of new ideas

Figure 7.1 **Brainstorm**

Brainstorming involves generating ideas and listing them as they come to mind. The process of narrowing your topic begins with writing down as many ideas as you can come up with regarding a specific topic. In true brainstorming, the strength lies in the spontaneous generation of ideas; initially, every idea is accepted. These ideas can be broad, narrow, specific, or general,

because at this point, it doesn't matter what they are. The list is then organized from general or broad to narrow and specific categories under the
broader labels. This helps organize your ideas into a more coherent model
for coverage of topics.

Figure 7.2 **Concept map**

In addition to, or perhaps even in conjunction with, brainstorming, there is
another tool you can use to help narrow and focus your topic: a **concept map**
(Figure 7.2). A concept map, also known as a mind map, is a visual representation of the potential areas you could cover in your speech. This more visual
model illustrates relationships between the ideas you generated as part of
brainstorming. In a concept map, you circle topics that have certain things in
common and draw a line connecting them to another group of ideas to which
they relate. This visual representation makes it easier for you to understand
your topic and eventually helps you organize your ideas into an outline for
your speech. Another strategy you can use is to analyze your ideas and choose
those that are most important or interesting.

Once you develop your concept map and have a better idea of what you plan
to talk about, you need to begin considering what aspects of the topic fit in
the time you have to deliver the speech. There are three ways to go about
making choices about what to cut and what to leave in the speech. You can
choose to cover the most important elements of the topic, you can choose the
most interesting or fascinating aspects of the topic, or you can combine the
important with the interesting.

A topic will likely have several elements, but it is unlikely they will be equally
necessary for the audience to know. For example, suppose you chose to deliver
a speech on the AIDS virus to your class. You brainstormed the topic and generated the following potential topics: history of the virus, biology of the virus,
affected populations, government treatment programs, famous people with
AIDS, and medical treatments for the disease. Any one of these is too large for

concept map
also known as a
mind map; a visual
representation of the
potential areas that
you could cover in your
speech

you to speak about to your class, so you then decide to brainstorm more and come up with Magic Johnson, Arthur Ashe, Mary Fisher, AZT, blood transfusions, the homosexual community, AIDS orphans, pre-exposure prophylaxis (PrEP), and contaminated needles. Now you are starting to see some links between broader and more specific ideas for your presentation.

This particular speech cannot cover all of these points, so you need to choose what to cover. You can elect to cover what you deem the most important elements of the topic, you can include the most interesting points about it in your presentation, or you can combine both. Looking at our example, the most important elements might be how the disease is transmitted and what segments of the population are most at risk.

On the other hand, it might be more interesting to the audience to hear about famous individuals who contracted the disease, such as Mary Fisher, Magic Johnson, and Arthur Ashe. Finally, you could decide that the best way to go would be to combine parts of both and talk about at-risk populations and then talk about how PrEP can be used to prevent HIV transmission in high-risk populations. Whatever route you choose, you have successfully employed brainstorming and concept mapping to appropriately narrow your speech's topic.

Knowing the elements of your speech topic is half the battle, and it was only made possible with a clear general purpose statement and time spent generating ideas for what to cover in the speech. Now that you have a narrow enough topic, some subpoints related to the topic, and a rough idea of how these all fit together, it is time to clearly articulate a specific purpose statement. In the next section of this chapter, we will discuss what this is and how you can effectively create one for your presentations.

Teacher Tips

When you are creating lesson plans, think about each class period as an informative presentation. You will probably know what your general purpose for each class period is based on your syllabus, but you will still need to narrow your general purpose to a more specific purpose statement that will allow you to develop a thesis statement and main points. Here are a few tips:

◊   Before you begin creating your lesson plans, brainstorm all of the things that you could teach about your topic.

◊   Choose the most important topics from your list to focus on.

◊   Organize your topics in a logical order. For example, if you are teaching elementary school students about clouds, you probably need to instruct students about the different kinds of cloud formations before they can understand how to predict the weather by looking at the clouds.

◊   Focus on quality, not quantity. It's better if students learn a few key concepts really well than to cover as many topics or textbook pages as possible in a class period.

Other contexts where these skills apply: Human Resources, Corporate Training, and Sales

DETERMINING THE SPECIFIC PURPOSE

The **specific purpose statement** is derived from both the general purpose and the topic of your speech. It is a far more concise statement than the general purpose and serves as a guide as you go forward developing your speech. Specific purpose statements are composed of one declarative sentence that notes what you will talk about, how you will talk about it, and what you want the audience to walk away with at the end of the speech. Look at your specific purpose as an umbrella; everything you do in your speech should fit under this umbrella. You might discover some interesting information, but if it doesn't fall under the specific purpose, then it probably should not be included in your speech. To include this information might be interesting to the audience, but it will also confuse them and detract from the central idea you wish to communicate. The specific purpose should have a sharp focus.

Let's look at an example of a specific purpose:

> "My speech will inform my audience that the process of hosting a dinner party requires a focus on detail that begins with determining when the party will occur, who will be invited, and what will be served."

As you can see, this specific purpose statement provides a sharp and clear focus for the speech. It indicates the general purpose of the speech (to inform), the topic of the speech (hosting dinner parties), and the main points you will cover (timing, invitations, and menu). This is clearly an informative presentation, but it also has a very sharp focus, making it easy for the audience to follow what you plan to say.

specific purpose statement
a narrower version of the general purpose statement that identifies what you will talk about, what you will say about it, and what you hope the audience will take away from the speech

Specific purpose statements for persuasive speeches are equally clear. Look at the following example:

> "My speech will convince my audience that Tiger Woods is the greatest PGA golfer of all time due to his short, middle, and long game, plus his ability to handle pressure and the sheer number of tournaments he has won."

Again, all three of the purposes mentioned above are accomplished. The central argument is clear (Tiger Woods is the greatest golfer ever), and the main points that support that claim also are indicated. This allows the audience to prepare to hear this information and think about how it connects to the central argument you make.

In commemorative speeches, the specific purpose statement is different from the two previous examples we have discussed.

Here is a commemorative speech specific purpose statement:

> "My speech will commemorate the occasion of Independence Day, a day when we celebrate the founding of our country, the principles that gave this country birth, and our development as a nation."

Here we notice the general purpose of celebration, the topic (Independence Day), and the main ideas that are to be celebrated in the speech. In each of these three examples, you see how specific purpose statements help ground speeches in a central idea, prevent you as the speaker from going off on tangents, and provide the audience with a sense of how the speech will unfold.

Health Care Help

Health care providers often give workshops to teach first aid or to teach people how to live well with a new health condition. For example, you might be invited to talk with a high school health class about nutrition, teach a roadside emergency class as part of a driv- er's education class, teach a workshop about living with diabetes, or teach a birthing class. When teaching these sessions, keep these things in mind:

◊   Be relevant. If you get to choose your topic, think about what is most important for your audience to know in their current situation.

◊   Don't overwhelm your audience with more information than they can take in at once.

◊ Keep solutions simple. Focus on things your audience can do to make the biggest difference.

If you are breaking your presentation into points based on the steps in a treatment, make them easy to remember. For example, you might remind your audience they just need to remember CAB (Chest compressions, Airway, Breathing) to do CPR, or to use RICE (Rest, Ice, Compression, Elevation) when treating common injuries.

Other contexts in which these skills apply: Management, Sales, and Government

The specific purpose guides you in developing your speech and also serves as the foundation for creating your thesis statement. The thesis statement, which is the core idea you wish to communicate to your audience, comes from rewording the specific purpose statement so that it makes sense to an audience. Let's examine how we would retool the specific purpose statements from above so they work as thesis statements.

Informative speech specific purpose statement:

"My speech will inform my audience that the process of hosting a dinner party requires a focus on detail that begins with determining when the party will occur, who will be invited, and what will be served."

Informative speech thesis statement:

"Hosting a dinner party requires a focus on detail that begins with determining when the party will occur, who will be invited, and what will be served."

As you can see, all three of the elements of the specific purpose statement are there, but the thesis statement is constructed to make sense to your audience. The topic and structure of the statement changed very little in this example, except that the first few words of the specific purpose statement were eliminated. Let's see what happens when we use the persuasive speech specific purpose statement.

Persuasive speech specific purpose statement:

"My speech will convince my audience that Tiger Woods is the greatest PGA golfer of all time due to his short, middle, and long game, plus his ability to handle pressure and the sheer number of tournaments he has won."

Persuasive speech thesis statement:

> "Tiger Woods is the greatest PGA golfer of all time due to his short, middle, and long game, plus his ability to handle pressure and the sheer number of tournaments he has won."

The same minor changes result in creating a clear thesis statement. Dropping a few words is all it takes to change one to the other. Let's see if the same holds true for commemorative speech specific purpose statements.

Commemorative speech specific purpose statement:

> "My speech will commemorate the occasion of Independence Day, a day when we celebrate the founding of our country, the principles that gave this country birth, and our development as a nation."

Commemorative speech thesis statement:

> "Today we celebrate Independence Day, a day that marks the founding of our country, celebrates the principles that gave this country birth, and marvels at our development as a nation."

Here the specific purpose statement and the thesis statement have more differences than a few simple words, but the essence of the idea is still the same. The changes only helped make the statement more appealing to the ear, rather than the eye; after all, the audience is hearing the statement, not reading it.

GENERAL GUIDELINES FOR SPECIFIC PURPOSE STATEMENTS

There are several things to keep in mind when creating the specific purpose statement. First, ensure that it is one statement. A specific purpose is just that: a statement, not a paragraph or an essay. The one-statement summary approach helps you stay focused and not put too much information in the speech. That said, just because it is a single statement does not mean it cannot have clauses embedded within it; in fact, if you look at the prior examples, there are several clauses in each specific purpose statement. These clauses also help keep you focused. Ultimately, if you have more than one sentence, you are trying to do too much in that speech, and it will confuse both the audience and you.

It is also important that this single statement be declarative in nature. This means that the sentence makes a statement and clearly says something. Go back and review the statements we used as examples, and you will find that all of them are direct, easy to understand, and declare something that will be done. This declaration weds you to the topic, and the supporting structure you state will support your comments about that topic. Your specific purpose statement is essentially a declaration of intent to the audience regarding what you will say.

Finally, understand that the specific purpose statement is not a rigid law by which you must abide but an evolutionary element of your speech. It can change based upon how you find the rest of your speech is coming together. In the end, the specific purpose statement must reflect how all the ideas fit together in your speech, but it can be adjusted as you craft the body of your speech.

Summary

Choosing and narrowing a topic can be a daunting task, even when the topic is provided to you in advance. It is a creative part of the speech-making process, and you must find a way to harness your creativity. In this chapter, we discussed how we invent or generate topics based upon identifying the general purpose of your presentation. We also discussed how to use brainstorming and concept mapping when developing ideas you think you might wish to include in your remarks. Finally, we showed you how to combine your general purpose and ideas generated through brainstorming to create a clear and concise specific purpose statement.

Key Terms

brainstorm 84

concept map 85

general purpose statement 81

invention 81

specific purpose statement 87

Activities

1   Take five minutes to brainstorm as many potential speech topics as possible. Write them down on a sheet of paper or inside the cover of your textbook so that you can refer back to this list throughout the course.

2   You will be preparing and delivering a speech in this class soon. While thinking about the guidelines for your next speech assignment, list three potential topics you might choose for that speech. For each topic,

explain why it would be appropriate for you, your audience, and the occasion.

3   For one of those three topics you chose in activity 2, write out your specific purpose statement. Next, convert your specific purpose statement into a thesis and preview of main points.

RESEARCH AND PREPARATION

Objectives

◊ Introduce aspects of what it means to be information literate

◊ Provide details of where to research specific types of information

◊ Detail tips for how to keep track of information gathered through research

Once you identify your topic, the next step in developing your speech is researching to find the information you plan to use in your presentation. In all but a few cases, speeches require some degree of research, which helps you appear credible and will increase your ability to impact the audience. The information you gather must relate to your topic and to your central idea, and, perhaps most importantly, be data the audience will respect.

On one hand, research has become easier today thanks to the internet, which provides people with access to vast stores of data. On the other hand, technology has made it much harder to differentiate between good, credible information and false data, or even opinions. The sheer amount of information available today makes the search for relevant and credible evidence more challenging. In this chapter, we address research and information used in speech construction. We will first explain information literacy, and then we will detail the general types of information you might encounter when researching. Next, we will discuss some places you might go to search for different types of information. Finally, we will cover the importance of keeping track of the information you find and plan to use in your speech.

INFORMATION LITERACY

Media, friends, and family deluge us with new information every day. Websites, blogs, videos, advertisements, commercials, banners, billboards, radio programs, and email constantly present us with new information. Navigating through this colossal amount of visual and verbal stimuli makes it essential for us to become critical consumers of information in our daily lives. The same skills are also necessary when looking for information while preparing a speech. For this reason, we need to familiarize ourselves with what it means to be information literate; the more clearly we understand information and how it works, the better we will be at crafting coherent arguments and evaluating the arguments of others. In this section, we detail the various skills necessary to become information literate.

CHARACTERISTICS OF INFORMATION LITERACY

information literacy
the ability to recognize when information is needed and to locate, evaluate, and effectively use that information

The American Library Association defines information literacy as the ability to "recognize when information is needed and have the ability to locate, evaluate, and use effectively the needed information."[1] There are five characteristics of information literacy that you should consider as you conduct research:

1   **Know why you want certain information for the speech.** You may want the information to catch the audience's attention, to provide background facts, or to make an argument and try to persuade an audience. What you wish to achieve helps you determine where you will go to get the material to help you create your speech.

2   **Know where to get the information you seek.** Today we can sit with our computer, tablet, or mobile phone and access much more information than we need, and this can make it difficult for a researcher, especially a novice, to sift through all of the information to find quality sources. Though internet searches are easy to do, they usually result in an overwhelming number of sources with questionable credibility, so they are not typically the best way to begin to gather relevant research information. Most university and college libraries contain expansive online databases that include sources ranging from scholarly journals to trade journals, encyclopedias, legal databases, popular magazines, legal references, and daily newspapers from around the world. If the databases feel overwhelming at first, reference librarians are available and ready to help you find sources. Always remember, though, that

---

1. American Library Association, *Presidential Committee on Information Literacy: Final Report* (Washington, DC: ALA, 1989) http://www.ala.org/acrl/publications/whitepapers/presidential.

print materials and interviews are also possible avenues for gathering evidence to use in your speech.

3 **Know how to assess the quality of the information you have found.** Simply stumbling upon information does not mean you should use it—even if, on the surface, it seems to fit what you plan to say. Before you use information, you need to evaluate the source and the information to make sure that the information is reliable, is relevant for your speech, and is a good quality source that will lend credibility to your presentation. In order to evaluate the quality of a source, use the five steps of the CRAAP Test (listed on pages 96–97), which was developed by librarians at California State University, Chico, to determine whether you should use a source.

4 **Create new knowledge.** One of the chief aims of research is to pull together information from various sources in order to create a coherent explanation of how those pieces of data fit together. This process creates new knowledge for the audience because they see something in a different, more complex light through your efforts to make connections between sources of information. This synthesis of ideas is one of the most important aspects of information literacy and is highly respected in academia and the professional world. Information literacy does not mean you know a lot of information, but rather, that you know how a lot of information fits together and can explain those connections to others.

5 **Be accountable for your use of information.** You are responsible for the things you say, and just as you should respect authorship and not misrepresent yourself in a paper, you should also not misrepresent yourself or someone else when you speak. You need to be honest with your audience about what you know, what you think, and what you do not know. It is important to avoid making broad claims when you speak that you cannot back up with the information you collected in your research. Make sure your audience also knows where they can go to get that information if they wish to locate it. Essentially, accountability in information use means you take ownership of what you say and respect the ownership of what others have said.

The CRAAP Test

C   Currency: How timely is the information? How recently was the article or book published? Has the source been updated, and does it use current references? Is this something that is likely to have changed since this article was published? For some topics, having the most up-to-date source will matter a lot, but for others, the information is unlikely to have changed much over time. For example, you probably need recent sources for a speech about current immigration policies, but older sources might be just as valuable for a speech about immigrants who arrived in the US at Ellis Island.

R   Relevance: Is this information important for your needs? Is the information in this source useful for your speech? Does it answer the questions that you have about your topic? Is it at an appropriate level for a college or university audience, or is it too simple or too advanced for your needs? Have you looked at several sources before determining that this is the best source to use? Even if a source is reliable and current, it might not be the best source for your presentation if it does not include the type of information that you need. For example, an article about the history of Ellis Island might be an excellent source, but it might not be relevant for a speech about current immigration issues at border between the US and Mexico.

A   Authority: Who is the source of the information? Who is the author or the publisher that is sharing the information? What are their credentials? Do they have expertise, experience, or institutional affiliations that qualify them to write about this topic? Is the publisher reputable? Will your audience view this source as a credible authority on this topic (i.e., a pediatrician is a much more credible source for information about vaccines than a celebrity blogger)? Keep in mind that some sources will be viewed as authorities by some audiences, but not others. For instance, while a Catholic audience might view the Catholic Pope as an authoritative source about religious issues, a Buddhist audience is far less likely to do so.

A   Accuracy: Can you verify that the information is reliable, truthful, and correct? Are there multiple sources that corroborate the information shared by your source? Did your source cite other credible sources and provide evidence for the conclusions that were shared? Was the source reviewed by other experts before it was published? What kind of language is used?

Does it seem like the author left out important information or is making a lot of errors (grammar and spelling errors, poor use of logic, etc.), or does the source appear to be unbiased and sharing well-supported information? If an article seems to be poorly researched, is full of errors, or contradicts other credible sources of information that you have found, then it might not be accurate and should not be used as a source for your presentation.

P **Purpose: Why is this source sharing this information?** What was the author's goal for writing this? Are they trying to inform, persuade, entertain, sell, or something else? Are their intentions clear? Is the author trying to share facts, opinions, or propaganda? Is the source clearly biased or pursuing an agenda, or do they appear to be objective and impartial? Will the author or organization benefit in some way from getting others to believe or do something? When doing research, it is helpful to regard any sources that have a clear political, institutional, ideological, religious, cultural, or personal bias or a vested financial interest with a bit of skepticism and to keep looking for additional sources. For example, you should not rely on a study about the effects of vaping if the study was paid for by a company that makes and sells e-cigarettes. Likewise, a website funded by a political candidate is not the best place to find current news.

bias
an unfair preference or distortion of information

American Library Association (1989). Presidential Committee on Information Literacy: Final Report. Retrieved from http://www.ala.org/acrl/publications/whitepapers/presidential

As you can tell, being information literate is not as simple as it sounds. It involves developing your research skills and your analytical abilities, as well as adhering to ethical standards as you look for and use evidence. Being information literate allows you to judge information for quality and thus use good evidence to construct stronger, more effective speeches. These standards for assessing quality of information apply to each of the general categories of data you might find in your research. In the next section, we elaborate on those different types of information.

TYPES OF INFORMATION

When conducting research, you will find information that fits into one of three broad categories: background information, unique information, and evidentiary information. Identifying what type of information you find is one of the core characteristics of a strong researcher.

Background Information

In many speeches, you will need to provide the context for your speech. This may involve providing the audience with the who, what, when, where, why, and how that are relevant to your topic. Background is often the first type of information you encounter when researching a topic with which you are unfamiliar, and finding it will help you refine your topic and could be useful when explaining the topic to your audience.

Unique Information

Another type of information you will encounter when researching is data that is unique. It could be statistics, quotations, or stories about people and events that are not common knowledge, but are nonetheless fascinating. This information can be valuable in capturing and maintaining the interest of your audience. Unique information gives your topic a personality by adding colorful facts, stories, or brief anecdotes, and it can also heighten audience appreciation and interest in the evidence you provide.

Practical Politics

If you are working in politics, you will need to spend a lot of time doing research that will prepare you for the situations you will face both during the campaign and after you or the candidate for whom you are working is in office. For example, here are a few things that you will need to have someone on your political team research thoroughly:

- ◊ **The issues:** Make sure you have the most accurate information about every issue that you will deal with. When you are in a position to make decisions that will affect others in significant ways, you have a responsibility to make sure your decisions are well-informed and are in the best long-term interest of your constituents and society as a whole. Be prepared to defend your statements and decisions!

- ◊ **The voters:** Who are they? What issues are most important to them? What information do they have?

- ◊ **Your opponents:** What are their policy proposals? Where do they stand on important issues? What are their voting records?

- ◊ **Yourself:** Someone on your team should conduct research to find out what your opponents might discover about you during their research.

This will give you the opportunity to correct any factual errors and be prepared to answer questions that will undoubtedly arise about your past.

Other contexts where these skills apply: Sales, Marketing, and Health Professions

Evidentiary Information

This type of information is the core of your speech and is what you set out looking for when researching a topic. It is information that lends direct support to both your thesis and the main points of your speech. Evidence can come in the form of statistics, testimony, examples, or a myriad of other materials that directly support the claims you make in your speech. What constitutes evidence varies depending on the topic of the speech, but for all intents and purposes, evidence is the guts of your speech. For example, businessmen trying to sell a product may use data on cost or performance, or even testimonials from current or prior users of the product. The key element is its central relationship to the topic.

Knowing what types of information exist and how to evaluate them are essential for any researcher. Another important aspect of successful research, which we will discuss next, is knowing where to go to get the information you need.

PLACES TO RESEARCH

As we mentioned earlier, technology has made information more readily available than it was in the past. This means that there are many more places for you to find research on your topics. In this section, we will discuss three sources of information you can take advantage of when researching: libraries, the internet, and people. Each of these can provide different types of information. Be aware, however, that both your topic choice and the outcome you desire will help determine where you should go to find your information.

Libraries

Libraries today do not operate anything like they did twenty years ago, let alone centuries ago. For instance, not too long ago, library patrons used physical card catalogues to search by author or subject, and learning the Dewey Decimal System was an important component of high school curricula. Today we can access research tools at our fingertips through computer databases and digital catalogues. This allows libraries to store even more information.

Although they vary in size and mission, most higher education libraries subscribe to electronic databases that contain an overwhelming number of books, encyclopedias, journals, and periodicals. EBSCOhost, for example, is an online system that can connect you to databases and indices for specific disciplines, providing easy, quick access to years of research. This search engine also provides source citations, abstracts, and many full-text copies of articles you can print, just as if the original source were right in front of you. When researching through this database and others, you can restrict your search to collect only entries that are available in full-text or in peer-reviewed publications.

Higher education libraries almost universally have access to search engines that comb through subscriptions to hundreds of journals with thousands of articles in the social sciences, humanities, hard sciences, education, engineering, law, and other disciplines. Many of these resources are in full text in either HTML or PDF format, making it easy to download copies of the material you need or want to your flash drive or desktop so you can open and read them later.

There are many databases that can help you refine your search to specific disciplines. One such search engine is the Education Resource Information Center (ERIC), which focuses on education. There are military and government databases, legal databases, and science databases. One jewel to take particular note of is LexisNexis. This search engine combs through newspaper and magazine articles from around the globe and can pull up a news article or op-ed piece in a local newspaper that may be miles away from where you are located. All of these search engines provide you with easy access to troves of information and include tools to help you find what you are looking for.

If you are having trouble deciding which database to start searching in first, you might also find that Google Scholar is a useful resource. On many campuses, if you are using a campus internet connection, Google Scholar will link directly to all of the library databases and will allow you to access any full-text articles to which your library has access. To try this on your campus, start by navigating to scholar.google.com. This will allow you to use a search function that is similar to a regular Google search, but it will limit your search to academic sources.

With all of this information located in different places, research can easily get frustrating. For that reason, when doing library work, seek out the librarians who work at your particular library before you get too irritated. Reference librarians are trained to search for material and know the library better than you do. You will also find that if you ask them for help, these dedicated professionals will, in all likelihood, save you time and emotional energy. Therefore, we suggest that you take advantage of this tremendous resource when seeking information on specific topics.

The Internet

In addition to searching the stacks of information available both on library shelves and in the databases to which they subscribe, you can also search the internet for information. There is a caveat: not all websites are created equal. Some are self-created and contain blogs that often consist of opinions, and thus are not a good source of scientific or factual data. One of the first steps in evaluating websites involves looking at the type of domain they exist on.

When using the CRAAP test to evaluate a website, you should pay special attention to the domain name that is designated at the end of the web address because this will tell you something about the source of the information. For example, websites that end in .gov are government-run, and those that end in .edu are managed by educational institutions. The information on these websites is usually reliable, and the source of the information is easy to identify. Historically, web addresses ending in .com were commercial websites, meaning that they are for-profit entities that make money from their websites. Websites ending in .org have typically been nonprofit and noneducation groups and organizations. While both of these types of websites might have accurate information, it is also possible that the information might be biased toward the goals of that company or organization, so careful scrutiny and additional research is necessary to decide whether you can trust the information on these websites. Finally, addresses ending in .net can be created by anyone and are not monitored by the Federal Trade Commission (FTC), so they are usually much riskier sources to trust. While these domain names are much less rigidly enforced and applied than they were in the past, and additional domain names have been created to designate other authors and sources of information, the domain name can be a useful part of your evaluation when applying to CRAAP test to determine whether a source should be trusted.

STEM Spotlight

Before you begin to develop a solution to an engineering problem, you will need to take time to go through the discovery process, which requires many of the same skills and steps you use when developing a speech. When you go through the initial discovery process, you will need to be prepared to do the following:

◊ Understand the problem.

◊ Identify the requirements for the solution.

◊ Understand the policies and obstacles that might limit your options.

◊ Learn about the context in which the solution will be enacted.

◊ Identify what other solutions have and have not been successful in other contexts.

Other contexts in which these skills apply: Management, Human Resources, and Performance Management

One of the most common places novice researchers go for information on the web is an online encyclopedia, but this should only be a starting point, not the bulk of your research. Wikipedia, perhaps the most universally known online encyclopedia, can be either an excellent source or a risky one, depending on the page.

Some of the pages on Wikipedia are well-researched and written by experts; you can usually identify these pages by the long list of peer-reviewed sources included in the reference page.

However, anyone can upload or edit information on Wikipedia, and anyone can change entries that were originally well-researched, calling anything found on the site into question. Information found there might be accurate, but it also might be fabricated, posted out of malice, or even uploaded as a joke. Be sure to check with your instructor before you use Wikipedia as a source. Generally speaking, Wikipedia is a good place to find background information before you begin your research, but you should rely on other sources for supporting materials when developing your speech.

One final tip regarding searching for information online relates to the use of proper search terms. Search terms are the keywords that you type into the search engine to help locate material. Understand that Google does a keyword search of the web when you use it to find information. This means that it will call up every website that contains the word or phrase you put in the search, resulting in a mountain of hits. One helpful way to minimize this pile of information and to focus it more succinctly around your topic is to use **Boolean operators** such as "AND," "NOT," and "OR" in all caps when typing in terms. As always, evaluate the returns using the website domain system we explained earlier.

Boolean operator using words such as "AND," "NOT," and "OR" when typing in search terms to focus the results

Interviews

People you know or whom you seek out can be great sources, but this depends upon the topic and your speech goals. One way to gather information from others is through interviews.

Interviews can be conducted in face-to-face meetings, over the telephone, through email, or even using technology such as Skype. It is often best to use a method in which you can see the other person during the interview so you can read the respondent's nonverbal communication, but this is not always possible. Using technology to see the other party in a discussion is becoming more and more commonplace in business, families, and even education with online distance courses, and it makes gathering information in a setting where you can see the person's nonverbal reactions much easier.

Regardless of what medium you use to conduct the interview, it is important to record what happens and what is said so you can relay accurate information in your speech. Make sure you have the respondent's consent when interviewing, as doing so without his or her knowledge would be unethical. Surreptitiously taping even a lecture without the instructor's knowledge is a grievous violation of someone's trust, and information gathered in this manner should not be used in a speech.

When you decide to conduct an interview to gather information for your speech, there are certain steps you should follow to make sure you get the most out of this tactic. First decide which type of interview testimony you want to collect. The two kinds of testimony are peer testimony and expert testimony. Peer testimony is provided by a nonexpert who gives an opinion or story regarding a particular topic. An expert, on the other hand, is someone with credibility and professional experience directly relevant to the topic you plan to discuss. It is distinctly possible that you might use one, the other, or both types of interviews for the same topic.

Suppose, for example, that you wanted to present a speech about the Great Depression. There are many sources of recorded economic, political, and social information available, but an interview with someone who lived through the Great Depression's hardships would be an excellent source. Another possible source would be someone who had researched the topic and written extensively about the Great Depression in books, newspapers, or journals. Both interviews would provide good information for your speech, and you might use one, the other, or both in your final presentation.

After you find someone willing to be interviewed, you must prepare for the interview very carefully. First, decide exactly what you want to learn from the interview. Then, compile a list of questions to ask in order to get at that information. Before the interview begins, ask the person how much time he or she has for your questions. During the interview, do not be afraid to deviate from your list of questions if the interviewee brings up an interesting topic. Much like exploring information in the library or online, what you find out through a person's answers may change the focus of your research, and that is not a bad thing. After all, interviewing and researching are about going where the information takes you.

When you finish the interview, be sure to thank the person you interviewed. You should also send a follow-up thank you email or card. These simple courtesies are professional, might help you if you need to speak to the person again, and are a good habit to form. Later, when transcribing your notes, make sure to clarify statements the person made if you are unsure what was said or what the person meant.

Interviews are not the only source of information people can provide; you can also sometimes gain access to personal correspondence. Personal correspondence includes emails people send to one another, collections of letters, and personal diaries or journals. Many libraries contain collections of these types of correspondences that may be available to you. These correspondences are generally considered rich data, as they are usually written from a personal perspective and reflect the feelings, opinions, and beliefs of the writers themselves. These primary documents can provide speeches with a degree of color that other information cannot.

Whether you conduct an interview, find an article in a journal or magazine, or use a website from a company, it is imperative that you track where you gathered your information. In the next section, we will provide some tips on doing just that and will supply some examples of common bibliographical techniques used to document sources.

Tips for Successful Research Interviews

1 **Do your research on your topic.** The first step to prepare for a research interview is to learn as much as you can about your topic. If you do not complete background research on the topic in advance, then you might end up asking questions that could have easily been answered with some research. This makes you look unprepared at best and shows disrespect to your interviewee because you are wasting their valuable time by asking questions that you could have easily answered on your own.

2 **Research the person you plan to interview.** Learn everything you can about the person that you plan to interview. Read their biography online, articles that have been written about the person and their research or organization, and anything that they have written that is publicly available (articles, books, etc.). What is their history, and what have they already said about your topic? What uniquely positions them to be able to tell you more?

3 **Plan your questions.** Only after you have done thorough research on your topic and your interviewee should you begin to write the questions that you will ask in your interview. Your questions should focus on information that you could not find while doing research and should be questions that could only be answered well by your interviewee. Your questions should also be open-ended and give the interviewee an opportunity to explain something that would be a helpful part of your research. For example, if you were interviewing Anne Wojcicki, the co-founder and CEO of 23andMe, you would be wasting both her time and yours you asked her to explain what DNA is—that information is easily available in any biology textbook. However, you might consider asking, "What motivated you to start 23andMe?" or "What effect do you hope that widely available genetic testing, such as that offered by 23andMe, will have on health care in the United States?"

4 **Send the interview request.** After you have planned your questions, you should send a request to the person that you want to interview. You will probably want to start by either calling the person's office or sending an email to ask for a short interview. Your communication should be professional and concise. For example, if you send an email request, you should include a

formal greeting and signature line, clearly and concisely state your request, explain how much time you are asking for, and add a formal subject line. See the example below:

Subject: Request for an Interview

Dear Dr. Wojcicki,

I am giving a speech about the effects of genetic testing on health care in the United States in my public speaking class. In my research, I have learned about some of the medical advances that have resulted from the availability of widespread genetic testing, such as that offered by your company, and I would like to interview you about your perspective on how genetic testing might impact health care in the future. Would you be willing to do a 20-minute phone interview with me sometime in the next two weeks? If so, what day and time would be most convenient for you?

I appreciate your time and consideration and look forward to talking with you.

Sincerely,
Melissa Broeckelman-Post

5   **Conduct the interview.** If you are doing an in-person interview, you should plan to arrive at the building early in case there are unexpected delays. If you are meeting in your interviewee's office, you might want to find a place to wait nearby, and then go to their office at the arranged time. If you are conducting an interview over the phone or using video conferencing software, you should call at the time that you scheduled the interview. Begin the interview by saying hello, introducing yourself, shaking the person's hand (if it is culturally appropriate to do so) and thanking the interviewee for their time. Listen carefully and take notes as you conduct the interview, and ask follow-up questions when it is appropriate to do so. Keep an eye on the clock so that you stick to your agreed-upon time frame. At the end of your interview, thank the interviewee for their time and for answering your questions.

6   **Follow up with a thank-you note.** After your interview is over, send a thank-you note to once again express appreciation for your time and to note something specific that you learned in the interview that was especially valuable. Sending a handwritten thank-you note is a timeless way to express gratitude that will usually make a strong impression, and is especially appropriate

for in-person interviews. If you choose to send a thank-you note via email instead, perhaps following a short phone interview, make sure that you follow the same conventions for professionalism as you did in your interview request email.

DOCUMENTING YOUR RESEARCH

Documenting sources is an important element of any paper or presentation. It is important to document sources in two ways in speeches: first, written in the outline or manuscript, and then verbally attributed when referencing them during the speech.

One of the most frustrating things about research is also one of the most avoidable. You will never be more irritated than when you reach the end of your preparation and realize that you need to go back and document all the places you found your information. To avoid this time-consuming concern, it is important to develop a way of documenting your research as you go. You may list some things you don't use, but it is easier to not use them than to repeat your search. Here are some ways to keep track of your research sources:

◊ Place notes on each piece of information you collect that lists the proper bibliographical citation for that piece of data. Later, when you are finishing your speech bibliography, go back and get the notes for the information you used and log it in your bibliography.

◊ Keep a notebook or Word/Google Docs document in which you log all your information and where you found it. This is a bit more detailed, in that you are annotating the bibliographical citations so you know what information came from which source, and this process can be instrumental in making decisions about what to include in your speech and what to leave out. As with the notes, once the speech is complete, go through the notebook and create the bibliography from the sources that you did end up using.

◊ Keep an ongoing bibliography in the document itself. Each time you encounter information you plan to use, log it in your running bibliography so that you already have it recorded. Then, when the speech is finished, go through the bibliography and delete the sources you did not use. This simple task will save time when you are preparing your speech and will ensure that you are making ethical use of the information you collected.

Generally speaking, there are three style manuals that are most often used to document sources. In English and some disciplines within the humanities, the preferred style manual is published by the Modern Language Association (MLA). In the social sciences and natural sciences, the preferred style manual is produced by the American Psychological Association (APA). Finally, in a few select humanities disciplines and in some areas of business, the footnote-heavy Chicago Manual of Style (CMS) is preferred.

Modern Language Association Style Guide (MLA)

There are two components to any style manual: referencing in the body of the text itself, and referencing in the Works Cited section, which is a list of all the sources used in a speech that generally appears at the end of the speech. MLA style generally prefers to use in-text citations that contain the author's last name and the page number where the information cited can be found. The year of the publication is not required for the parenthetical reference, but the title should be included if you have more than one source by the same author or do not know who the author is. This is required for all references, even when the information is paraphrased. Here are some examples of in-text citations using MLA:

One author, not mentioned in sentence:

> In the United States, having a standardized time became important when the railroad made faster travel possible (Gleick 44).

One author, mentioned in sentence:

> Gleick notes that having a standardized time became important when railroads made faster travel possible (44).

Multiple authors, not mentioned in sentence:

> Entertainment programs can also educate viewers about social issues (Singhal and Rogers 289).

Multiple authors, mentioned in sentence:

> Singhal and Rogers point out that entertainment programs can also educate viewers about social issues (289).

Unknown author:

> People tend to take smaller bites and eat less when their food has a stronger aroma ("Smaller Bites" 43).

Website without an author, not mentioned in sentence:

> The first blood donation programs began during World War II (www.
> redcross.org).

In addition to including parenthetical references throughout the narrative of the speech outline, you also must include a "Works Cited" page at the end of the document. Here are some examples of common entries in an MLA "Works Cited" page:

Magazine/Newspaper Article with Single Author:

> Smith, John. "Form and Style." *The Detroit Free Press,* 8 Nov. 2010, p. A8.

Magazine/Newspaper Article with Multiple Authors:

> Smith, John, Stephanie O. Billbrook, and Melvin Cooper. "Form and
> Style." *Dayton Daily News,* 2 Jan. 2008, p. A9.

Magazine/Newspaper Article with No Author:

> "The Form is Not Right." *The Sacramento Bee,* 18 Mar. 1994, p. A14.

Journal Article:

> Smith, John. "Bibliographies Can Be Fun." *Canadian Journal of
> Communication*, vol. 17, no. 3, 2004, pp. 88–124.

Chapter in an Edited Volume:

> Smith, John A., and Gene Lyle. "Chapter 3: The MLA Style Guide." *Fun
> with Citations,* edited by Harold Johnson, Cedric Levi, and Jiwani
> Jones, Routledge, 2012, pp. 101–111.

Book:

> Jones, Penelope. *Correctly Tracking Sources.* Chicago, U of Chicago P,
> 2010.

Website:

> "Life and Stuff." *wuemudr.com.* North Southern University, 12 Oct.
> 2002, wuemudr.com/articles/101202/life-and-stuff. Accessed 12
> Jan. 2004.

A Letter to the Editor in a Newspaper:

> Smith, John. Letter. "People like food." *Miami Herald,* 17 July 2010, p. A9.

Government Reports:

> United States, Department of Health and Human Services, National
> Institutes of Health. *Citations are Important.* Government Printing
> Office, 2006.

Notice that some of the titles of articles are placed within quotation marks,
while names of journals, newspapers, books, and magazines are italicized.

American Psychological Association Style Guide (APA)

APA, the style favored by the social and natural sciences, is different from
MLA style in several respects. For instance, although both MLA and APA
require in-text parenthetical citations, the format in APA differs from that of
MLA. Here are some examples of APA parenthetical citation styles:

One author, not directly quoted:

> In the United States, having a standardized time became important
> when the railroad made faster travel possible (Gleick, 1999).

Multiple authors, not directly quoted:

> Entertainment programs can also educate viewers about social issues
> (Singhal & Rogers, 2003).

Author in text, directly quoted:

> Gleick (1999) noted, "With the century ending, some towns and
> cities resisted the onslaught of precise and standardized railroad
> time" (p. 44).

Website with author, not directly quoted:

> This is the first year that people living in the US will watch more mov-
> ies online than on DVDs (Pepitone, 2012).

Website with no author, not directly quoted:

> The first blood donation programs began during World War II ("Red
> Cross blood program," 2012).

Website with author, directly quoted:

> "That's a 135% year-over-year increase for online video" (Pepitone,
> 2012, para. 4).

There are several things to note here as well. First, if a work has three or more authors, you should use the last name of the first author and then the phrase "et al." to refer to the rest of the authors. When using the author's name in the sentence, you only need to put the year in the parentheses, or the year and page number if the material is directly quoted. Last, when the author is listed as "Anonymous," reference it by using the word "Anonymous," followed by the date in the parenthetical citation.

APA, like MLA, calls for a list of all sources used in the speech to appear at the end. However, their list is called a "Reference List," not a "Works Cited" page as it is in MLA. Like the other style manuals, the list is organized alphabetically. Let's look at how entries for some common sources are formatted in APA:

Magazine/Newspaper Article with Single Author:

Smith, J. (2010, November 8). Form and style. *The Detroit Free Press*, A8.

Magazine/Newspaper Article with Multiple Authors:

Smith, J., Billbrook, S. O., & Cooper, M. (2008, January 2). Form and style. *Dayton Daily News*, A9.

Magazine/Newspaper Article with No Author:

The form is not right. (1994, March 18). *The Sacramento Bee*, A14.

Journal Article:

Martin, J. N., & Nakayama, T. K. (2015). Reconsidering intercultural (communication) competence in the workplace: A dialectical approach. *Language and Intercultural Communication, 15*, 13–28. https://doi.org/10.1080/14708477.2014.985303

◊ Include the issue number for all journals that have issue numbers.

◊ Include the Digital Object Identifier (DOI) or URL at the end of the reference. Write both DOIs and URLs as hyperlinks in your reference list (i.e., beginning with either "http://" or "https://"), even if you are referencing an older work that uses a different DOI format. If you cannot find the DOI for the journal article on the article itself, try looking it up online at http://www.crossref.org/guestquery/. Some older articles do not have DOIs.

Chapter in an Edited Volume:

> Smith, J. A., & Lyle, G. (2008). Bibliographies are difficult to master. In H. Johnson, C. Levi, & J. Jones (Eds.), *Fun with citations* (pp. 101–121). Routledge.

Book:

> Jones, P. (2010). *Correctly tracking sources*. University of Chicago Press.

◊ Do not include publisher location when citing a source's publishing information.

Website:

> Simpson, H. (2002, October 12). *Form and style: Bibliographies are difficult to master*. Online Style Dictionary. https://onlinestyledictionary.com/form-and-style-101202

A Letter to the Editor in a Newspaper:

> Smith, J. (2010, July 17). People like food [Letter to the editor]. *Miami Herald*, A9.

Government Reports:

> Office of Communications (2006). *Form and style* (AHRQ Publication No. 12-0630). Department of Health and Human Services, Agency for Healthcare Research and Quality. https://ahrq.gov/reports/2006/form-and-style.pdf

Pay close attention to the capitalization and punctuation schemes in APA, as they can be tricky. Notice, for example, that in most cases, only the first words of titles and subtitles are capitalized, while the others remain in lowercase. Also note that the full name of the author is not listed; the first name is initialed only.

Chicago Manual of Style (CMS)

The *Chicago Manual of Style* is the third style guide accepted in parts of academia and business. This style, unlike that of APA or MLA, does not use in-text parenthetical citations, but requires footnotes in the text. As you can see, this is not the only difference in the guidelines for footnotes, which we placed above the bibliographical entry examples below:

Magazine/Newspaper Article with Single Author:

Footnote:

> 1. John A. Smith, "Form and Style," *U.S. News and World Report*, April 12, 2006, 30.

Bibliography:

> Smith, John A. "Form and Style." *U.S. News and World Report*, April 12, 2006.

Magazine/Newspaper Article with Multiple Authors:

Footnote:

> 2. John A. Smith and Joanne Doe, "Form and Style," *Financial Times of London*, June 1, 2000, 17.

Bibliography:

> Smith, John A., and Joanne Doe. "Form and Style." *Financial Times of London*, June 1, 2000.

Magazine/Newspaper Article with No Author:

Footnote:

> 3. "Footnoting Correctly," *Economist,* December 7, 1999, 19.

Bibliography:

> "Footnoting Correctly." *Economist*, December 7, 1999.

Journal Article:

Footnote:

> 4. John Smith, "The Works Cited Page is Awesome," *Geopolitics* 9, no. 4 (2002): 38.

Bibliography:

> Smith, John. "The Works Cited Page is Awesome." *Geopolitics* 9, no. 4 (2002): 35–60.

Chapter in an Edited Volume:

Footnote:

> 5. John Smith, "Footnoting in Alphabetical Order," in *Proper Citations and Works Cited Pages*, ed. Susan Clark, John M. Thompson, and Percy L. Jones (Boulder, CO: Westview Press, 1987), 10.

Bibliography:

> Smith, John. "Footnoting in Alphabetical Order." In *Proper Citations and Works Cited Pages*, edited by Susan Clark, John M. Thompson, and Percy L. Jones, 8–14. Boulder, CO: Westview Press, 1987.

Book:

Footnote:

> 6. John A. Smith, *The Value of Footnotes* (Wilmington, DE: Scholarly Resources, 1981), 212.

Bibliography:

> Smith, John A. *The Value of Footnotes.* Wilmington, DE: Scholarly Resources, 1981.

Website:

Footnote:

> 7. "Pregnancy and Amniocentesis," WebMD, accessed July 19, 2008, http://www.webmd.com/baby/guide/amniocentesis.

Bibliography:

> WebMD. "Pregnancy and Amniocentesis." Accessed July 19, 2008. http://www.webmd.com/baby/guide/amniocentesis.

A Letter to the Editor in a Newspaper:

Footnote:

> 8. John Smith, letter to the editor, *Las Vegas Review-Journal*, August 14, 2007.

Government Reports:

Footnote:

> 9. United States, Department of the Treasury, *Citations and Taxation, 2006* (Washington, DC: GPO, 2007).

Bibliography:

> United States, Department of the Treasury. *Citations and Taxation, 2006.* Washington, DC: GPO, 2007.

Note that the title of the list at the end of the document is called a "Bibliography," which is a different title than that used in either MLA or APA style. The list, though, is still organized alphabetically. One of the quirks associated with Chicago style is that once you do a complete footnote for an item, you need not repeat the full entry on the next use of the same source. Rather, that note should give only the author's last name and the page number.

We want to emphasize that these are short guidelines that by no means encompass all the requirements of each style manual. They should, however, provide you with a good, solid foundation for sources you may encounter and need to document. We encourage you to also think about obtaining copies of the manual that is appropriate for your discipline so that you can follow all the conventions expected in your particular field.

Oral Citations

In addition to listing and citing sources at the end of your outline or manuscript, you also need to verbally attribute sources when speaking to your audience. You should include these citations exactly the way that you plan to say them during your speech in your preparation outline. Verbal attribution does not mean that you read the entire bibliographical reference, or even tell the audience the page on which you found the information, but it does mean that you let the audience know that the information came from someone other than you. This is important, as it is an ethical practice that also builds credibility with your audience. Ideally, your oral citation should include (1) the author or person who was the source of information for the article, (2) that person's credentials, (3) the name of the publication, and (4) the date that the source was published. However, you won't always have all four of these pieces of information, so you should share as many of these details as you can to let your audience know where you found the information. Here are several ways in which you could adequately attribute source material during a speech:

> According to Dr. Sanjay Gupta on June 15, 2009, on cnn.com, people who receive email reminders with health tips are more likely to make healthy choices throughout the day.

> According to a 2016 Gallup Poll, increasing numbers of Americans are worried about the housing market.

> In his 2003 book *Lamb*, author Christopher Moore offers an account of Jesus from the perspective of his fictional childhood best friend, Biff.

> Some people, such as *Washington Post* columnist George Will in the June 3, 2016, *Washington Post*, argue that baseball should not add another wild card team to its playoff structure.

> The *9/11 Commission Report*, completed in 2004 by a team appointed by President Bush and members of Congress, recommended a series of changes in government policy to respond to the threat of modern terrorism.

All of these statements verbally attribute information gleaned through research to their sources. These statements help increase credibility and also let the audience know where they can find information you used.

Summary

Solid research on your topic is the backbone of a strong speech. Conducting good research was the focus of this chapter, and we introduced you to the five characteristics of information literacy so that you can understand what it takes to gather quality information on your topic. We also explained the different types of information you will encounter in your research, as well as where you can go to locate such information. Finally, we detailed the importance of documenting and attributing the sources you use and briefly explained the three major style manuals used in academics and the business world.

Key Terms

bias 97   information literacy 94
Boolean operator 103

Activities

1   Think about the topic that you are likely to use for your next speech. Using your university's library website, find a book, a newspaper article, a peer-reviewed journal article, and a credible website that are related to that topic. Write out an APA-format citation that you would include in your references page for each of those sources.

2 Search your library website to learn more about the resources that are available. Where can you go for help if you have questions? What is the name of your reference librarian?

3 Who are three experts you could potentially interview about your topic? What unique perspectives and experiences could each person contribute?

AUDIENCE ANALYSIS

Objectives

◊ Learn basic methods for analyzing an audience before a speech

◊ Understand how audience analysis continues during a speech

◊ Familiarize yourself with ways to gather audience information

Speaking may seem like an act conducted by an individual, but it actually cannot be done without others. The audience is just as important in the speech process as the speaker. This chapter focuses on how to analyze the audience as a speaker so you can craft messages that work with the specific groups to whom you speak. We will first talk about some basic audience analysis methods that can take place before a presentation. Next, we will explain how analyzing the audience does not stop with the start of your talk but rather continues during the entire presentation. Finally, we will discuss different ways to gather audience information using some common interpersonal and social scientific methods.

BEFORE THE SPEECH

The amount of time you have with your audience before a speech can vary quite a bit. For instance, you might be delivering a quarterly update on sales figures to your supervisor, in which case you roughly know when you will be asked to speak with your team. On the other hand, you might be asked to develop a presentation on plans for a new engineering project to three different investment companies with only a few days advance notice. In each of these scenarios the phrase "before the speech" means something very different. In the first situation, you have a great deal of time to consider your audience, analyze them for relevant information, and ultimately make adjustments. In the latter, you have precious little time and even less information on your potential audiences. In both situations, there are methods for gathering information on your audience before you give your presentation. In this section, we will discuss direct observation and the collection of demographic data.

Business Basics

When preparing for a sales presentation, work to identify what the customer needs (also sometimes called "identifying their pain") so that you don't waste everyone's time trying to sell a solution that won't fix the problem. Find out what the client cares about BEFORE you walk into the meeting, and take some time early in your first meeting to make sure that you fully understand the problem. Here are a few ways to find out about your client:

◊ Look at the client's website. Find out what the company does, and look for key terms or a mission statement that sums up the company's values.

◊ If you have an opportunity to do so, talk to someone within your client's company to find out about its goals and concerns.

◊ Search for news articles to find out whether anything has happened at the company recently that caught the media's attention (positive or negative).

◊ Try to find newsletters, white papers, research reports, and any other documents that might be available that will help you find out what your client has been working on recently.

◊ Talk to others in your own company who have worked with this client in the past.

Other contexts where these skills apply: Engineering, Job Seeking, and Counseling

Direct Observation

One tool for audience analysis is your perception of the situation in the moment. Through direct observation you can collect a great deal of information on your audience. Let's look at a few things you might observe and how they could quickly be incorporated into your presentation.

First, if the speech is at a company's office or complex you can examine the walls for photos, slogans, and materials that are prominently displayed. Companies post information about upcoming events as well, and this data can be easily added to your speech in the form of an offhand reference. Acknowledging the company and the importance of its information demonstrates that you pay attention to detail.

In addition to environmental cues, you can get a fairly accurate read on how many people will be in attendance for the presentation and who they might be. It is not difficult to take a quick mental count of people in the room as you move about before the meeting or presentation. You can also tell who the people are by examining name badges, paying attention to introductions, and watching where people sit and how they dress. All of these behaviors can provide you with important data you might be able to use in your talk.

Finally, through direct observation you can get a feel for the emotional disposition of the audience toward you and your talk. Look at facial cues, eye movement, whether people have notepads, or if they seem excited. This information can give you a heads-up on what to expect when you begin your speech. If the audience looks bored, tired, or disengaged, you may need to begin with great energy or come up with something early in the speech to cause them to want to listen to what you have to say. On the other hand, if they seem interested, tap into that excitement from the beginning.

Demographics

Collect simple demographic data on your audience to help provide a picture of to whom you will be speaking. **Demographics** are categories of definable characteristics of groups of people, such as age, race, religion, socioeconomic status, education level, and sexual orientation. It is not hard to imagine how such data might be useful to a speaker.

demographics
categories of definable characteristics of groups of people, such as age, race, religion, socioeconomic status, education level, and sexual orientation

Demographic data is commonly collected by a variety of institutions. Political candidates make use of this data to know which segment of the audience to target and which message to present to that audience. The same commercials do not air in Oregon as do in Ohio, for example, where different issues matter more to particular demographic groups that reside there. Demographics allow candidates to tailor one message for one group of potential voters and another for a different section of the audience. Elected officials also use demographic data via polling to assess how the public feels about policies that have been passed or policies that are being presented in Congress.

Marketers use demographics to evaluate particular strategies about sales. For example, a marketing team for a luxury car manufacturer could analyze Census Bureau demographic data and determine whom they would like to target. Because they are more likely to target those living in high-income zip codes, they will consult the Census Bureau information to find out where those zip codes are located. The Census Bureau report also provides information on religious practices, ethnic origins, and other such data. The one caveat to using Census Bureau data is that it is only collected every ten years, so be sure to get the most current and relevant information from them.

Demographic data is used in education by teachers as well as administrators. Administrators need to track performance by demographic groups and report it to their accrediting agencies. Students and professors frequently look around on the first day of class and note the number of females versus males, the age of students, and perhaps even ethnic or racial breakdowns of those present. This is in some ways an automatic reflex and illustrates how direct observation can also be used to gather demographic information about an audience.

In the United States some demographic categories are protected by federal government laws. For example, protected categories include age, race, gender, sexual orientation, religion, and disability. The law forbids treating people differently because they belong to a particular group within one of these categories. This illustrates the power of demographic categories and data and the information and policies they shape in society. Knowing the reach and influence of demographics can be helpful to speakers who gather data about their audiences ahead of time and make specific adjustments to their messages so they are more likely to resonate with those particular audiences. Ultimately, demographic information can show differences in values, beliefs, and opinions among people—and it is there where the true power of this information resides.

As you learned in Chapter 6, demographic characteristics can provide some valuable insight into the likely experiences, expectations, beliefs, values, and attitudes of your audience. However, each person is a part of several cultures and co-cultures, and an individual's experiences and perceptions are influenced by numerous factors that impact their position in their community, so it is important to recognize that individual experiences likely vary from the general assumptions that you might make based on a group's overall demographic characteristics.

METHODS OF ANALYSIS DURING THE SPEECH

The process and usefulness of audience analysis does not end as you begin your speech. In fact, perhaps the most helpful form of audience analysis occurs during the presentation as you observe and adapt to how the audience receives your message. In this section, we will discuss two elements involved in conducting audience analysis during the speech, including the continuing role of direct observation and polling the audience.

Direct Observation

As we mentioned when covering audience analysis before the speech, there is no more valuable tool than your own ability to observe the audience. During a speech, it is more likely that a speaker will react to nonverbal cues from an audience than to anything else. Generally, nonverbal behaviors tell how the audience is truly reacting to the message. This is because nonverbal reactions are very hard to control, and so audience members tend to let them go, especially when they are not the one in the so-called spotlight. These actions are spontaneous and more accurate indicators of how audience members are receiving your message. If the speaker notices certain things about the audience, he or she then has an opportunity to take advantage of that information, often without the audience even knowing it.

You might notice that your audience is increasingly more engaged with you and your topic as the speech continues. Certain indicators of this may be head nods, smiles, raised eyebrows, clapping, or even cheering. This is, of course, a positive sign and means you are on the right track with what you are saying. This does not mean you should rest, however, because in their enthusiasm is an opportunity for more emotional connections between them, you, and your topic. You can increase the tone of your voice, use hand gestures more emphatically to make a point, or even reference someone in the crowd or some action taking place. These observations will solidify your identification with the audience and enhance the success of your speech.

Another powerful indicator of audience engagement is eye contact. First, as the speaker you should make as much eye contact with the audience as possible. The audience also should be making eye contact with you throughout your speech. This indicates respect and interest in you and/or your topic. If they are not making eye contact, then consider changing the energy of the delivery or the cadence and rhythm of your voice to get their attention and bring them back to the content of your presentation (Table 9.1).

Table 9.1

AUDIENCE INTEREST AND DISINTEREST	
GAINING AUDIENCE INTEREST	**LOSING AUDIENCE INTEREST**
• Making eye contact • Varying tone, pitch, and pace • Using gestures to make a point • Using pauses effectively • Referring to someone in the crowd • Involving your audience (e.g., polling)	• Poor delivery skills • Not varying your tone, pitch, or pace throughout your speech • Reading your speech • Talking about things that are not relevant to your audience

Lack of eye contact, however, is just one way an audience can indicate a lack of interest in your speech. The audience may show a decreased level of interest in a variety of ways, including shifting in their seats, talking to neighbors, reading, sleeping, or even leaving the room. Another key indicator is if you notice members of the audience looking at their watches or cell phones. This can mean they are impatient and want the speech to end. All these behaviors should communicate to you that the time has come to put some energy into your delivery to help refocus the audience's attention and try to get them engaged with the speech (Table 9.2).

As you can see, direct observation of audience behaviors is a powerful tool for audience analysis that speakers can take advantage of and use to help deliver a successful presentation. It is not, though, the only strategy for audience analysis in their tool kit.

Table 9.2

AUDIENCE ENGAGEMENT AND DISENGAGEMENT	
SIGNALS OF AUDIENCE ENGAGEMENT	**SIGNALS OF AUDIENCE DISENGAGEMENT**
• Nodding heads • Smiling • Raising eyebrows • Clapping or cheering • Making eye contact	• Shifting in their seats • Talking to neighbors • Reading • Sleeping • Leaving the room • Looking at watches or cell phones

Polling the Audience

Direct observation is something any speaker can use in virtually any situation; however, other strategies, such as polling the audience, may not be feasible in certain circumstances. Nevertheless, it is important to understand how to employ this technique for gathering information about an audience during a speech. Polling the audience is considered informal because it does not follow the rules of the scientific process, but its results are very helpful to any speaker. There are also different moments when you might consider polling the audience.

The first moment when you might poll the audience is during the introduction of your speech. In fact, this could be a creative attention getter. Not only do you get immediate feedback, but it is also a good way to get the audience engaged by asking them to respond and thus invest themselves in the outcome their answer produces. Even if the audience does not verbally or physically respond, they will likely mentally consider the question. Whether they answer or not, polling them has produced both data and attention. Generally, the best way to poll is by asking a question, or series of questions, and requesting that the audience members raise their hands if they agree or disagree with your statement. This can help introduce a topic and give you information about what parts of your topic might be the most relevant to cover.

The other instance when polling the audience can come in handy is during the speech when you cover something complex or difficult. This approach allows you to determine if the audience understands the points you are making. If they are following along, then continue as planned, but if they are not, slow down and readjust your coverage of the material so the audience can understand it. It is acceptable, as the speaker, to query them if you have any concerns about their comprehension of the issue, and the information you gather from this analysis holds tremendous value.

There is one important caveat to polling the audience to gather information: you cannot control the outcome of your question. Things could go as planned, and that is always a good thing, but they also might not. The audience members could turn to each other to discuss your question, thus taking their attention away from you as the speaker. They also might not answer the way you expect them to, and this may rattle your nerves because you are not prepared for their answer. To this end, be sure your questions are purposeful and get at the information you want to gather. Do not ignore what you receive from the audience, but rather find the most effective way to use it in your presentation.

OTHER WAYS OF GATHERING AUDIENCE INFORMATION

Although we have focused on a few audience analysis methods, there are several others that you can employ, depending upon the time you have to prepare your speech. Some of these methods include talking to a contact person, conducting a statistically valid survey of potential audience members before the presentation, and interviewing people who might attend your talk. As you can imagine, each of these is dependent on quite a few variables but nevertheless can provide you with valid and vital information as you prepare to speak.

Contact Persons

In many instances in which you deliver remarks to people outside your organization, there is a contact person responsible for making arrangements regarding your presentation. This could be the person who manages the event at which you are speaking, the person who invited you to deliver a sales presentation, or simply a colleague at another company. If the speech is at a neutral site, such as a hotel conference room, then this contact person likely reserved the room where you will speak, arranged the seating style, and is in charge of the audio-visual equipment. This contact person should be able to give you some insights into the makeup of the audience and the environment in which you are speaking. If audience members are required to reserve seats in advance, you might even be able to get a list of potential attendees. If the list is not available, the contact person should be able to provide their background, their values, and possibly even their disposition toward the event at which you will be speaking. No matter what the situation, it can only help to have a healthy dialogue with your contact person regarding the event and the audience.

Scientific Surveys

Previously, we mentioned polling the audience, and we told you it was not scientifically rigorous. Of course, scientifically rigorous polling is not possible during a speech; however, if you have enough advance time you can accurately survey your potential audience. These surveys help to gather demographic data as well as people's feelings toward particular issues or topics. To do this you need to develop Likert scale questions that help people numerically gauge their feelings regarding a specific idea or object.

Likert scales provide a statement to which people circle a number indicating the strength with which they agree or disagree. Individuals must choose only one answer to each statement. Likert scales vary in terms of the ranges from which they ask people to make a selection, but generally they go from either 1 to 5 or 1 to 7, with the middle number representing a neutral opinion. This allows a researcher to see how strongly the population being measured feels regarding an issue. As you can tell, such information would be invaluable for a speaker in advance of a presentation.

An audience's answers to these questions can often be broken down by demographic category, thanks in large part to the inclusion of such questions on the survey. The larger the audience, the more segmented the data becomes when broken into demographic groups. For instance, the Nielsen rating system, which is used to measure television audiences, breaks down surveyed populations according to demographic categories and provides advertisers with information regarding which programs they should advertise during.

Scientific surveys are not restricted to gathering demographic data or asking Likert scale questions; they can also contain open-ended questions that ask audience members to use their own words in response to a question. Open-ended questions allow audience members the opportunity to provide their reasons for feeling a certain way or their impressions of a specific idea or object. How they describe these things also tells you what is important and what might resonate with them. This type of information can be quite helpful, so some surveys ask people both forced-choice and open-ended questions. Ultimately, the success of surveys depends on what information you are trying to gather. Scientifically surveyed data can be rich and provide speakers who plan well with much-needed information as they prepare their speeches.

Teacher Tips

Polling the audience (your students) is one way to determine if your students understand the lesson and are ready to move on to the next subject. Checking for understanding is also sometimes called *formative assessment* and can include any strategy that allows you to find out what students know so you can use that information to adapt your teaching. Here are several ways you can check for understanding:

◊ Give a quiz.

◊ Ask direct questions about the content.

◊ Ask students to give examples that illustrate the concepts (in words, drawings, or role-playing activities).

◊ Give students examples and ask them to identify the concept.

◊ Do a think-pair-share. Ask students to *think* about and write down their answers to a question, then talk about their answers in *pairs*, and then call on several groups to *share* their answers with the rest of the class.

While getting answers from a few students is helpful, you can more effectively assess your class's understanding by getting responses from all of your students at once. In any class, you can ask students to raise their hands to indicate which answer they think is correct, but if the resources are available you should also consider using technology such as clickers or interactive programs/apps like Poll Everywhere. As a bonus, these strategies help keep your students engaged and interested throughout your class!

Other contexts where these skills apply: Human Resources, Marketing, and Project Management

Personal Interviews

Perhaps you do not have a contact person or do not have the time to create, implement, and analyze a scientifically valid survey instrument. This does not mean there is nothing you can do to gather more data on your audience. One final strategy you may employ is to personally interview potential audience members to allow you to gauge their interest in your topic and, perhaps, their actual opinions on the matter. If you know the person whom you interview, you also might get information on other potential audience members that can be quite useful—especially in a sales situation.

Interviews also have the added bonus of allowing you to get to know someone who will be in attendance at your talk. Knowing someone in the audience can help reduce tension and anxiety when you actually deliver your remarks. It also allows you to catch up with that person at the event before you talk to see if there is any other information he or she can relay to you.

Interviews are an intensely personal matter for several reasons. First, you are asking people to give time from their day to speak with you, and this in and of itself is a big commitment. Second, you are asking them to use that time to share their personal attitudes, beliefs, and ideas with you, so you should respect them for sharing that information, even if it might not be what you wanted or expected to hear. Finally, interviews occur in intimate settings, whether they are in person, over the phone, or even via Skype, so nonverbal behaviors that convey information regarding a person's personality will be available. This information must not be abused.

Health Care Help

Patient questionnaires (e.g., the forms that everyone must fill out during a first visit to a new doctor or dentist, at a blood drive, etc.) are a survey method for quickly obtaining information about individual patients as well as aggregating data about all of the patients in your practice. To make sure that you get the most accurate information possible and that your patients are comfortable answering the questions honestly, keep these tips in mind when writing your questions:

◊ Make your questions as straightforward as possible.

◊ Choose a font and format that are easy to read, yet allow the patient to maintain some degree of privacy from nearby wandering eyes.

◊ Use familiar, everyday language your patients will understand.

◊ Choose neutral language that does not imply that a positive or negative value judgment is associated with particular answers.

◊ Questions should be comprehensive and relevant to your medical specialty.

Other contexts in which these skills apply: Marketing Research, Human Resources, and Government

Summary

In any speaking situation, even those with no advance preparation time, audience analysis is a key component to a presenter's success. Information about the audience can help you tailor your message in a way that increases the likelihood of success. In this chapter, we have discussed audience analysis from several perspectives, all designed to illustrate how analyzing audience data can help you in crafting and delivering a successful speech. We covered different methods of audience analysis before the speech. We then provided strategies for audience analysis during the speech. Finally, we went over some specific ways of gathering information about an audience that might provide you with even more insight into their beliefs, attitudes, and personality. Audience analysis is the key to success in any speaking situation.

Key Term

demographics 121

Activities

1   Watch a recent product advertisement. Who are three audiences that you think the message is trying to reach? How did the product advertisers adapt their message to try to connect with each audience?

2   Think about the audience that you will be speaking to in this class. How would you summarize your audience's demographics?

3   Write three survey questions you would like to ask your audience that would give you information allowing you to better adapt your speech for your specific audience.

SUPPORTING MATERIALS

Objectives

◊ Become familiar with three different types of supporting materials that can be used in a speech

◊ Understand the advantages and disadvantages of each type of supporting material

◊ Learn guidelines for using supporting materials for maximum effect

Introductions capture the audience's attention and conclusions leave the audience with something to remember, but the real action is in the body of your speech, where you provide materials to support the claims made in your presentation. These supporting materials are the key to successfully influencing an audience. Successfully incorporating strong supporting materials into your speech helps demonstrate your credibility on the subject and supplies the rationale behind why you are telling the audience what you are telling them. It is in finding the best evidence for your speech and connecting it through the reasoning process that you deliver a smooth and effective presentation.

In this chapter, we will explore some common supporting materials you might use for any speech, whether it is informative, persuasive, or delivered on a special occasion. First, we will cover examples and how they can be used at different points in a speech. Then we will explain statistics and offer advice on how to effectively incorporate them into your presentation. Third, we will explain testimony and its appropriate place in a speech. Finally, we will offer some guidelines for successfully incorporating and using supporting materials in a presentation.

EXAMPLES

Examples can be useful as attention getters when beginning the speech, or they can help explain how data connects to the everyday experience of the audience. In this respect, good examples can enhance your credibility and help connect your audience with the topic by making seemingly abstract information relevant to their lives.

In fact, examples are one of the most common forms of supporting materials. We use examples in dialogue every day when talking with friends and family. We use them to make decisions in business, and we use them in small group scenarios. They are the most ubiquitous and versatile form of supporting material available to speakers. Examples are instances we use to help our audience think of an entire category of objects or events. Examples can be used to help define or clarify concepts, draw attention to a particular feature of an experience, or elicit memories and emotions in our audience. Examples can be of a specific object or event and can even include narratives that illustrate a common experience. Whether it's examples of television shows we enjoy, music we like, or athletes we think epitomize good models, we compare people and make judgments based in part upon examples of the best and the worst of a similar event, object, or scenario. One of the powers of examples is that they humanize information, grounding ideas to a concrete reality.

real example
an example that is factual

There are two types of examples, real and hypothetical, and they come in two forms, brief and extended. A **real example** is one that is factual, and you will often encounter real examples during the research process. Real examples can be employed as attention getters to open a speech, but can also help support claims within the body of your speech. If you use them for evidence, however, they should be coupled with other forms of information, thus enhancing their appeal. Using only one case or example to illustrate a point opens up the possibility of employing a reasoning fallacy such as the hasty generalization (see Chapter 14).

hypothetical example
an example that is fictional

A **hypothetical example** differs from a real example in that it is not found during the research process. Hypothetical examples are fictional, though believable and relevant, stories that serve to make a point. Like real examples, hypothetical examples can be used to get the audience's attention at the start of the speech and as supporting evidence within a speech. It is even more important to supplement hypothetical examples used as evidence with other data; otherwise the claim you make can be easily dismissed as based upon a fabricated, unrealistic example. If you are using a hypothetical example, you should not present the example as real, and you should ensure that your example is germane to the point you are making.

Both real and hypothetical examples can be brief or extended. A brief example makes a very quick point and can be effective at any point in a speech. These stories require little detail and focus on the connection between an aspect of the example and the argument or claim you are making. They are often only two or three sentences. Brief examples can be especially useful when you have a time limit for your presentation and need to find a way to connect with your audience and humanize your topic.

brief example
an example that makes a very quick point and can be effective at any point in a speech

Extended examples require more information than brief examples. These stories take time, and the importance of them lies in the details. Extended examples can be used as attention getters, but they are more useful within the speech as a means to provide the audience with an opportunity to visualize what you are saying and hopefully remind them of what you are talking about. Extended examples can be quite interesting to an audience, but they can also be risky. The danger is that they can encourage speakers to go off on tangents and make it difficult to stay on point. It is also important as a speaker to carefully consider how much time it will take to deliver an extended example to the audience and whether that time is too much of the total presentation. Remember that the extended example is not the speech focus but rather a means to support your overall purpose.

extended example
an example that takes time; the importance lies in the details

Examples are powerful when used appropriately, but they cannot and should not be the crux of your entire argument. They help to humanize your argument, enhance your credibility, and connect the audience with the topic of your speech. Ultimately, however, examples alone will not win the day in your presentation.

STATISTICS

Whereas examples provide color and a means to personalize information for an audience, statistics seemingly represent cold hard facts. Statistics summarize and organize sets of numbers to make them easier to understand or visualize. People generally "want the numbers" and believe numeric data are incontrovertible truths they cannot debate. This data gives your claims an aura of legitimacy and logical appeal. Like examples, statistics come in many forms and can be quite influential on an audience, but they also need to be carefully deployed because statistics can be manipulated, disputed, and used

statistics
numbers that summarize and organize sets of numbers to make them easier to understand or visualize

unethically. Perhaps the reason statistics are so powerful is that they surround our lives. Think how much of your academic life is statistically explained: your grade point average (GPA), cost of tuition, cost of fees, enrollment numbers, open seats in classes, GPA to graduate with honors or to get off probation, number of absences, and student loan calculations are just a few examples. Statistics provide an air of objectivity and certainty to an otherwise chaotic world, and so audiences tend to appreciate them when offered in support of an argument. Some of the most commonly used types of statistics include **measures of central tendency** (including the mean, median, and mode), the standard deviation, and percentages.

measures of central tendency
statistics that indicate where the middle of a distribution lies, including the mean, median, and mode

One of the most common statistics used to quantify our experiences is the average, or **mean**. The average is calculated by adding up all the numbers in a specific group, then dividing that total by the amount of entries added together. We use averages to describe things such as unemployment, salary, temperature, crime rate, and even performance in sports. Averages provide a picture of the tendency of a group of like things, but they by no means indicate the certainty of an event's occurring. Just because a ballplayer has a batting average of .300 (meaning he gets a hit on average three out of every 10 times) does not mean he will always get that many hits in that period of time. It just means that, over time, that is what you can expect to occur. Averages are just one type of statistic that we can use to explain numeric data to an audience, and it is not always the best piece of information.

mean
the average in a distribution of numbers

Another way to make sense of a group of numbers is through the **median**, or the middle number of a group of numbers. To determine the median point, rank the numbers in the group from high to low, or low to high, and locate the middle number of that group. If the total number of numbers is odd, it is easy to ascertain. For instance, if you have eleven numbers you would select the sixth number, as there would be five numbers above and five numbers below it. In a case where there is an even number of numbers, as with the example provided in Table 10.1, you compute the median by combining the two middle numbers and then dividing by two. The median can be better than the average in certain situations, such as when discussing real estate. For example, home sale prices are reported as both average sale prices and median sale prices. If there are a few homes that sell for much, much more than the typical home in an area, those homes would skew the average so that it is higher than someone would typically pay for a home in that area, whereas the median gives you a better idea of the typical price of a home. The median gives you an idea of the spread from low to high of a group of numbers. Medians are helpful at providing a more complete picture when offered

median
the middle number in a distribution of numbers

along with the average of the same group of numbers, but one more statistic can aid even further in explaining a set of data to an audience.

The **mode** is the most frequently occurring number within a group of numbers. As in the real estate example, sometimes averages and medians can be skewed by outliers. The mode helps paint a picture of which numbers occurred the most often, thus showing whether the average and median were in the center or if they were skewed because of outlying numbers. The example in Table 10.1 illustrates this point.

mode
the score that appears most often in a distribution of numbers

Note that the mean and median are more than $80,000 apart. This is because the mean and median have been skewed by three houses sold for way above average prices. Additionally, the mode of $275,000 is more than $120,000 less than the mean, demonstrating that most people paid below what the numbers indicate was typical.

Table 10.1

SOLD HOUSES IN A CERTAIN METROPOLITAN AREA	
PROPERTY NUMBER	SELLING PRICE
1	$800,000
2	$770,000
3	$700,000
4	$350,000
5	$330,000
6	$330,000
7	$300,000
8	$275,000
9	$275,000
10	$275,000
11	$250,000
12	$100,000

Here are the measures of central tendency:

Mean	=	$396,250
Median	=	$315,000
Mode	=	$275,000

One way to explain the spread of numbers in a group like the one we just explored is to calculate the **standard deviation**. The standard deviation is a measure of variability that shows how far apart the numbers are that create the average. The smaller the standard deviation, the closer the group of numbers is to the average, and thus the more accurate the average. A higher

standard deviation
a measure of variability that indicates how spread apart the numbers are in a distribution

standard deviation indicates a group of numbers that are significantly spread out, and so the average becomes less useful. For example, if the standard deviation in home prices is $10,000, then that suggests that most homes are selling for a fairly similar price, whereas a standard deviation of $100,000 would indicate that there are much larger differences in home prices.

Finally, many speakers use percentages or proportions to help audiences understand the data being presented. When comparing large numbers it is easier for audiences to visualize what 50 percent of a group looks like, rather than to think what 345 out of 690 looks like. Percentages are often useful when presenting demographic data or comparing the likelihood of two different events happening, such as comparing the likelihood of being in a car accident versus a plane crash.

margin of error
a measurement of the potential sampling error in polling; it provides a likelihood, not a certainty, that the result of the poll will be within a certain range

One other statistic that is important to be familiar with is the margin of error. The margin of error is a measurement of the potential sampling error in polling. It provides people with the likelihood that the result of a poll will be within a certain range. The smaller the margin of error, the more accurate the poll. When using survey data it is essential to understand what the margin of error is for the poll you choose to use.

No matter how you explain statistics, though, there are risks. You must use the most appropriate statistic for your topic, and present that information as accurately and fairly as possible. Think of the example of the home prices. What if you constructed your argument using the mean and median as supporting materials? Someone could easily refute your argument by pointing to the mode and the standard deviation, thus making your statistics questionable and damaging your ability to connect with your audience. What if you tried to convince your audience that your hometown needed more police officers because crime had doubled in the previous year, and an audience member pointed out that the increase had been from two petty crimes to four petty crimes? While it might be true that the number of crimes doubled, it would not be especially fair to make your audience believe the danger is substantially higher and their lives are in far greater danger. There is one more type of supporting material in addition to statistics and examples, and we will discuss it next.

TESTIMONY

Testimony, the third type of supporting material we will discuss, includes the words of other people. There are two types of testimony you can use in a speech: expert testimony and peer testimony. One of the powers of testimony is that it uses people's words, whether quoted or paraphrased, to lend support to an argument. It provides a perspective other than your own, and, like examples, serves to humanize your position.

testimony
using the words of other people as evidence

The first type of testimony, **expert testimony**, can also be the most powerful. To be considered expert testimony, the information must come from someone who is an expert on the topic. This means the person has conducted extensive research on the topic, has significant experience with the topic, or holds a position that lends credibility to his or her ideas on the subject matter. Remember, however, that just because a person is an expert in one area does not make him or her an expert in every area. For example, consider a scientist who is an expert on the properties of physics. You would use his or her testimony or words to support an argument about the way things work in the natural world, but the scientist's ideas on constitutional law, for instance, would be no more expert than those of the average citizen.

expert testimony
testimony from someone who has conducted extensive research on the topic, has significant experience with the topic, or holds a position that lends credibility to his or her ideas on the subject matter

It is also important to consider how the audience will view the person whose testimony you use. No matter the qualification of the person, if the audience does not see the person as credible, then that person will not be nearly as powerful as he or she could be. Experts need experience and knowledge about the topic as well as good character for the audience to see them as unbiased.

Not all testimony you use as supporting evidence comes from experts. It is also effective to use testimony from those in the same peer group as the audience. This helps them connect with the ideas you present in a more meaningful way because they identify with the person whose testimony you provide. **Peer testimony** requires no advanced degrees or experience with the topic, but it is important for the audience to identify with that peer. They also need to provide testimony relevant to the topic of the speech and the specific claim you are making. Peer testimony can be useful when you are explaining a similar group's opinion on your topic or showing how your audience might be affected by your topic. For example, you might use peer testimony to show how students are affected by increases in tuition.

peer testimony
testimony from someone who is in the same peer group as the audience, but who is not necessarily an expert on the topic

Expert and peer testimony can serve as powerful pieces of supporting material if they fit the topic and the situation. They also help connect you and your topic with the audience by enhancing emotional connections and logical assertions with perspectives other than your own. However, as with examples and statistics, testimony alone cannot be the sole evidence upon which you stake your claims. It is, after all, circumstantial evidence if it is used alone. In the next section, we will provide some guidelines for effectively incorporating supporting materials into your presentations.

STEM Spotlight

When putting together a research proposal or project plan, supporting materials are critically important, especially in the STEM fields. Of the types of evidence that are discussed here that are usually used in speeches, it is likely you will be expected to rely on statistics and other quantitative data. Additionally, your proposal will likely need to include the following types of evidence to show that your proposal is feasible and will fully address your research problem:

◊ formulas and calculations

◊ measurements

◊ materials specifications

◊ references

◊ project timeline

◊ budget

◊ other relevant support materials

Other contexts in which these skills apply: Sales, Performance Management, Engineering, and Accounting

GUIDELINES FOR USING SUPPORTING MATERIALS

During the research process you are certain to find more information and supporting materials than you will need in the speech itself. This is a good thing, but it can be frustrating when you decide what should go, what should stay, and where support is best used in the speech. So, when putting your speech together, carefully analyze what will assist you in getting your ideas across to the audience. In this section, we provide some helpful guidelines for doing just that.

◊ **Be sure to have balance between your types of supporting materials.** As we have noted throughout the chapter, you cannot rely solely on any one of the three types of supporting materials to make your speech. Using all three types of supporting materials demonstrates a broad knowledge of the topic and its applicability to the audience and also creates emotional and logical dimensions for your presentation.

◊ **Only use supporting materials relevant to your topic and argument.** You may encounter information during the research process that is fascinating and interesting. This information may also be something you really want to share with your audience simply because of its "cool factor," but it has little to do with your topic. Do not include such data in your speech if it does not help you achieve the purpose of your speech. Use only supporting materials that connect to the claims you make within your speech.

◊ **Make sure you stay focused when using examples.** As we mentioned earlier, an extended example can be risky, especially within speeches with tight time limits. Examples need to directly relate to the topic and help achieve identification with the audience, but you must also be able to quickly return from the example to the speech itself. In other words, it should not be a digression from the speech purpose but rather a piece of evidence in support of that purpose. When this happens, it allows you to stay focused on your goals. This is especially critical when using examples as attention getters, because if they are too long, you and your audience will quickly lose focus.

◊ **Choose the type of testimony to use based upon the goal you are trying to achieve.** Not all testimony functions equally in a speech. If you want to personalize information to help an audience identify with the topic and with you as a speaker, then it is best to use peer testimony. On the other hand, if the testimony is meant to provide credibility to the information you just provided or to support a claim you are making with objective information, then it is better to use expert testimony. You should never use peer testimony to justify a claim but rather use it to illustrate its applicability to the audience.

◊ **Use supporting materials ethically.** Don't mislead the audience with your supporting materials, as this will alienate them and weaken your speech. The supporting material should be presented honestly, and you should not ignore statistics that weaken your argument or change information for the purpose of influencing the audience. Audiences actually respect honesty and openness, as these are qualities of a good speaker, and so you should be candid about any potential shortcomings with your information.

These are just a few guidelines to help you make judicious decisions regarding the placement and use of supporting materials within your speech. Many of your choices obviously depend upon the goals of your speech, the audience you will be speaking to, and the topic you are addressing.

Summary

Supporting materials are both the evidence for your claims and vehicles through which you can connect with an audience. As we illustrated in this chapter, there are three primary forms of supporting materials, each with a role to play in any speech. Good speakers balance their use of examples, statistics, and testimony when articulating a position to an audience.

Key Terms

brief example 133	median 134
expert testimony 137	mode 135
extended example 133	peer testimony 137
hypothetical example 132	real example 132
margin of error 136	standard deviation 135
mean 134	statistics 133
measures of central tendency 134	testimony 137

Activities

1   What are three specific support materials that you can use for your upcoming speech? How will each of these support materials help your audience better connect with and understand your message?

2   Do some research and find several statistics or numbers from credible sources that will help your audience better understand your topic.

3   Who are some potential people who could provide expert and peer testimony that would help to support your speech? What experiences or expertise do they have that would be beneficial?

CONTEXT AND THE SPEECH SITUATION

Objectives

◊ Understand the differences between various environments in which you might speak

◊ Appreciate how different media influence speaking environments today

◊ Learn how to effectively adapt to and use elements of the speaking environment when delivering a presentation

You may ask yourself when you will ever need to give a speech. You might have to deliver a toast at a wedding or give a report as part of a class project, but those might be all the situations you can envision. The fact of the matter is that in many different professions you will be called upon to deliver a speech, and all of those instances will present different environments in which you must effectively deliver your message. Most, if not all, professions have national associations, business meetings, and client presentations. Each of these different scenarios requires public speaking skills. In fact, media has expanded the potential venues through which you might deliver a speech or presentation.

In this chapter, we will first explain some of the basic elements found in any speaking situation. We call these the components of the speaking environment. We will then discuss how media has changed and expanded the idea of a speaking environment in many ways—ways very relevant to you, regardless of what career path you choose. Third, we will cover the different types of live audiences and rooms that you may encounter when speaking. Finally, we will provide some basic tips for using the speaking environment to your advantage when addressing an audience.

BASIC COMPONENTS OF THE SPEAKING ENVIRONMENT

Every speaking situation can be described in three different dimensions. The first is the physical location in which the speech is being delivered. The second dimension details the speaking tools available in that location, and the final dimension of any speaking situation is the speaker. Each of these dimensions is relevant to understanding any speaking environment, and in this section we will explain how these dimensions can manifest differently in various speaking situations.

Teacher Tips

The size of your class and classroom, along with the experience and knowledge of your students, will have a large impact on how you teach. Here are some considerations for common scenarios:

◊ **Large lecture.** Large lectures (one hundred or more students) are usually taught in classrooms with stadium or auditorium-style seating that is higher in the back of the room than in the front of the room. In this type of class, the teacher will need to rely primarily on lectures and will need to use a presentation technology, such as PowerPoint, to ensure that all students in the room can easily see visual cues used throughout the class. These classes typically include the most prepared, formal presentations.

◊ **Standard classroom.** Standard classes usually include twenty-five to thirty students, and students are usually seated in individual desks on level ground. In these classrooms, teachers use a variety of instructional strategies, including lecture, discussion, small group activities, and more. When lecturing, instructors should use some type of visual cues, but can be effective using either PowerPoint or a whiteboard. In this kind of classroom you might teach using a balance of formal presentations and informal discussions.

◊ **Small seminar.** Seminars are usually classes with fifteen or fewer students and are often taught with everyone seated around a large conference table. These classes are usually intended to be conducted primarily in a discussion format, so it is common for instructors to remain seated at the table through most of the class and to avoid using any type of presentation technology. When you are teaching in this situation, your presentation will be very conversational.

◊ **Online classes.** In *asynchronous* online classes, in which students can do the coursework at any time, instructors often need to record video lectures that are posted online, so the class is sometimes taught using strategies similar to those of large lecture classes. *Synchronous* online classes, in which students and the instructor are in a videoconference at the same time, can be taught more like a standard class or small seminar with a variety of instructional techniques, and discussion can even be done on a discussion board throughout the class.

Other contexts where these skills apply: Sales, Management, Group Facilitation

Physical Location

The **physical location** of a speech refers to the immediate environment in which the speaker will be speaking. Locations vary from large rooms to small rooms, from outdoors to the comfort of your office or home. It is important, however, to stress that the location refers to a physical environment and not the medium through which a speech is delivered. In that respect, the internet is not a location but rather a medium through which a message is transmitted. The location would be the actual location in which the video or audio file was recorded. Now that we have made that distinction clear, let's explore a variety of physical locations in which you might deliver a speech and discuss the challenges and advantages inherent in each.

physical location
the immediate environment in which the speaker will be speaking

One of the most common venues for a speech of any kind is indoors. The majority of sales presentations, company updates, conference panels, wedding toasts, and eulogies occur inside. "Indoors," however, is a broad description with a lot of variance. Indoors can refer to a small, intimate setting in a conference room; it can mean a classroom; auditoriums and churches are also both indoors, as are large arenas or even a living room in someone's home. Indoor speaking in any of these environments provides some very basic, but important, advantages for a speaker. First, the lighting and air temperature can usually be adjusted for your comfort. Being indoors also minimizes certain types of distractions by blocking out the outside world and its associated sounds, such as airplanes, cars, wind, weather, and even people talking. The contained nature of an indoor room, regardless of how big or small, is generally the most comfortable situation in which speakers may find themselves.

Indoor speaking does not encompass all possible speaking environments, as occasions do arise when you might be called upon to speak outdoors. These situations could include company picnics, family reunions, golf tournaments, building dedications, political rallies, or facility tours for prospective clients. Compared to indoor presentations, outdoor speaking is more challenging because there are significant distractions for the audience and you, but there are also some unique advantages as well.

One prime example of a possible advantage to outdoor speaking situations is the opportunity to adjust the setting in advance of the presentation. In many cases outdoor speech locations are set up before the speech, and so the actual seating style, arrangement, and design of the environment can be influenced in advance with a site trip. When a speech is indoors you have no chance to knock down a wall or create more space, but outdoors you have space to play with, thus allowing you to somewhat customize your speaking situation.

Even so, many of the advantages of speaking indoors are challenges when presenting outdoors. For instance, you cannot control the weather outdoors and thus must have backup plans to compensate for rain, wind, or other unforeseen nature-related obstacles that might present themselves. You also might not have some of the comforts available in a conference room, such as electricity, thus inhibiting your ability to project your voice to a large crowd or show slides or videos to your audience. If the weather is nice or the setting is scenic, your audience may easily lose focus on you and your message. For these reasons, outdoor speaking can be more challenging than presenting indoors.

When considering indoor or outdoor presentations, here are some basic questions you should ask when preparing to speak:

Indoor Presentations

◊   How many people can be seated in the room?

◊   Are you on an elevated platform?

◊   Is the audience elevated above you?

◊   What is the temperature of the room?

◊   What is the lighting like?

◊   How much noise from the outside can be heard in the room?

Outdoor Presentations

◊ How is the seating arranged?

◊ Can I influence or change the way the venue is designed?

◊ Is electricity available?

◊ What will the weather be like?

Whether you find yourself indoors or outdoors when delivering your speech, location is just one of the primary components of the speaking environment. Next, we will discuss a second aspect of the speaking environment relevant to both indoor and outdoor speech delivery: speaking tools.

Speaking Tools

There will usually be some type of **speaking tool** to assist you when delivering your speech. These tools include a microphone, a podium, a lectern, lighting, and projectors. Each of these tools can help improve the delivery of a speech in a variety of ways, but you must become familiar with the nuances of the available tools before trying to incorporate them into your presentation.

speaking tool
device that assists speakers, such as a microphone, podium, lectern, or lighting

The most common speaking tool is a microphone. Some voices project well, carrying throughout even large rooms, but many people do not have that powerful a voice and need to amplify it. Even those with a booming voice will sometimes need a microphone in large areas or where there may be background noise that interferes with the audience's ability to hear the speaker. Microphones can allow for this to happen, but not all microphones are created equal.

Microphones primarily come in three types. The first is a fixed microphone, which may be on or attached to a podium. These microphones are often placed at the top of a stand and can be adjusted to the height of the speaker. This is convenient for speakers, but it is important to adjust the height before the presentation, if possible, so as not to take up time determining how to adjust the stand when you should be speaking to the audience.

The second type of microphone is portable and wireless, enabling it to be carried around the room by the speaker. This type is especially advantageous if a speaker or moderator wants to interact with the audience because it allows the presenter to hand the microphone to individuals and allow them to speak. If you choose to do this, be aware that when you pass the microphone to someone you have lost some control over the situation. Most often this is not a problem, but sometimes individuals who are given a microphone go on rants or do not relinquish the microphone when you want them to. Overall, though, wireless microphones give you more freedom to move about a large room when addressing an audience.

The third type of microphone is also portable but is not handheld; rather, it takes the form of a small receiver on your lapel that picks up and amplifies your voice. This device is usually called a hands-free microphone and also comes in the form of headset microphones. These are very useful when the speaker wants to present visual aids or to make demonstrations with products. Sometimes you see people in grocery stores or at conferences who wear these types of microphones to demonstrate how to use a product while also speaking to an audience.

podium
a raised platform on which the speaker stands

The next tool is a **podium**, which is a raised platform that can vary in size that the speaker stands on. As mentioned earlier, it is advantageous to both the speaker and the audience if both are not on the same level, and podiums create this type of atmosphere. Sometimes a podium is in the center of a room, as in an arena, while other times it is at the front of the room. In larger rooms, or in situations when there are multiple speakers, a **dais** may be used, which is a raised platform similar to but larger than a podium.

dais
a raised platform similar to but larger than a podium, often on which multiple speakers can stand

lectern
the stand behind which people speak and on which they place their notes

People commonly confuse a podium with a lectern. A **lectern** is the stand behind which people speak and on which they place their notes. Lecterns are usually placed on a podium or dais so that there is a designated place from which a person will speak.

Another tool available in speaking situations is the lighting of the area. Obviously, in most cases, indoor lighting is more easily controlled than outdoor lighting. The lighting can help create a certain mood, can spotlight the speaker or someone in the audience, or can even be dimmed so that visual aids are more visible to the entire audience. In most cases if the lighting is not uniform the speaker is more brightly illuminated than the audience members.

Outdoor speeches are trickier to manage with regard to lighting, as there is often natural light with which a speaker must compete. Natural light, though, is unpredictable, and when the sun goes behind clouds it can significantly alter visibility for a crowd. Many outdoor venues will supply additional lighting if the weather indicates it might be needed. Always pay attention to weather forecasts and stay in touch with the site coordinator to determine what, if any, adjustments are needed for lighting.

The final tool that you might use in a speaking situation is a projector. Projectors are often used to display PowerPoint slides, video clips, websites, or other audiovisual resources. You will read more about how to use these resources effectively in the chapter on presentation aids, but when planning your speech, you should find out whether you will have access to this resource.

The Speaker

The last aspect of the speaking environment we will discuss is perhaps the most important and that is you, the actual speaker. You have the ability to influence how your message is received through the construction of three components of your speech. How you carry yourself, your posture, and your dress all communicate a message to the audience. Your appearance and how you conduct yourself adds importance and influences the mood of the situation. Your choices in clothing and demeanor must convey the same emotional attachment and feeling you want to create for that moment. In this part of the chapter we will first address the three creative elements you bring to the speech as a speaker, and then we will cover the elements of posture and dress that influence the effectiveness of your message.

artistic proofs
constructed by the speaker for the occasion; concerns *ethos, pathos,* and *logos*

Aristotle, a famous Greek philosopher and teacher, identified the artistic and inartistic proofs that speakers wield when delivering a presentation to an audience. **Artistic proofs** consist of three things: *ethos, pathos,* and *logos. Ethos* refers to the credibility that you have on the topic you discuss, and it is considered artistic because you, as the speaker, choose how to explain your credentials and expertise to an audience (we will address credibility in more detail in Chapter 16). *Pathos* refers to the emotional dimensions of your appeal, how you try to speak with the emotion that you wish the audience to feel, and how you construct stories to support your points that generate that emotional response in the audience. *Pathos* is most effective when you use a single object or individual to which the audience can relate, much like commercials for the ASPCA use pictures of a single dog to engender a feeling of pity and sympathy for all dogs housed in kennels. *Logos* refers to the logical organization of the evidence you present, and Aristotle considered it artistic and creative because as the speaker you choose when to lay out certain arguments instead of others and what evidence to use in support of your claims (we will cover elements related to *logos* in Chapters 14-16). In contrast to

ethos
the credibility of the speaker

pathos
the emotional dimensions of the appeal, which can influence an audience's disposition toward the topic, speaker, or occasion

logos
the logical dimension of the appeal

inartistic proofs
all the evidence, data, and documents that exist outside of the speaker and the audience but nevertheless can aid in persuasion

artistic proofs, Aristotle defined inartistic proofs as those which the speaker does not create, like statistics, testimony, and other forms of data. The development of artistic proofs and the choice of which inartistic proofs to use in any given context are decisions you make as the speaker, as are other things, like the way you dress.

Practical Politics

Knowing the environment you will be speaking in and what resources will be available in that space are important for helping you tailor your speech to the audience. A keynote speech in front of thousands of people is very different from a town hall meeting, which is very different from a small coffee gathering in someone's living room. Here are several contexts in which you should be prepared to speak:

◊ large keynote address

◊ televised debate

◊ public interview (on television or in front of an audience)

◊ town hall meeting

◊ after-dinner speech at fundraisers of various sizes

◊ one-on-one conversations in coffee shops or walking down the street

◊ speeches to energize your supporters

◊ speeches to persuade undecided and oppositional voters

◊ commemorative speeches, tributes, eulogies, and other special occasion speeches

Other contexts where these skills apply: Engineering, Academia, and Human Resources

Your choice of clothing can communicate your level of respect for the audience and the situation, so you should take care in how you appear when you speak. Both women and men should be well dressed. If you are unsure of how to dress, remember the old axiom that it is better to overdress than to underdress. Often the situation itself will dictate the type of clothing to wear, but when in doubt it is always helpful to ask.

Guidelines on Dressing

Here are some general guidelines on dressing for some common speaking situations:

◊ Wedding toast—Formal

◊ Eulogy—Semiformal or formal

◊ Sales presentation—Semiformal

◊ Classroom as teacher—Semiformal

◊ Classroom as student—Business casual

Dress is the only element of the speaking situation that you will always have total control over, so it is important to take advantage of this. As the speaker you will be the focus, and you always want the audience to see that you respect them and the situation; the first thing they will notice about you is the way you are dressed. If you dress inappropriately or in a distracting fashion then the focus shifts from your presentation to your attire, and the audience will not receive the message you intend them to.

When you are the speaker, you should dress at least as formally as your audience. Make sure your clothes fit well and are comfortable; if you are constantly tugging at a garment that doesn't quite fit then both you and your audience will be distracted throughout your presentation. Likewise, avoid wearing accessories or clothing with busy patterns that will distract attention from what you are saying, unless you have a specific reason for that particular accessory or garment.

So far we have covered the three basic elements of any situation, but, as we mentioned earlier, technology has drastically altered our understanding of speaking situations. In the next section, we will discuss mediated speaking situations and how they might arise in your chosen career.

MEDIA

The last several decades have seen a great change in technology and thus a corresponding change in our ability to communicate. In particular, we can now hold conference calls with people across the globe, upload presentations to YouTube to watch at a convenient time, and use videoconferencing software such as Skype. In this section, we will discuss using media to enable presentations through these various programs.

Perhaps one of the most common media through which businesses present materials is conference calling. Conference calling allows multiple parties to communicate on one telephone line, thus allowing for a larger audience and increased audience interaction. To be successful, however, conference calls must be carefully arranged and monitored.

Over the last several years conference call software has developed to the point that we can now see the people with whom we are talking, thus creating the possibility for videoconferencing. Even classes on college campuses utilize this software for distance education courses in which students watch lectures or presentations live from places other than the classroom and can be seen by and interact with the instructor and other students. Two common programs that facilitate this are WebEx and AdobeConnect. This software also adds the ability to post comments and pose questions online to those presenting in the room, and allows many people to interact from different locations at once. Outside of the classroom, videoconferencing can be valuable in business situations where distance is a factor. For example, suppose a software development team wanted to demonstrate a new feature to clients located in different cities. With videoconferencing, the team's clients would all watch the same demonstration at the same time regardless of their location.

In addition to these videoconferencing services that have become increasingly popular in business and educational settings, there are also several simpler videoconferencing tools that are often used for personal communication. Some of these videoconferencing tools include Skype, Zoom, FaceTime, WhatsApp, Portal, Amazon Echo Show, and many others. This software allows you to see the person who you are talking with as though you were in a face-to-face conversation, despite being located in geographically dispersed places.

Webcams can also be used to tape presentations and demonstrations for upload to the Web. One popular site where video blogs, or vlogs, are posted is YouTube, a repository for hundreds of thousands of video compilations. These video diaries, journals, or presentations are there in perpetuity, so be careful what you choose to upload. Uploading videos to YouTube is easier than actually giving a speech because you do not see your audience. That said, you never know if what you post will go viral!

These technologies are becoming more and more popular. In an increasingly connected world, they save companies and individuals a great deal of money and time, both because traditional communication tools can be quite expensive as compared to VoIP solutions and because travel is not required. These technologies can enhance productivity and accomplish much the same thing as face-to-face meetings; however, although these technologies are popular, people still speak to groups in live settings.

Conference calls, whether via phone or video, should be treated with a similar level of formality as an in-person meeting. Below are some tips for a successful conference call.

◊ Create a clear agenda that is appropriate in scope and manageable within the time frame established for the call.

◊ Test your audio and/or video prior to the call to ensure you can be heard and can hear others clearly.

◊ If you are leading the call, dial in a few minutes early to welcome the other participants and make note of each person who dials in so you know when everyone is present.

◊ If any person is unfamiliar with any others on the call, offer introductions to everyone, including information about their role in the call.

◊ If you are leading the call, ensure that each participant has an adequate opportunity to share their thoughts.

◊　Appoint someone to take notes and create a list of action items to circulate to participants after the call.

◊　When you are not speaking, place your line on mute so that background noise does not interfere with the meeting.

◊　If your conference calling tool has the capability to record audio, first ask permission from everyone to record the call. Then, with permission, you can share the recorded conversation with anyone who may have been unable to join the call.

ROOM SIZE VERSUS AUDIENCE SIZE

Because outdoor venues can vary a great deal depending on geographic location, we will provide some suggestions for indoor locations for speeches that have a bit more stability. There are several indoor scenarios in which you may find yourself, and each has its challenges and opportunities.

Small rooms, the most common speaking environment indoors, include conference rooms and classrooms, and they allow more intimacy with audience members. It is unlikely that you will need a microphone in these situations, as everyone should be able to hear you easily; however, some moderate-sized rooms might be packed with people and require a microphone for those in the back to adequately hear you. Generally, these settings allow you to move around or sit to deliver your remarks.

Business Basics

If you are preparing to give a sales presentation, tailor your presentation to the situation as much as possible, and be prepared to adapt if you find yourself in a slightly different speaking context once you arrive on site. Here are considerations for some common scenarios:

◊　**Presentation for a large number of stakeholders.** Begin with a formal presentation, and allow the stakeholders to ask questions at the end after they have heard all of the relevant information.

◊　**Conference room with a few people.** You should have some presentation materials ready to use, but if possible, treat the presentation more like a discussion. Ask questions, and focus your presentation on your client's needs instead of covering every possible feature you could speak about.

◊ **One-on-one sales pitch.** If you are meeting with someone in a one-on-one situation, begin by asking questions, and treat the sales pitch as a conversation. Listen to the client, ask questions, and address his or her most important concerns.

◊ **WebEx or other online presentation.** Prepare an outline of your presentation, along with any relevant slides and demonstrations. Plan your presentation around the number of people who will participate in the call, using similar guidelines for in-person presentations with an audience of a similar size. Because you will not be able to see the audience's nonverbal reactions you should provide occasional opportunities for verbal feedback to make sure you are addressing your client's concerns.

Other contexts in which these skills apply: Interviewing, Engineering, and Social Work

Small rooms can sometimes contain a small audience. If you are expecting a much larger audience this can be a letdown, but as the speaker you have the obligation to put as much energy into the speech as you would if the group were large. If the audience is small consider being more informal and presenting your ideas in a conversational manner. This may also allow you to ask the audience for their feedback during your presentation. Small settings with small audiences can create an opportunity for more interaction with your audience, but also remember that the smaller the audience, the larger the focus on you as the speaker.

Small rooms are not the only indoor locations for presentations, as you may deliver remarks in a big room with a large audience. In this setting a formal delivery is required, and you are restricted in your ability to interact with the audience. This situation requires a strong delivery and a very clear organization of your ideas. Since this venue is less intimate than a smaller setting, it is easier for the audience to drift away and become disengaged. Such an obstacle requires you to be prepared and to deliver your remarks with enthusiasm to minimize the risk of losing the audience.

Large rooms, however, do not always guarantee large audiences. In fact, it is possible that you may find yourself speaking to a small audience in a very large room. This is a challenging environment, even for experienced speakers, as the size of the room can be intimidating and the number of attendees can be disappointing. There are some ways you can turn the situation to your advantage. First, you may want to acknowledge the discrepancy between attendance and room size to the audience that is present. Usually in these circumstances audience members are scattered throughout the room or auditorium, and this increases the challenge. If this occurs ask the audience members to move down front and sit as a group. This allows you to focus on them and creates an intimate environment, thus mitigating the distraction of a large room. You can also engage them in much the same way you might in the smaller room scenarios we discussed earlier.

The ratio of room size to audience size can create challenges and opportunities for you as a speaker, but remember all the tools available to you and use those that will enhance your presentation and allow you to adapt to the situation. Regardless of the room in which you find yourself, remember that different environments create both opportunities and challenges, and as a good speaker you must not only adapt to the situation but also know how to use it to your advantage.

Summary

We often have little control over where and when we are asked to speak, so it is essential to understand the different nuances of the variety of situations in which you might find yourself asked to present. In this chapter, we explained some fundamental characteristics of speaking situations and how the media has influenced the ways in which we communicate in those situations. We also provided some practical suggestions for handling these different contexts so that you can maximize the impact of your presentations. Situations can create stress, but we can also use them to create success for ourselves.

Key Terms

artistic proofs 147	*logos* 147
dais 146	*pathos* 147
ethos 147	physical location 143
inartistic proofs 148	podium 146
lectern 146	speaking tool 145

Activities

1   What challenges do you expect to face in the physical location in which you will deliver the speeches in this class?

2   List all of the possible speaking tools that will be available for you to use when you give your speeches in this class. What pitfalls do you need to avoid? How can you use those tools to help enhance your speech?

3   How can you use *logos*, *ethos*, and *pathos* together to build an effective presentation?

OUTLINING

Objectives

◊ Understand the principles that serve as the foundation for any good outline

◊ Appreciate the difference between a preparation outline and a speaking outline

◊ Become familiar with other forms of speaking materials

Any good speech is carefully prepared and organized before its delivery. This organizational process begins with sifting through the information you gather when researching, but the structure of your speech really takes shape when you draft your outline. The development of an outline is not a one-time task. Rather, it is a process in which you create a full-sentence outline that illustrates the points you want to make and from which you practice your speech. As you practice, you become more familiar with the material and thus can pare it down to shorter phrases, which in turn constitutes your speaking outline.

In order to successfully use this process, it is important to understand the principles that guide the construction of a good outline. In this chapter, we will first cover the principles of outlining, then discuss the characteristics of a preparation outline and how to turn that outline into a proper speaking outline. Despite the emphasis on outlining in this chapter, we recognize an outline is not the only type of speaking material you might use, so the chapter concludes with a brief exploration of other types of speaking materials.

OUTLINING PRINCIPLES

Outlining is a systematic method of organizing your ideas. This approach ensures that your argument is clear and that your information is in an appropriate place within the speech. There are three key tenets to outlining: subordination, coordination, and division. Each of these three principles helps you create an organized presentation that your audience can follow.

Subordination

subordination
process of creating
a hierarchy of ideas
in which the most
general ideas appear
first, followed by more
specific ideas

All outlines work to create what is essentially a hierarchy of ideas through the use of symbols and indentations. This process of creating a hierarchy of ideas in which the most general ideas appear first, followed by more specific ideas, is called subordination, and it is a key principle of outlining. In an outline, each level has a different symbol set, and those symbols correspond to items such as main points, subpoints, and sub-subpoints. The first or broadest level is a main point, and it is represented by a capital Roman numeral. The second, slightly more specific level is a subpoint, and it is represented by a capital letter. The third level, if needed, is even more specific than the second level, and is denoted by an Arabic numeral. The following shows what the system looks like:

I. Main point

   A. Subpoint

   B. Subpoint

   C. Subpoint

      1. Sub-subpoint

      2. Sub-subpoint

II. Main point

Notice how indenting different levels creates the perception of a hierarchy of points. The main point is the most general and does not include specific evidence or data, but rather, sets up an entire section of a speech that provides data and evidence in support of the main point. The subpoint is a more specific aspect of the main point and can include specific evidence or information in support of the main point. Sometimes this information can take several sentences of explanation, and in those cases another level of the outline, the sub-subpoint, is created.

Each time you move to a new level, the information should support the level above it. So if you have a subpoint indicated by a capital letter and need to explain it further, you do not use another capital letter; rather, you move down a level to numbers so you can visually see that that explanation relates to the particular subpoint it is under. In essence, the deeper into the levels one goes, the more specific the information gets, but it always relates to the level under which it appears.

Coordination

The hierarchy created by an outline that adheres to subordinated points naturally creates coordination of information. By **coordination** we mean that all information on the same level has the same significance. In other words, all of your main points are equally important, and each subpoint is of similar importance to the other subpoints. The same types of statements appear on the same level, and when you find yourself making a claim in a place where you should be providing data in the outline, it should indicate that you are at the wrong level of the outline and need to make a change. This coordination helps you and your audience stay on track and provides expected and relevant information when it is needed.

coordination
all information at the same level has the same significance

Division

The final principle of outlining we will discuss is the notion of **division**, and it is just as important as the ideas of subordination and coordination. If you are going to divide a point, such as a main point, into subpoints, you need to have two or more subpoints in order to do so. The same is said for dividing subpoints as well—you must have two sub-subpoints if you plan to create a new level for the outline. More succinctly: if you have a main point I, you must have a main point II, and if you have a subpoint A, you must have a subpoint B, and, of course, if you have a sub-subpoint 1, you must have a sub-subpoint 2.

division
principle that if a point is divided into subpoints, there must be two or more subpoints

The principle of division ensures that you give adequate attention to each line and claim you make in a speech. If you have too many claims and not enough evidence, the speech needs more attention to the supporting materials. Division ensures balance, explanation, and organization within the hierarchy of ideas and should not be discarded as unimportant.

Outlining helps you logically organize your ideas by adhering to the three principles of subordination, coordination, and division. Because of the structured nature of an outline and the use of these ideas, it is easy to see how an outline serves a speaker better than bullet points or random notes. It affords you the ability to lay the main points out and logically put the subpoints and sub-subpoints neatly into the hierarchy. Additionally, the earlier you start the outlining process, the better your speech will be, and the more you get into the practice of outlining, the more you will realize that it is a valuable tool, whether you are preparing a speech or writing a research paper.

PREPARATION OUTLINE

We have repeatedly noted that developing a speech is a creative and fluid process, and the development of an outline is no different. We mentioned a few moments ago that organizing your speech begins when you start gathering information, but it accelerates when you sit down to prepare an outline. The earlier you do this, the more time you have to make changes and work through different ways to deliver your material. The preparation outline is a tool that facilitates such changes in a smooth fashion by visually illustrating the information you collected and the arguments you wish to make.

Preparation outlines follow several rules. The first is that each symbol of the outline is followed by a full sentence. For example, we show a main point and subpoint:

I.   Main point stated as a full sentence

    A.   Subpoint stated as a full sentence

    B.   Subpoint stated as a full sentence

II.   Main point stated as a full sentence

    A.   Subpoint stated as a full sentence

    B.   Subpoint stated as a full sentence

Full sentences help demonstrate what you want to say and also allow you to make specific connections between points and evidence. Additionally, they allow you to practice your speech in its entirety, which, as you will see when we discuss how to create a speaking outline, is very helpful.

The second rule for preparation outlines is that you should only have one major idea per symbol. In your subpoints, you will probably need two or three sentences to explain each idea, but each subpoint should be a distinct idea that is separate from the other subpoints. By doing this, you can break a speech down to its component parts and ensure that your information appears where it should. This makes it easier to spot information that is out of place and to cut or move that information to another, more appropriate location in the outline. If you find you cannot create a properly divided point, then this may indicate that the statement should be moved or discarded.

A third rule of preparation outlines pertains to in-text citations. Preparation outlines should contain proper citations for material drawn from sources. This enables you to cross-check the source and make sure you verbally attribute information when you share it with your audience. In your outline you should cite your source the same way you plan to cite the source verbally. Generally speaking, you will briefly cite a source and then provide the corresponding information (details about what to include in oral citations appear in Chapter 8, Research and Preparation). When you write a research paper, you will probably use parenthetical citations for your sources, but parenthetical citations are not useful in speech outlines since your audience cannot look up information in your references page while you are speaking and you are likely to forget to cite your sources if you do not include what you plan to say about the source in the text of your outline.

Rule number four pertains to the difference between a preparation outline and an essay. Remember that a speech is not written like an essay even though it is typed into an outline. Instead, you should write the outline just as you actually plan to say the speech when you deliver it. When we write a formal essay we use different language, grammar, sentence structure, and even lengths of sentences. When you prepare and deliver a speech you should use language that is not too complex and with which you feel comfortable. Essays and speeches have different flows and different expectations. Remember that a speech is closer to a conversation in terms of language use than it is to an essay, so prepare your outlines with this in mind. If you choose to write a draft, this same rule applies because the ultimate product is to be spoken, not written.

A strong preparation outline is essential for preparing a successful presentation, but it is not the last outline you'll create. After practicing with the preparation outline and making any adjustments you deem necessary to organization and wording, you should begin to reduce it to a usable outline from which you will deliver your speech. This is the process of creating a speaking outline, which is the actual outline you will speak from when delivering your remarks.

Example Preparation Outline

Below is a sample outline for an informative speech.

Notice how it follows all the requirements for a strong preparation outline.

Informative Speech (Object)

General Purpose: To inform about an object

Specific Purpose: To inform my audience about George Washington, the first president of the United States of America

Central Idea: George Washington's ability to handle difficult circumstances in war and government grew out of experiences in his early life and his dedication to detail.

Introduction

I. *Attention Getter:* Despite what your teachers may have told you, George Washington never chopped down a cherry tree and he did tell quite a few lies when shaping the founding of this nation, but who wouldn't when faced with the series of events he confronted throughout his life?

II. *Central Idea:* In fact, George Washington's ability to handle difficult circumstances in government grew out of experiences in his life and his dedication to detail, not some mythic promise to always tell the truth.

III. *Preview #1:* As a young adult in the British colony of Virginia, Washington sought the respect and pride that accompanied an aristocrat, but that desire almost led him to bankruptcy and forced him to pay closer attention to the economic environment around him in future business dealings.

IV. *Preview #2:* Later, when fighting the Revolution, he understood how important seemingly simple tasks were to having any hope of success in fighting the British.

V. *Transition:* Throughout his life, Washington exhibited that vision all leaders must have, and it eventually served him well when he became our first president.

Body

I. *Main Point #1 Topic Sentence:* Washington almost never became president, or even fought in the Revolution, because as a young aspiring Virginia gentleman he almost bankrupted himself.

A. *Subpoint #1:* Washington inherited most of his land from his family and friends, and the bulk of it was farmland in Virginia.

B. *Subpoint #2:* Like many upper-class aristocratic farmers in his day, Washington farmed mostly tobacco and had it sold in England, but the profits were not large.

C. *Subpoint #3:* Even in the face of limited profits Washington paid a lot of money for dozens of dessert glasses, a hogskin hunting saddle, a custom-made mahogany case with sixteen decanters, engraved stationery, and many other expensive items he could barely afford.[1]

---

1. Joseph J. Ellis, *His Excellency: George Washington* (New York: Random House, 2004), 49.

D. *Subpoint #4:* The costs got so high that in 1763, Washington almost ran out of money and was notified by his broker that he was short 1,800 pounds, and that interest would begin to accrue immediately.[2]

E. *Subpoint #5:* Quickly Washington realized he would never be able to pull himself out of debt because of the system, and he blamed the British Empire for his problems.

F. *Subpoint #6:* One of the saving graces for Washington was his getting out of tobacco as his main crop, and this move saved him from ruin, because tobacco taxes became one of the major contributors to economic problems in the colonies.

Transition: The experience of almost losing his money contributed to his fiscal discipline later while president, and the vision that saved his money in this episode was also evident in other areas of his life.

II. *Main Point #2 Topic Sentence:* Washington lost more battles than he won, but because of his attention to detail and ability to figure out the right risks to take he ended up winning the war.

A. *Subpoint #1:* Perhaps the most important battle Washington fought was, according to historian Richard Brookhiser, "the battle for sanitation."

1. **Sub-subpoint #1:** In Washington's time, troops did not always build latrines and often took to relieving themselves in the ditches at the foundation of the fort.[3]

2. **Sub-subpoint #2:** Only when a German soldier who helped train the Americans arrived at Valley Forge was the practice of building latrines institutionalized in the Regulations for the Order and Discipline of the Troops of the United States.[4]

B. *Subpoint #2:* In addition to the latrine issue, Valley Forge also represented another serious problem for Washington: enlistments for most of his men ended in December.

1. **Sub-subpoint #1:** Wars during Washington's time took winter breaks, much like colleges do, to take a break from bad weather and regroup, and the winter of 1776 was no different.

---

2. Ellis, 50.

3. Richard Brookhiser, *George Washington on Leadership* (New York: Basic Books, 2008), 14.

4. Brookhiser, 14–15.

2. **Sub-subpoint #2:** In need of a dramatic victory to keep his troops from leaving when enlistments ran out, Washington staged a successful surprise winter attack on a mercenary camp in Trenton on Christmas that year.[5]

Transition: Almost losing his money made Washington financially responsible, almost losing his army made him a more efficient strategist, and, as I will discuss next, recognizing the talent of others made him a stronger leader.

III. *Main Point #3 Topic Sentence:* The forces Washington commanded during the Revolution did not contain a lot of seasoned fighters, so the general was forced to look for skill sets in the unlikeliest of places in order to fight the war.

A. *Subpoint #1:* One of those Washington identified early on as having the necessary skills and drive to make things happen was Henry Knox.

   1. **Sub-subpoint #1:** Knox was a bookseller from Boston whose only qualification was that he was well read on engineering.[6]

   2. **Sub-subpoint #2:** Knox used that knowledge to become the chief artillery officer in Washington's army and a future confidant during Washington's administration as president.

B. *Subpoint #2:* In addition to a bookworm, Washington also found a close ally and dependable lieutenant from the ranks of the pacifist Quakers.

   1. **Detail #1:** Nathaniel Greene of Rhode Island was a Quaker, but he supported the war against the British and quickly rose in favor with Washington.[7]

   2. **Detail #2:** Washington thought so much of Greene that he named Greene his successor if he should fall in battle.[8]

Transition: Washington had a knack for knowing when to change crops, how to strike the enemy, and who could be entrusted with difficult tasks, all skills he needed to be successful when he later became president.

Conclusion

I. *Signpost:* In conclusion, George Washington's early years and time conducting the Revolution gave him the experiences he needed to be successful as president.

---

5. Kathryn Moore, *The American President: A Complete History* (New York: Fall River Press, 2013), 10.

6. Ellis, *His Excellency*, 81.

7. Ellis, 81–82.

8. Ellis, 81–82.

A. *Summary #1:* When he ran up debt trying to become a Virginia gentleman, he demonstrated vision by diversifying his crops and learned the fiscal discipline necessary to lead.

B. *Summary #2:* During the war, his ability to seize the right moment at Trenton illustrated his knack for understanding the importance of timing.

C. *Summary #3:* Finally, as a general with few competent soldiers in his army, he showed an ability to identify talented people who could accomplish the tasks the army needed to be done.

II. *Restate Thesis:* All in all, Washington's time early in life and as a general gave him the necessary experiences to develop important skills he needed when he was elected president.

III. *Clincher:* Now, the next time you see his face on a quarter or a dollar bill, you know that George Washington's life is more than myth or folklore; it is the story of a man with judgment and vision learned through hard experiences.

SPEAKING OUTLINE

After you practice and become familiar with the material in your preparation outline, you prepare the speaking outline. The speaking outline is a truncated form of the preparation outline and does not have full sentences, unless you are citing a direct quotation from a source. There are several reasons to reduce the information and words on a preparation outline when developing the speaking outline:

1 If you speak from a preparation outline, it becomes a manuscript speech, and you are less likely to adapt to audience feedback.

2 Speaking from a preparation outline encourages reading to, and not conversing with, the audience, thus resulting in the perception that you are reading an essay instead of delivering a speech.

3 You are more likely to stare at the outline, thus dramatically reducing eye contact with the audience.

Speaking outlines maintain several features of the preparation outline, so it is not as if you are developing a brand new outline from scratch. You still use the Roman numerals, capital letters, and numbers, and you still follow the principles of subordination, coordination, and division. This helps you clearly understand the hierarchal nature of your speech while delivering it and provides you with visual representations of the importance of information so that if you run short on time, you can quickly see what you can skip. In essence, the speaking outline is a shorthand version of the preparation outline. You should find the speaking outline much easier to compile than the preparation outline. One important thing to remember is not to add anything new to the speaking outline—keep it close to the preparation outline in this respect because that is what you have been practicing with and know best.

Health Care Help

Outlining isn't just for presentations; it can also be a valuable tool for ensuring that appointments with health practitioners are as successful as possible. Most medical appointments are relatively short, so it is important for you to come prepared. Before your appointment, create an outline of what you want to discuss with your doctor, including:

◊   symptoms and concerns,

◊   any lifestyle changes or plans, and

◊   questions about treatment.

If you're a medical practitioner, having an outline of topics to discuss with patients and a checklist (a simple type of outline) of things to review can help you make sure you do not overlook something simple that points to a serious condition. As Atul Gawande argues in *The Checklist Manifesto*, a simple checklist can help eliminate medical errors and reduce the number of deaths during surgery by more than a third.

Other contexts in which these skills apply: Interviewing, Performance Management, and Event Planning

The speaking outline also provides the opportunity to do a few things relevant to your presentation that you need not do in a preparation outline. For instance, you can add delivery cues for yourself based on your practice with prior outlines. For instance, let's suppose you want to emphasize certain points during your speeches. On a speaking outline you can add a few reminders in the margin of your outline to give yourself a visual cue, such as a hand-drawn megaphone, or simply write in bold, "LOUDER!" Or suppose you want to make sure you slow down to explain a specific point. Again, you can use a visual cue, such as drawing a sign that says SLOW and coloring it yellow. The speaking outline is more flexible in this regard than a preparation outline, and you can modify it to meet your particular needs.

OTHER FORMS OF SPEAKING MATERIALS

While we strongly recommend outlining a speech, we also recognize that there are several other strategies and approaches speakers can take when preparing their remarks. Two such approaches we will briefly discuss here are note cards and a teleprompter.

Some students like to use note cards, as they allow you to put a finite portion of your speech in one easy-to-find place. If you use note cards, ensure that you do not run main points together on a card, but keep ideas separate. You should still use Roman numerals, capital letters, and numbers to help you understand the hierarchy of your points. You also can put delivery cues on the cards. If you use note cards, be sure to number them sequentially. It is very uncomfortable if you drop your cards and have to reorder them in front of your audience. Also, make sure you know if your professor limits the number of cards you may use. Note cards can be seen as less professional than having a speaking outline on regular-sized paper, as you are constantly shifting between cards in front of the audience. If you use note cards, be sure to practice with them so they feel natural to you as you are speaking.

Example Speaking Outline on a Note Card

Introduction

I.   **AG:** Silverstein: "Intercultural dialogue is the best guarantee of a more peaceful, just, and sustainable world."

II.   **B&AR:** Define culture, connect to GMU

III.   **Cred:** COMM 305

IV.   **Thesis:** Learning about co-cultural theory will help us better understand the communication strategies that marginalized groups use in intercultural interactions.

V.   **Preview:** research evolution, co-cultural theory, example

Body

I.   **MP1:** Research evolution

    A.   Moon—early 90s pop culture; Smith—2000s identity and globalization; Leeds-Hurwitz—2009, intercultural dialogue

    B.   Leeds-Hurwitz: 1980s move toward studying cultural phenomena

II.   **MP2:** Co-cultural theory (Orbe)

    A.   Philosophical assumptions

    B.   Strategies & preferred outcomes

III.   **MP3:** Example

    A.   Poor accommodations for hearing impairment

    B.   Response: assertive communication

Conclusion

I.   **Thesis**

II.   **Review:** evolution, theory, example

III.   **Closer:** Silverstein

Another option for delivering prepared remarks is the electronic teleprompter. The teleprompter loads the draft of the speech, word for word, into its memory and scrolls slowly through the speech as you speak. The device is placed on a stand that can adjust to eye level. Teleprompters are very expensive and are used most often by politicians who do not have time to practice long speeches. As such, when speakers use teleprompters, they deliver manuscript speeches and have little to no room for adapting to audience feedback or going off-script. If you use a teleprompter, remember that technology can fail, and having a speaking outline or note cards prepared just in case is a smart thing to do.

To illustrate why it is important to have backups with you in case of technology failure, consider the case of Mary Fisher in 1992. Fisher was asked to speak about AIDS at the Republican National Convention and was afraid that the organizers of the convention, who did not want her to speak, would turn off her teleprompter. So, rather than back down, she prepared for the worst and went on stage with a copy of her speech in her pocket in case the teleprompter failed. Thankfully, it did not, but if it had, she still would have been able to deliver her remarks.

Summary

In this chapter, we discussed the fundamental principles behind outlining: subordination, coordination, and division. We illustrated how these principles help you organize your speech throughout the development process. Then we explained how to construct strong preparation outlines and how to turn those into good speaking outlines after you practice. Finally, we covered two other ways in which you might prepare and deliver speeches: using note cards and using a teleprompter. We cannot stress enough the importance of organization in the speech development process, and a properly prepared outline is one of most powerful tools you can use to ensure a successful presentation.

Key Terms

coordination 159   subordination 158
division 159

Activities

1   Why is it a good idea to develop both a full preparation outline and a speaking outline before giving an extemporaneous speech?

2   Find a video of a speech, such as a TED talk, online, and share the link. Can you identify the main points made in the speech? Did the speaker spend about the same amount of time on each point?

3   Why is it important to use the appropriate outlining symbols and indentions in your outline? How does this help you as a speaker?

INTRODUCTIONS, CONCLUSIONS, AND CONNECTIVE STATEMENTS

Objectives

◊ Learn how to properly format an introduction to a speech

◊ Discover how to connect segments of your speech in a seamless manner

◊ Understand the different components of a speech conclusion

The two most important moments of any speech are the introduction and the conclusion. They represent the only chance to make a first impression and the final opportunity to remind the audience about the key aspects of your speech. This is not to say that the body of the speech is unimportant, but rather to emphasize the importance of starting and finishing a speech. This chapter addresses these two key parts of the speech and provides suggestions for how best to craft effective introductions and conclusions. It also provides some tips for connecting all the parts of the speech so the audience knows when you move between points.

To do this we first cover the structure of the introduction, followed by the structure of the conclusion. In doing so, we provide some guidelines for developing these two vital speech components. Finally, we discuss the use of connective statements, which are also known as transitions, and demonstrate how they can be deployed effectively to move between points within a speech.

STRUCTURE OF THE INTRODUCTION

Introductions follow a fairly standard approach, but despite the common elements contained in any good introduction, it is important to remember that you can and should be creative in how you choose to style them. This creativity enhances the ability of an introduction to accomplish what it needs to, so do not view the goals of an introduction as a restrictive and boring set of rules. There are six goals that the introduction needs to accomplish within the introduction itself.

Get the Audience's Attention

The first thing that you need to do is to get the attention of the audience and make them want to listen to the speech. It is important to engage the audience early so they don't miss important information. Gaining the audience's attention may sound easy, but it involves effort. Simply stating a quotation or statistic is not enough; you need to connect that data to the speech itself so that the audience is dialed in to your topic right away.

There are numerous ways to grab the audience's attention, but you must carefully examine which strategy best suits your speech topic and your audience. For instance, providing a startling statistic or personal story might draw in an audience that is predisposed to disagree with you and what you plan to say. On the other hand, posing a rhetorical question or quoting someone famous might be a good way to gain the attention of an audience that might already agree with you. These are not hard and fast rules but rather ideas meant to get you to think about how best to make a first impression with an attention getter that is relevant to the speech topic and the audience.

One way to get an audience's attention is to ask a question. Speakers usually ask a rhetorical question, that is, a question that relates to the topic but does not require an answer from the audience. Suppose you were giving a speech about ways to live a healthy lifestyle. One way to start the speech is to ask the audience, "How many of you would like to live a long and healthy life?" Would anyone answer "no" to this? Highly unlikely. Rhetorical questions like these are not the only form of inquiry that can be used to start a speech and gain the audience's attention.

Another opening strategy is to ask the audience a question that requires a verbal answer. These questions help you gather data from the audience while also orienting them toward you and your topic. This question should be simple, and it is best if it's a question with a yes/no answer. The more detailed the query, the less time you will have to speak because you will be busy listening to the audience's comments. The question also should not spark much of a debate, because that opens the opportunity for audience members to confront each other directly, which results in your losing control of the speaking situation. Remember that questions are a strategic way to get the audience's attention and are not intended to open the floor to dialogue, debate, and discussion.

A third way to get the attention of the audience is with a famous quotation that aligns with your topic. For example, suppose you wanted to speak about community service. You might consider using someone else's words to begin your speech; perhaps President John F. Kennedy's words summarize your topic best: "Ask not what your country can do for you—ask what you can do for your country." Most everyone can attribute this statement to the former president. Regardless of whom you quote, whether the speaker is famous or not, the statement should be tied to the topic, or the audience may anticipate your speech going in another direction. You can easily focus the quotation by providing an explanation following it, and always be sure to verbally cite the person who made the statement you quoted.

> **"Ask not what your country can do for you—ask what you can do for your country."**
>
> John F. Kennedy

A fourth way to creatively gain the audience's attention is through the use of startling statistics. Startling statistics surprise an audience and make them curious about what the data would mean to them. Suppose you had done research and found some unique information that provoked your interest. You might begin your speech by sharing that figure with your audience. Obviously, you would need to not only provide a source for these numbers but also cite that source. This not only helps get the audience's attention but enhances your credibility as well.

The fifth way to garner the attention of the audience is through a narrative or short story that relates to the topic. Humans are story-telling creatures. Stories make things real to us and organize our experiences into something that makes sense. The danger with using a story as an attention-getting device, though, is that stories sometimes take up too much time. Stories can be personal, fictitious, or factual, but they must be relevant to the topic of your speech.

Stories also present an opportunity to connect the introduction and conclusion by starting a story at the beginning of a speech but leaving its conclusion for the end of the speech. Suppose a student was giving a speech about how an education changes a woman's life for the better. The speech could begin with the story of hardship as a means to focus the audience on a theme. Then, at the conclusion, the speaker could finish the story with a happy ending, illustrating that despite the hardship, getting an education changed her life for the better.

The sixth potential strategy for gaining attention is one of the most common ones prescribed by people with little training in speech—it is also one of the riskiest ways to open a speech. Beginning a speech with a joke can be either effective or a disaster. Effective jokes, like the other attention getters we have discussed, must be appropriate for the audience and related to the topic of the speech. Just opening with a joke for the sake of a joke does not help the audience prepare for your message. Additionally, jokes should not be offensive or contain inappropriate language, because this sets a poor standard of expectations for the audience and damages your credibility. When you choose a joke to tell an audience—particularly an audience of people you do not know—you do so with the expectation that the audience will respond by laughing. But what if they do not? This would create a very awkward situation for you, and it is not the way you want to begin your speech. For this reason, jokes should not be the first choice for an attention getter, despite what the general public may say.

Clearly State the Relevance of Your Topic

After you gain the audience's attention the important work of your speech begins. The human attention span is short, and so once you get the audience to focus on your speech you need to work to keep their attention. The first step in doing so is also the second thing you need do in your introduction: establish the relevance of your topic. Or, to put it another way, tell the audience why they should care about this topic. If you cannot justify the topic, then you must consider why you chose it. Most topics have real-world significance and can be justified with some research and consideration.

This process need not be a long explanation; in fact, it should be no more than a sentence or two at the most. One of the best ways to establish the significance of your topic can be to share a statistic or other information that illustrates how many people are affected by the issue or why it is a serious concern. Your relevance statement (or audience significance statement) should explicitly lay out your topic, help focus the audience on a particular area of knowledge, and explain why it matters. Stating the topic also blends into the next task of an introduction: establishing your credibility on the topic.

Establish Your Credibility

Now that you have the audience's attention and have established the topic of your speech, you need to explain to them why they should listen to your comments about this topic. This answers the question, "Why am I qualified to speak on this topic?" There are two easy ways to answer this question. First, the topic may be one with which you have experience or expertise. For example, a mechanic delivering a talk on how to change the oil in a car has experience and expertise on this topic. All he or she needs to do to establish credibility is explain their vast experience with oil changes and cars. This type of experience, however, is not always easy to come by—especially when delivering a speech in class for an assignment. Even in these situations, though, you can establish your credibility. Just be careful not to exaggerate your knowledge and experience.

In classroom situations, you can establish credibility by noting the research you conducted on the topic. Let's say you have decided to deliver a speech on human trafficking. You do not have any experience with this activity and no firsthand knowledge, but you did a great deal of research on it for weeks leading up to the assignment. All you need to do is tell the audience about the time spent looking into human trafficking, and you have given them reason to listen to you. Another option is to explain why the topic is especially important to you. For instance, perhaps your family has been personally affected by human trafficking. Establishing credibility is essential in an introduction because even if an audience gives you their attention and is interested in your topic, they will quickly move on to something else if they do not believe there is a reason to listen to your comments on the issue.

State Your Argument

Once you have focused the audience's attention firmly on your topic and convinced them you are qualified to speak on it, it is time to let them know what you intend to say about the topic. This means it is time to state your argument, or thesis, for them. This is the fourth part of an introduction. The **thesis**, or argument, is a carefully worded one-sentence summary of exactly what you will cover in your speech. You can see your thesis statement as the anchor for your speech because everything that follows it is related to it in some way. The claim you make and the focus you establish with this statement guide the rest of your speech. See Table 13.1 for some examples of thesis statements.

thesis
a carefully worded one-sentence encapsulation of exactly what you will cover in your speech

Table 13.1

THESIS STATEMENT EXAMPLES
INFORMATIVE SPEECH THESIS EXAMPLES
• Dropbox is a great tool that will back up your files online and make them available from any Internet-connected device. • Becoming a vegetarian benefits your health and the environment.
PERSUASIVE SPEECH THESIS EXAMPLES
• Due to growing enrollment and limited space, the university should build a central parking deck for student use. • Congress should work to develop a more equitable tax code.
SPECIAL OCCASION SPEECH THESIS EXAMPLES
• George Smith was a loving father and a loyal friend who will be greatly missed. • The winner of this year's Community Betterment Award has worked tirelessly to make sure that children have a safe place to do homework and play after school.

Connecting the rest of your speech to your argument helps ensure that your speech is sharply focused and does not go off on tangents. In short, it provides the destination of your speech—where you want the audience to be at the end of the presentation. As with any journey, knowing where you are going is nice, but knowing how you will get there is equally important, and so we will now turn to the next task of an introduction.

Preview Main Points

Once you tell the audience where you are headed, you need to explain how you plan to get there, and so the fifth element of an introduction is providing a preview of your main points. A preview can be one statement or a few, depending on how you wish to explain the roadmap of your speech to the audience. In either case it must contain all the main points you will cover in your speech in the order in which you plan to cover them (see Table 13.2). With a one-sentence preview, your main points appear as several different clauses within the sentence. For example, a student is going to give a speech about the historic Battle of the Bulge in World War II. The student could break down the speech into four points and have the following preview statement: "The Battle of the Bulge occurred in four primary segments: first, the German attack that created the bulge; second, the courageous stand of the 101st Airborne at Bastogne; third, General Patton's historical march to lend support at the bulge; and finally, the clearing weather that made the Allied air campaign possible." This lets the audience know there are four parts, or four main points, that will be covered in the speech. This roadmap makes it easier for the audience to comprehend and follow the speaker throughout the speech and also keeps the speaker sharply focused.

Table 13.2

PREVIEW STATEMENT EXAMPLES
First, I will explain why public transportation is better for the environment. Second, I will tell you why using public transportation improves your community. Finally, I will describe how taking public transportation will help to improve your health.
You should do three things to make sure you're ready next time an emergency strikes. First, build an emergency preparedness kit. Second, create a family emergency communication plan. Third, make sure your legal documents and insurance plans are up to date.
You can take charge of your health by doing three simple things more often: Move more, sleep more, and eat more nutritious foods.
To save a life with CPR, remember to check your ABCs: airway, breathing, and circulation.

For novice speakers, the one-sentence approach to a preview may be a bit challenging. In that case a slower, but just as effective, method is using several statements. These statements usually begin with "First, I will explain . . . Second, I will cover. . . Next, I will detail . . . Finally, we will explore . . ." These numeric indicators specifically indicate the order of main points and are helpful for both the speaker and the audience. This method obviously takes longer than a one-sentence approach, but it achieves the same end result. At this point the introduction is almost complete, save for one small, but important, task.

Transition to the Body

When you have established the topic and explained how you plan to approach it, all that remains is getting on with your speech. To do so, however, requires a subtle move to let the audience know you have finished introducing the topic and will now get into the details of your speech. This move is a transitional statement at the end of the introduction. A **transition** is a connecting statement that lets the audience know you are leaving one point and moving to another. If your preview statement and the transition are constructed properly, this should be apparent to the audience. See Table 13.3 for examples of transitional statements.

transition
connective statement that signals you are finished with one point and moving on to another

Table 13.3

TRANSITIONAL STATEMENT EXAMPLES
To understand why a border collie is a great dog to have if you want a furry running partner, we need to begin by exploring the history of border collies.
When you begin a new exercise regimen, it is important to start slowly.
First, we need to understand the factors that led to the housing crisis.
Let's start by learning about the need for organ donors in the United States.

One last thing to note about introductions: Even though they are the first thing the audience hears, they are the last thing you write. The reason for this is that when constructing the body you may want to change the order of main points, thus impacting the preview and the transition. You also might want to use what you planned as an attention getter as data for a main point, especially if it is a statistic or quotation. So it is always best to prepare the body of the speech and the conclusion before constructing the introduction.

TRANSITIONS BETWEEN MAIN POINTS

Throughout your speech you will need to ensure that the audience follows your argument and understands when you are changing topics. Similar to travelers who use road signs to know when to change course and billboards to find places to eat and stay the night, speakers supply connective statements throughout their speeches so that their audiences know they are shifting topics. Some of the most important connective statements in a speech are transitions between main points. Transitions between main points are easy for speakers to forget, but they are necessary for a successful presentation because they keep the speaker on track and aid the audience in understanding the direction the speech is going. A transition between main points should include three parts: an internal summary, a signpost, and an internal preview.

internal summary
a statement that summarizes what you already have covered and precedes transitions

Internal Summaries

An **internal summary** reviews the point that you just covered and indicates to the audience that you are preparing to move to another point. Internal summaries serve to keep ideas well organized in the minds of both the audience and the speaker. They remind audiences about the important connections you made within a main point and also help push your argument along at the same time. For example, the blue portion of this statement is an internal summary a speaker might say: "I just discussed the second stage of wine-making, which consisted of testing with a hydrometer, adding chemicals and stirring, then allowing the wine to set for a period."

Signposts

Signposts are key words that signal to the audience that you are moving from one part of the speech to another. Signposts catch the audience's attention and, like traffic signs, help show the audience what is ahead and keep them on track while listening to your speech.

Signposts can help divide the speech into obvious parts for you and your audience. Some of the more common signposts are words such as "next," "additionally," "secondly," "third," and "finally."

signposts
key words that signal to the audience that you are moving from one part of the speech to another

Internal Previews

Like the preview of main points at the end of the introduction, an internal preview provides a roadmap of what is ahead for the audience. An **internal preview** informs the audience of the elements of the next main point. For example, the blue portion of this statement is an internal preview: "Now that we have seen the initial stage of making wine, let's move into the second stage, which includes taking tests with a hydrometer, adding some chemicals and stirring, then letting the wine sit for an extended period of time." These are especially helpful when moving to a more complicated point because they foreshadow information for the audience.

internal preview
serves as an outline of what is to come next in a speech and is often combined with transition statements

STRUCTURE OF THE CONCLUSION

Once you have gone over everything in the speech body that you said you would do in the introduction, it is time to finish your speech. In finishing your speech, remember it is the last thing the audience will hear from you, thus increasing the likelihood they will remember it. Much like introductions, conclusions also have some essential elements: a signpost, a summary, and a clincher (or memorable closer). In this section, we will discuss these three parts of a good conclusion.

Signal the Conclusion

After explaining your main points in detail and connecting them to your overall argument, you need to indicate to the audience that the conclusion is approaching. Just as you use a signpost to signal to the audience that you are moving from one point to another in a transition between main points, you should use another signpost to signal to your audience that you are beginning the conclusion. Signposts that signal you are about to conclude your speech include phrases such as, "To summarize," "Finally," "To conclude," and "Let's wrap up." These simple statements clearly indicate to audiences that the conclusion is here, and the speech is almost at an end. The signpost, however, is not the indicator that the speech is over, just that it is almost finished. There is still some work to do.

Provide a Summary

After the signpost, you need to revisit the main ideas and central argument of your presentation. There are two parts to this task: restate the thesis and review the main points. In reviewing the main points, you want to remind the audience of the evidence and information you provided in the body of the speech. It is important that you do not include new information or cite new evidence at this point. The summary should recap the highlights of the speech and be as brief as possible. It does not need to detail everything you just told the audience, but rather should generally summarize what you spent time talking about.

After summarizing the main points it is also important to remind your audience about the central argument or thesis of your speech. This is accomplished by briefly explaining how the main points substantiate the overall position you articulated in the presentation. In other words, explain how the roadmap got you and the audience to the destination. This restatement should not use the exact same words as the initial statement of your argument from the introduction but should be similar to it. You also should create it so that if the audience remembers any one thing from your speech, it's the main argument.

Memorable Closer

Obviously, even though your argument is the most important part of your speech—it is, after all, why you spoke—you need more than that to end the presentation. The **clincher**, or the final statement of your speech, is an additional statement that follows the summary of your main points and argument. There are numerous forms of clinchers, and many are the same devices we shared as a means of getting the audience's attention. If you began the speech with a short story, you can finish the story at the end of the speech, giving a nice sense of fit and closure. You also may end with a famous

clincher
the final statement of your speech

quotation, personal reflection, or even a call to action for the audience. You do not have to revisit the same form of attention getter used in the introduction, but you might want to. No matter which route you choose to follow, it is important that you remind the audience why they listened in the first place.

Summary

This chapter explored the requirements of introductions and conclusions within your speech and provided information on how to connect main points and move smoothly from one part of the speech to the next. These structural aspects of a speech are important, as they directly influence an audience's ability to follow your speech. Introductions get the audience's attention and establish a roadmap for the way you plan to cover a topic. Transitions between main points help audiences understand when new points will be covered and how they relate to your overall argument. The conclusion represents the last opportunity for you to emphasize the core components of your speech.

Key Terms

clincher 180   signposts 179
internal preview 179   thesis 175
internal summary 178   transition 177

Activities

1   At this point, you probably have a pretty good idea what the topic of your next speech will be. For that topic, write out two different potential attention getters. Which one do you think will be most effective? Why?

2   Write the thesis statement and preview of main points that you intend to use at the end of your introduction. Revise it a few times and work toward using careful language that draws in your audience's attention, and then work with a friend to see if you can help to improve each other's thesis statements.

3   Now, write the transitions you will use between the main points that you just identified above in question 2. Make sure that each transition has a clear summary, signpost, and preview. Can you use more ornamental language to help draw your audience's attention?

REASONING

◊ Understand the two different types of reasoning

◊ Learn the different forms of reasoning used in argument

◊ Identify the many different errors in reasoning that are common in arguments

Many believe that because we have reasons for doing or believing something, we have sound reasoning. Unfortunately, reasons are not the same as reasoning. Good reasoning is the foundation of any speech, and in this chapter we will explore how to logically organize ideas within a speech so that they maximize their ability to connect your message with the audience. We will also illustrate some common errors of reasoning, or fallacies, that creep into our justifications and attempts to persuade others, thus tricking us into believing someone's reasons are based on sound judgment.

We begin our discussion by differentiating between the two different types of reasoning: deductive and inductive. We then explore some common forms of reasoning used to make arguments every day. Finally, we will detail a number of common reasoning fallacies that infect our speech.

TYPES OF REASONING

The reasoning process is different from providing reasons for something. It explains how the reasons you supply connect to the conclusion that you make, and there are generally two ways these connections can be accomplished. One of these, deductive reasoning, deals with providing structurally certain conclusions. The other, inductive reasoning, focuses more on probability.

Deductive Reasoning

deductive reasoning
an argument that reasons from known premises to an inevitable conclusion

Deductive reasoning uses specific premises to reach an unavoidable and certain conclusion. Deductive reasoning relies upon a formal structure that comes in three parts. That formal structure is a **syllogism**, which lays out claims that build upon each other to reach a conclusion.

syllogism
a logical argument consisting of at least two claims that build upon each other to reach a conclusion

The first part of the syllogism is the major premise, which is the statement of a general truth or fact. After the major premise, a minor premise, or specific instance of the general truth in action, is provided. Taken together, the major and minor premises result in the third statement, the conclusion, which is the logical result of both the major and minor premises. Here is an example of perhaps the most famous syllogism.

Major premise:	All men are mortal.
Minor premise:	Socrates is a man.
Conclusion:	Socrates is mortal.

categorical syllogism
a syllogism in which the argument is based on membership in a group

This syllogism illustrates that Socrates, the specific instance, is a manifestation of the major premise, man, and thus, like all members of that group, is mortal. This conclusion is both logical and certain, as the only way for this to fall apart would be for someone to prove that Socrates was not properly categorized as a man. This is an example of what is called a **categorical syllogism**, because it deals with minor premises belonging to a category established in the major premise.

disjunctive syllogism
a syllogism in which the major premise includes two or more mutually exclusive alternatives

A second form of syllogism that is also deductive in nature is the **disjunctive syllogism**. Rather than making claims about categorical membership, disjunctive syllogisms provide either-or scenarios. For instance:

Major premise:	This key will unlock either my house or my car.
Minor premise:	The key does not unlock my house.
Conclusion:	Therefore, this key unlocks my car.

Notice that this syllogism still deduces the proper conclusion by excluding one of two alternatives stated in the major premise. It is called disjunctive because the two aspects of the major premise are mutually exclusive and cannot coexist.

A third and final type of syllogism found in deductive reasoning is the conditional syllogism, which proposes if-then scenarios in the major premise. This is usually used for hypothetical situations or planning for the future. Let's look at an example.

conditional syllogism
a syllogism in which the major premise contains a hypothetical condition and its outcome

Major premise:	If I take the bus home, then I will save money on transportation.
Minor premise:	I will take the bus home.
Conclusion:	Therefore, I will save money on transportation.

Here we see an alternative in a hypothetical situation eliminated in the minor premise. The if-then statement provided the conditions resulting from the stated action in the minor premise. When used correctly, each of the three syllogisms we discussed provides structurally certain conclusions. Unfortunately, few things in life are certain, so we deal more often in probabilities, and that is where inductive reasoning comes into play.

Inductive Reasoning

Inductive reasoning is much different from deductive reasoning because it is based upon probabilities rather than absolutes. With inductive reasoning, you begin with particular pieces of evidence and use them to construct probable conclusions. This is the inverse of deductive reasoning, which begins with general certainties and applies them to specific cases.

inductive reasoning
an argument that comes to a probable, instead of an absolute, conclusion

One of the more common applications of inductive reasoning is the use of polling data to make assumptions about group behaviors. For example, if you know that 75 percent of students support a fee for a new recreation center on campus, and you are in a class with twenty students, then it is probable that five of them disagree with that position. This is not certain, because you might be in a class in which everyone either supports or does not support the fee, but it is likely given the evidence. With inductive reasoning, the more evidence we provide in support of a claim, the stronger the probability that the claim is accurate—but we can never be certain.

Both inductive and deductive reasoning are useful, but the far more commonly used reasoning process is inductive. Few things in life are certain; after all, we are not even certain the sun will rise tomorrow. We know it is highly probable, but we are not totally certain. In the next section, we will explore some specific argumentative structures that employ both deductive and inductive reasoning.

FORMS OF REASONING

Whether you are delivering an informative or persuasive speech, you will always need to make strong connections between the information you provide and the claims you make. Properly employing solid reasoning enables your audience to understand the points you are making, while also bolstering your credibility with the audience. On the contrary, not using sound reasoning will cause the audience to disregard much of what you say and will damage your credibility. In this section, we will discuss four different reasoning forms: cause, example, analogy, and sign.

Reasoning by Cause

reasoning by cause
arguments that claim one event or factor produces an effect

The first type of reasoning we will go over is by cause. **Reasoning by cause** occurs when you claim that one occurrence creates a specific effect. When making a claim such as this you must keep several things in mind. First, consider if the cause you present is necessary and sufficient for the effect to be produced. A **necessary cause** is one that must be present for the effect to happen, such as it must be lower than 32 degrees Fahrenheit for water to freeze. That temperature is necessary to produce freezing. A **sufficient cause** is one that can produce the effect in question, such as drinking water is sufficient to quench your thirst. It is not necessary, as there are other beverages that can quench thirst, but drinking water is sufficient for the effect to take place.

necessary cause
arguments in which a cause must be present for an effect to happen

sufficient cause
a cause that can produce the effect in question

Causal reasoning is also one of the foundations for many superstitions we hold. In sports, athletes will often wear the same clothing or perform the same rituals during a game because they believe they have a causal relation to a positive outcome. There is little to no evidence to support these beliefs, yet they believe them nonetheless.

Reasoning by Example

Another way to reason is by example. This form of reasoning is quite common, as we often look for instances that help us make more general conclusions. When reasoning by example, you take a number of specific realities and arrive at an overall conclusion about them.

Example one:	My biology class was tough.
Example two:	My chemistry class was hard.
Example three:	My astronomy class was difficult.
Conclusion:	Science classes present a real challenge to me.

reasoning by example
the process of inferring general conclusions and making general claims from specific cases

When **reasoning by example**, the occurrences must be related. This argument, for instance, would not be as strong if we replaced biology with art and chemistry with philosophy. The reason for this is that the examples then lose their relationship to each other. The more relevant examples you provide, the stronger the conclusion.

Reasoning by Analogy

reasoning by analogy
comparing two similar cases in order to argue that what is true in one case is also true in the other

Reasoning by analogy occurs when we use analogies to support a claim. An analogy is when you argue that what is true in one situation is true in another. Analogies differ from examples because they do not need to have more than one similar instance. Essentially, reasoning by analogy tries to argue for common elements between different cases. These analogies also can be either literal or figurative.

literal analogy
when the two cases being compared are classified the same way

Literal analogies take place when the two cases being compared are from the same classification. For example, you might argue that a certain crime prevention tactic effectively used at one school should be adopted at your school because the student population and campus environments are similar. This analogy takes a real occurrence in a similar classification and applies it to another real situation, trying to emphasize the commonalities between the two situations to argue for similar results in both cases.

figurative analogy
when the two cases being compared are from completely different classifications

Figurative analogies are different from literal analogies in that they compare cases from entirely different classifications. For example, an argument that a successful businessperson would make a good elected official is a figurative analogy. The reason it is figurative is because the business world and the political realm are two entirely different classifications, with very few similarities. Business is not policy making, but the figurative analogy seeks to make the comparison based on leadership experience in two different classifications. Just because the two examples are from different classifications, however, does not make the analogy false or even illogical—it requires you to be more explicit about the areas of comparison and reasons they are relevant. Both of these types of analogies are effective means of making a reasoned argument to an audience.

Reasoning by Sign

reasoning by sign occurs when the presence of one thing indicates the presence of another

The final type of reasoning we will discuss is **reasoning by sign**, which occurs when the presence of one thing indicates the presence of another. The classic example of this type of reasoning is when you see smoke in the air, it is a sign there is a fire somewhere. Or, if you see footprints in newly fallen snow, it is a sign that someone has walked across the area since the snowfall ended.

Reasoning by sign can also be more than observation of simple natural occurrences, as it can apply to characteristics as well. For example, to run for president you must be at least thirty-five years old. Therefore, being president is a sign that the person in the office is at least thirty-five years old. Be careful with this type of reasoning, however, because the inverse when reasoning by sign is not always true: Being thirty-five or older is not a sign that you are president.

As speakers, we must ensure that our reasoning is sound so it can have the desired impact on the audience. It is easy for speakers to err when reasoning, and some unethical speakers all too often employ reasoning fallacies to convince the audience to believe or do something. Additionally, as audience members, we have a responsibility to detect errors in reasoning so we can better assess the messages we receive. In the next section, we will examine several different examples of errors in reasoning, or reasoning fallacies.

Practical Politics

Many political ads rely on reasoning fallacies in an attempt to sway voter opinions on candidates or issues. As a voter, it is important for you to listen carefully to the types of reasoning being employed in political ads, and to beware of fallacies. Any time an ad tries to represent another candidate's position on an issue, you should take time to research the candidate to find out whether those representations are accurate. Whenever someone advocates for a policy, do some investigating on your own to make sure there is evidence to support that policy. As a politician, you have a responsibility to be ethical in your use of reasoning.

Other contexts where these skills apply: Marketing, Sales, and Management

REASONING FALLACIES

A **fallacy** is an error in reasoning. Some are easy to detect, yet others are more elusive to identify. In this section, we will cover ten of the more common reasoning fallacies that speakers use in presentations. You will also undoubtedly recognize that many of these fallacies are exhibited in advertisements and our interpersonal interactions.

fallacy
an error in reasoning

Ad Hominem

The first fallacy we will address is the **ad hominem**, which is attacking the opposing person's character instead of his or her argument. An ad hominem attack is simply name calling and does not address the ideas and reasoning of the attacked person. When we refute another person's position by calling him or her names or focusing on personal history when it is irrelevant, we employ an ad hominem attack. These types of attacks are unethical, inappropriate, and not grounded in logic, but unfortunately society uses them quite often.

ad hominem
fallacy committed by attacking the opposing person's character instead of his or her argument

Ad Verecundiam

Another reasoning fallacy with a Latin name is the **ad verecundiam** fallacy, which is an appeal to authority. This fallacy asserts that positional authority, such as being a parent or a boss, makes someone's argument correct and accurate. When a child asks a parent why he or she should take out the trash, and the parent responds, "Because I am your mother/father," the parent is using a reason based on an appeal to authority instead of giving a logical reason. Authority-based appeals can be made using parents, bosses, God, teachers, doctors, or any other position of authority as the reason that someone should do something. These do not assert logical reasons but rather assume that authority equals correctness. This is not to say that we should not follow instructions from people in authority, because refusing them can carry heavy consequences, but an argument based on an appeal to authority is not a logical argument and is not a good type of argument to use in your speech.

ad verecundiam
appealing to the arguer's authority as the thing that makes his or her argument correct or accurate

Slippery Slope

Perhaps the most famous logical fallacy is that of the **slippery slope**. This fallacy relies on the belief that once a course of action is taken, other unavoidable events will inevitably occur. More succinctly, once we start down a path there is no turning back. You can think about a slippery slope as being similar

slippery slope
asserting that once a course of action is taken, other unavoidable events will inevitably occur

to a domino effect—the speaker is arguing that once an initial event or action takes place, others will follow, just as pushing over the first domino can cause the others behind it to fall. These fallacies are often very subtle and seem to make sense, but they make unsupported assumptions about an end outcome based on an initial action. The slippery slope is a perverse version of a conditional syllogism, in which there is a series of unsupported assumptions made with either explicit or implicit if-then statements. Politicians often make such cases to pressure public support for certain policies, but if we are more attuned to the structure of the slippery slope, then we can avoid being misled.

Non Sequitur

non sequitur
making an unjustified move from one idea to another

The next fallacy we will explain is yet another Latin term, **non sequitur**. Non sequitur means "not in sequence," and the fallacy thus refers to making an unjustified move from one idea to another. This is a very common fallacy, and some instances of it are harder to detect than others. Assuming that someone is wealthy because he or she owns expensive furniture or drives a nice car is an unwarranted jump from one idea to another. While it is possible that someone who has nice furniture or drives an expensive car is wealthy, it is also possible that someone inherited the furniture, is renting the car for a day, or bought an expensive-looking car by accruing a lot of debt while barely making ends meet. There is not enough data to make the assertion logical, and thus the conclusion does not follow from the observation. Think of all the times you may have made an unwarranted assumption about a person or an idea without enough evidence.

straw man
fallacy committed when the speaker misrepresents the opponent's position by oversimplifying that position, taking comments out of context, or representing an entire group's position with bad arguments from one person in that group

Straw Man

The fifth type of fallacy is that of the **straw man**, which happens when the speaker distorts the actual position of an opponent. In a straw man fallacy, the speaker misrepresents the opponent's position by oversimplifying that position, taking the opponent's comments out of context so that they don't represent the opponent's position at all, or representing an entire group's position with really bad arguments from one person in that group (who might be real or fictitious). The speaker then attacks this misrepresented position or one piece of problematic evidence, and then claims that the entire argument or position must be thrown out. However, even if one piece of evidence used in an argument is problematic, it does not necessarily mean that the entire argument is wrong. For example, some people who believe that warnings about climate change are a hoax might use an example of a single study that was found to have flawed data as evidence that the entire theory that the climate is changing is wrong, despite the mountains of evidence scientists around the world have collected indicating that climate change is a real, serious concern. Buying into a straw man argument is evidence of a lazy thinker who does not pay attention to the larger case being made.

Hasty Generalization

The **hasty generalization** is the next type of fallacy we will address, which refers to drawing conclusions about broad principles or categories based upon a small sample of evidence. Basing a decision about an entire group or category on just one or even a few examples of it is not a valid, logical argument, yet we do this all the time. Consider how many times you have tried one dish from a particular culture's cuisine, or one movie from a specific genre, and did not enjoy it. Then, as a result of that experience, you refused to try anything else from that cuisine or movie genre because you did not enjoy that one experience. These are examples of hasty generalization because you made a judgment about an entire large group or category based on a ridiculously small sample. Similarly, if you asked five students on your campus whether they think *The Daily Show* is the best show on TV, and then use this to claim that everyone on your campus thinks *The Daily Show* is the best show on TV, then you have used hasty generalization.

hasty generalization drawing conclusions about broad principles or categories based upon a small sample of evidence

Either-Or

The seventh fallacy we will cover takes place when we assume there are only two alternatives, when in actuality there are more. This is called the **either-or fallacy**, and people sometimes use it to limit alternatives and force choices in a specific direction. These arguments, which are erroneous applications of a disjunctive syllogism, assume the audience must "either" do this, "or" do that. The argument proceeds to eliminate one of the two alternatives, leaving the audience to believe that the other action is the only one left, when really there are more possibilities to consider. For example, when former President George W. Bush said, "Either you are with us, or you are with the terrorists" in his address to a joint session of Congress following the September 11 attacks, he was committing an either-or fallacy. Eventually, one of the two options that you present might be a good choice, but limiting the options to only two from the beginning is not the best manner in which to make a

either-or fallacy assuming there are only two alternatives when in actuality there are more than two decision, and arguing that only two options exist is not a valid way to make an argument.

False Cause

false cause
fallacy assuming that
one event causes
another unrelated
event to occur

The eighth fallacy is the false cause, which assumes that one event causes another unrelated event to occur. Remember earlier in the chapter, when we discussed reasoning by cause, we mentioned superstitions. Superstitions are the result of false cause, which is an error in the application of that reasoning form. This is why it is always important to seek a connection between an event and what the speaker believes causes the event. If evidence cannot support that there is a necessary or sufficient relationship between the two, then we determine that false cause has been applied.

Red Herring

red herring
introducing irrelevant
ideas to focus
attention away from
the real issue

Ninth in our list of reasoning fallacies is the red herring, which happens when the speaker introduces irrelevant ideas to focus attention away from the real issue. This fallacy is very common on political news programs when a commentator questions a politician or candidate for office about prior actions or statements, and the politician tries to avoid responding. This type of reasoning fallacy essentially tries to change the topic of discussion from one matter to another. When people cannot, or do not, want to respond to an argument, they will try to change the topic to more favorable ground by introducing a red herring to the discussion. In doing so they hope to avoid directly confronting what they have been asked. There is no logical connection between the red herring and the topic under discussion, but they can be introduced in a fashion that makes it seem like a connection is there.

Begging the Question

**begging the
question**
assuming certain facts
that have not been
proven

The tenth and final fallacy we will address is begging the question. We beg the question when we assume certain facts that have not been proven. These types of fallacies often are prefaced by statements such as "it begs the question," "it goes without saying," "everyone agrees," and "let's just say for the sake of argument." All of these phrases tell the audience to assume things to be true without offering proof of their accuracy. They are then followed with a series of other claims built from that false understanding until the end, when the audience agrees to the entire proposition without evidence supporting its foundation.

As speakers, you should carefully craft your messages to ensure that the reasoning supporting your claims is sound and fallacy-free. If audience members detect fallacious reasoning, then you will lose credibility. Even if the audience does not detect the fallacy, it is unethical to use a fallacy to gain agreement. As audience members, we should pay close attention not just to the evidence provided and the claims made but also to how the evidence and claims relate to each other. That is the fundamental characteristic of a good consumer of information.

Summary

In this chapter, we began moving from information gathering and organization to the way we articulate our claims and argument to the audience. Reasoning is both organizational, in that it helps direct us to the best way to connect our evidence with our claims, and inventional, because it helps demonstrate and enhance our personal credibility with the audience. We covered the two types of reasoning, deductive and inductive, as well as provided four forms of reasoning in arguments. We concluded with an exploration of the various ways reasoning can be corrupted and falsely applied.

Key Terms

ad hominem 189

ad verecundiam 189

begging the question 192

categorical syllogism 184

conditional syllogism 185

deductive reasoning 184

disjunctive syllogism 184

either-or fallacy 191

fallacy 189

false cause 192

figurative analogy 187

hasty generalization 191

inductive reasoning 185

literal analogy 187

necessary cause 186

non sequitur 190

reasoning by analogy 187

reasoning by cause 186

reasoning by example 187

reasoning by sign 188

red herring 192

slippery slope 189

sufficient cause 186

straw man 190

syllogism 184

Activities

1   Find an example of a commercial that relies on a fallacy to persuade viewers. Share the link to that video. Explain which fallacy you believe is being illustrated, and provide a rationale for that choice.

2   Write out an example of a syllogism (not one included in the book). Label the major premise, minor premise, and conclusion. Which type of syllogism did you create?

3   Give an example of a statement that uses inductive reasoning. Which type of inductive reasoning does your statement illustrate?

INFORMATIVE SPEECHES

Objectives

◊ Recognize the four different types of informative speeches

◊ Learn five different ways to organize the body of an informative speech

◊ Become familiar with the goals and strategies for each of the four types of informative speeches

Now that we have covered the basics of research, organization, and how to make reasoned claims, we turn our attention to the first of three types of speeches you might find yourself delivering one day. We often equate speeches with political candidates making appeals to an audience, or perhaps a sermon on morality from a preacher, but not all speeches are designed to persuade a person. In fact, one of the most common types of speeches is an informative speech. Informative speeches are presentations in which speakers explain a topic to an audience without trying to convince them of anything. These speeches of explanation occur in a variety of formats, but the one you may be most familiar with is a classroom lecture by a teacher or instructor. These presentations are designed not to convince you to believe or do something but rather to explain something to you so you understand it. These are informative speeches.

Informative speeches are intended to teach the audience something new and have two key purposes: to **inform**, which is to make the audience aware of a phenomenon, and to **explain**, which is to deepen the audience's understanding of that phenomenon. When you are simply informing an audience, you are likely to be using the linear model of communication, which you will recall treats communication as a one-way process whereby a speaker gives their audience information, while there is no response from the listeners. For example, if you are reporting the morning's headline news, sharing information about the day's stock prices, or telling someone the year that you were born as part of an identity security check, you are simply sharing information with someone else. However, explaining goes much further.

inform
make the audience aware of a phenomenon

explain
deepen the audience's understanding of that phenomenon

Speeches that seek to explain something to an audience provide deeper details about how and why something is a certain way and take care to pay attention to whether an audience accurately understands what is presented. Evidence of this understanding, or lack thereof, comes through nonverbal reactions and answering questions during or after the presentation.

Explanatory, or informative, speeches typically cover one of four broad topics and are often organized in one of several different ways to help the audience understand the subject in question. In this chapter, we will first discuss the four different types of informative speeches. Next, we will explain five of the most common ways to organize informative speeches. Then we will explore different ways to explain difficult concepts, before providing strategies for facilitating audience understanding. Finally, we will discuss the goals of an informative speech and provide some strategies for best delivering information to an audience.

TYPES OF INFORMATIVE SPEECHES

There are four different topics you might explain to an audience, and these topics help differentiate between the four types of informative speeches. In this section, we will explain each of these four types of informative speeches. We will begin with speeches about objects, which are perhaps the most common informative speeches. Then we will discuss speeches about processes, which include things like recipes and installation directions. Third, we will cover speeches about events, such as vacations or historical occurrences. Finally, we will detail informative speeches about concepts, such as religious beliefs or laws.

Speeches about Objects

The first form of informative speeches we will discuss are those which address objects. A speech about an object concerns a tangible item, such as a piece of sports equipment, a memento, a souvenir, a building, or even a country. These speeches are often found in the classroom and internal business meetings where new products are being developed. However, the term "object" can also refer to people. When you stand and introduce yourself at the start of a new class or at a company or church function, you are the topic being explained, and as something tangible, you are classified as an object for the purpose of identifying the type of informative speech you are delivering.

Informative speeches about objects can include any person, living or deceased, fictional or factual. For example, you might deliver a speech about Harriet Tubman, a prominent figure with the Underground Railroad during the mid-nineteenth century. You might also deliver a speech about the fictional character Sheldon Cooper, who appears on the television show *The Big Bang Theory*. Both are people, and as such, they are considered objects.

Speeches about objects could also pertain to particular places. Suppose you visited the Statue of Liberty in New York City and wanted to inform your audience about the characteristics of this historic landmark. You could explain to your audience how to get there, tell them when the site is open, and highlight a few must-see places neighboring Ellis Island. Or, you might be tasked with explaining a larger space to an audience. For example, if your company is planning to introduce a product to a new market, you might be asked to explain the characteristics of that market to the senior staff. These could include demographic characteristics, economic prosperity, and geographical issues relevant to that new market. In either instance, you are delivering a speech about an object.

Speeches about Processes

Informative speeches are not always about objects. In fact, many times they are more of a how-to type of speech. The next form of informative speech is about a process. These speeches are generally easier to construct and deliver than other speeches, as they pertain to a sequence of events presented in chronological fashion. However, processes vary in terms of complexity.

A very simple process could be baking a cake or changing the tire on a car. In the latter example you would explain each stage of changing a tire, beginning with setting the parking brake, then moving on to blocking the wheels, loosening the lug nuts, jacking up the car, removing the flat tire, replacing the spare tire, tightening the lug nuts, lowering the jack, and checking the lug nuts again, before finally unblocking the wheels and releasing the brake. Each step depends upon the completion of the preceding one for the process to be completed correctly.

Informative speeches about processes can be more complicated as well. Consider a doctor explaining the treatment plan for patients suffering from cancer. This can include radiation schedules, chemotherapy plans, surgeries, and rehabilitation requirements. The process can be very complicated and confusing to patients, so doctors need to effectively explain how the recovery process will unfold. In business, marketing plans are also often complex initiatives with various components, and in order to move forward with those initiatives they need to be carefully explained in a step-by-step process to the staff responsible for their implementation.

Speeches about Events

The third type of informative speech includes those presentations about an event. Speeches about events can unfold in a variety of ways, but they focus on something that has happened, is happening, or might happen in the future. The central focus of informative speeches is to explain the characteristics of the event, and so it might take shape chronologically or topically.

You are probably familiar with informative speeches about events presented in chronological order from your time in history classes. History is the progression of events that already happened. For example, when history teachers and professors lecture about the World War II Battle of Pearl Harbor, they probably explain it in the chronological order in which the events happened. This makes sense and helps the audience of students understand how the battle unfolded. Even so, sometimes events are best presented in a topical format.

Consider the possibility of working for a company that is about to host a conference. During a conference many different things happen at the same time, and a large staff is responsible for administering the event. In this instance, someone will need to address the staff and explain what will simultaneously happen in different locations during the conference. For example, a wedding planner might talk about what needs to happen as the wedding ceremony unfolds and what needs to be done at the same time to set up for the reception that will take place immediately afterward in a separate location. This is not a chronologically sequenced presentation but rather one that is delivered around topics or locations.

Speeches about Concepts

The last type of informative speech covers concepts. Concept speeches are the most abstract of all the informative speech types, as they are about ideas and not concrete constructs. The speaker's task when delivering information about concepts is to take something abstract and ground it in reality through the use of real-life examples, illustrations, and vivid depictions. Concept speeches can be about religion, economics, politics, relationships, or any theory or idea that is not tangible.

Informative speeches about concepts can be about seemingly simple theories, such as evolution, or more complex philosophies like existentialism. It is important to remember that all products and tangible items we encounter once started out as ideas with no concrete dimensions, so try to think about these types of informative speeches as pertaining to the inception of an idea. If you have an idea for a new product, you first need to explain the concept of the product before getting approval to create it.

Of course, speeches explaining concepts also appear in non-business enterprises. For example, preachers in churches explain religious principles to their congregations by illustrating principles in action. Lawyers argue about the law, which is abstract, by applying it to particular real-life cases. All productions in the entertainment fields and advertising begin with conceptual frames and drawings. Speeches about concepts explain these initial ideas before they ever become tangible, as once the topic is tangible it becomes a speech about an object.

Each of the four types of informative speeches can be about the same topic; they simply approach it in different ways. For example, if you want to speak about Buddhism, you could speak about Buddha as a person and describe his life, thus delivering a speech about an object. You could also focus on how to become a practitioner of Buddhism, thus delivering an informative speech about a process. The speech also could focus on a specific Buddhist ritual, thus coming at the topic from the angle of an event. Finally, it could be about the central beliefs of Buddhism, which would be a speech about a concept. What matters is that your specific purpose statement clearly articulates which type of informative speech you plan to deliver. Once you determine the type of speech you are giving, you can then organize the body in a way that makes the most sense to the audience.

ORGANIZATIONAL PATTERNS

When explaining complex information to people who are unfamiliar with it, proper organization of your speech is essential. In the development of the speech, you must determine the most effective way to present complicated information to the audience. Sometimes it's as simple as laying out a sequence of steps, but often it is more complex. In this section, we will discuss five different ways to organize an informative speech. Treat these organizational patterns as tools in your speech toolkit that you can turn to at any time when they make the most sense. In short, let the information dictate the pattern; don't choose the pattern and then make your information fit it.

Chronological

The first organizational pattern we will present is chronological, which sequences events in the order in which they occur in time. This pattern illustrates to the audience not just what occurs at each step but also how the central focus of the speech is changed by each move forward. Take, for example, a speech about a medical treatment program. This is a fairly complicated subject; however, if the speaker explains what is involved at each treatment step, why it must go in that order, and how the patient will respond and feel after each step, then the topic becomes easier for an unfamiliar audience to follow.

You may believe that chronological patterns are restricted to informative process speeches, but in fact they are more versatile than that. For instance, they could also be used to organize a speech about an object, such as an airplane. A speech about airplanes could discuss their historical development and major moments of change in their appearance and use. Chronological organization is easily understood by an audience and can be used with many different speech topics, not just processes.

Cause-Effect

A specific form of the chronological organizational pattern involves causes and effects. The cause-effect pattern discusses one or more causes that result in a specific event. It is important when discussing this organizational strategy that you remember that just about everything has more than one cause, and so you must be careful when arguing that something caused something else. Now that the reminder is out of the way, let's talk about how to structure speeches like this.

Cause-effect speeches begin by explaining one or more things you claim cause a resulting event. For instance, a speech about a business plan for a company could have several different causes for the specific effect of monetary growth or loss. The causes could be a creative marketing plan for a new product, an expanded sales force, and more investment in product training. Each of these causes could then be linked to the specific effect of raising revenue for the company. Such an approach illustrates the complexity of multiple causes for one desired effect in a way an audience can follow. The cause-effect pattern is generally easy for the speaker to organize and easier for an unfamiliar audience to understand. The key element to a good cause-effect speech lies in making the connections between the causes and the effects explicit and obvious for the audience.

Problem-Solution

A third way to organize your speech involves focusing your explanation around a problem and its solution. As with the cause-effect pattern, it is important to make the link between the two explicit for the audience and also to focus on the past. We say focus on the past because with an informative speech such as this, you are not proposing a specific solution to an existing problem but rather explaining how a past problem was solved. Doing this is what makes the speech informative and explanative, rather than a persuasive speech, in which you try to convince an audience to enact a solution to an existing problem.

Teachers often employ problem-solution organization in their lectures and discussions with students. For example, when discussing the Civil Rights Movement they might set up their lecture by establishing all of the problems faced by African Americans in society during the 1960s. The teacher could then talk specifically about the nonviolent resistance of Martin Luther King, Jr., and how it influenced the passage of legislation protecting the rights of the African American community. Such a speech is not persuasive but rather explains several problems and a way they were solved.

Spatial

Sometimes we cannot effectively explain something to an audience in a clear chronological sequence, so we need an organizational pattern that does not rely on time sequencing. Instead, spatial organization explains material to an audience by emphasizing how things are physically related to one another in a defined area or space. Here location, not time, creates the structure of points. Like time, however, spatial organization must follow a logical pattern in which the subject of each subsequent point is located near or adjacent to the location of the previous one.

Suppose a student wanted to deliver a speech about their native city of New Orleans and, after examining the city's geography, decided to organize the speech by regions of the city. The speech could have these spatial areas as its main points: the French Quarter, the Central Business District, the Downriver District, and the Uptown area. In each main point of the speech the prominent characteristics of each area would be explained. It would be important, however, to order the regions in a way that mirrors the way they are connected on a map.

Topical

The final organizational pattern we will discuss is topical, or categorical. In this pattern, you look at the particulars of the topic and find a theme for the topic in a certain category. This pattern often takes shape when you want to focus on a specific aspect of a topic, so that aspect becomes the organizing theme for the speech. Topical organization is also employed when the other organizational patterns do not seem to fit what you want to do.

If you wanted to explain different modes of dealing with interpersonal conflict to an audience you would most likely do so topically. In this speech, you would cover the five ways to handle conflict: withdraw, accommodate, force, compromise, and collaborate. Each one of these strategies represents a topic, or category, related to managing interpersonal conflict and is also logically linked. If the information were presented in this way, an audience would easily be able to follow the explanation of this complicated material.

Topical organization, however, is not restricted to speeches about concepts. You also might want to focus a speech about a person this way as well, as opposed to doing it chronologically. For instance, you could speak about comedian Stephen Colbert topically by organizing the speech's main points around the categories of his family life, his comedic career, and his social activist activities. This is not chronological, but topical, and still allows the audience to follow along with your speech points.

When it comes to choosing an organizational pattern you should always remember not to be too rigid. There will be topics that will require you to combine some of these five patterns. Take the Stephen Colbert example. The main points are ordered topically; however, the discussion of each of those main points might make the most sense if presented chronologically. This allows you to have an overarching organizational pattern for main points and also the flexibility to organize the subpoints of those main points differently so they make better sense.

Teacher Tips

When you are teaching, each class period is basically an extended informative speech. As you develop your lesson plans, think carefully about which key ideas you want to focus on during your class period and which pattern of organization will be most effective for helping your students understand those concepts. To help enhance your students' understanding, try incorporating some of the following into your lesson plans:

◊ live or video demonstrations

◊ models or pictures of the objects

◊ diagrams and idea maps that show how topics are related

◊ activities that allow your students to apply and build on ideas

◊ questions or assignments that allow you to check for understanding

Other contexts where these skills apply: Corporate Training, Sales, Accounting, and Health Professions

EXPLAINING DIFFICULT CONCEPTS

In many informative speeches, you will be explaining concepts that are difficult for your audience to understand, particularly if your audience is not composed of experts in the subject about which you are speaking. There are many reasons that an idea might be difficult for an audience to understand, but according to Dr. Katherine Rowan[1], there are three primary reasons that it is hard for a nonexpert audience to understand a complex idea: (1) the language or concepts are difficult, (2) the structure or process is hard to envision, or (3) the idea is difficult to believe. When explaining difficult concepts in your informative speech, you should first identify why the concept is difficult to understand, and then choose the explanatory strategy that best helps audiences overcome that particular challenge. In this part of the chapter we will discuss ways to overcome these three challenges to effective explanation.

---

1. Katherine E. Rowan, "A New Pedagogy for Explanatory Public Speaking: Why Arrangement Should Not Substitute for Invention," *Communication Education* 44, no. 3 (1995): 236–50.

elucidating explanation

helps your audience understand the definition term by distinguishing the essential characteristics that are always present from the associated characteristics that are only sometimes present in the objects, concepts, or processes that are examples of the term that you are defining

Difficult to Understand

When a concept is difficult to understand because the language is unfamiliar to your audience, you should use an **elucidating explanation**. Your goal in an elucidating explanation is to help your audience understand the definition of a term and to be able to distinguish the essential characteristics that are always present from the associated characteristics that are only sometimes present in the objects, concepts, or processes that are examples of the term that you are defining. Rowan explains that elucidating explanations should include four parts: (1) a common *exemplar*, or ideal example, of the concept; (2) a *definition* that explains the essential characteristics of the concept; (3) several examples of the concept, along with some *nonexamples* that might commonly be mistaken as examples of the concept; and (4) opportunities for your audience to *practice* identifying examples and nonexamples of the concept.[2]

Take the case of the term "immediacy," which might be unfamiliar to some people who have not studied instructional communication or psychology. If you used an elucidating explanation to help your audience understand the concept of immediacy, you might say:

> "In *Dead Poets Society*, Mr. Keating, who is played by Robin Williams, seems to draw his students in and connect with them by doing things like calling on them by name, moving around the classroom, using a lot of vocal variety and gestures, using humor during class, and having a relaxed posture. All of these behaviors show that Mr. Keating has a high level of immediacy. Immediacy is 'the degree of perceived physical or psychological closeness between teachers and students. Immediacy represents a set of verbal and nonverbal communication behaviors that indicate a teacher's willingness to approach and be approached by students.'[3] Some examples of teacher immediacy behaviors include making eye contact with students, having a relaxed body posture while teaching, allowing for small talk, using words like 'we' and 'us,' and using vocal variety and gestures. However, sarcastic humor, telling stories that embarrass students, and reading from PowerPoint slides are not examples of teacher immediacy."

Here you see how each of the components of an elucidating explanation are included. Not all elucidating explanations need all of these components, but

---

2. Rowan, "A New Pedagogy," 236–50.

3. Virginia P. Richmond, Derek R. Lane, and James C. McCroskey, "Teacher Immediacy and the Teacher-Student Relationship," in *Handbook of Instructional Communication: Rhetorical and Relational Perspectives*, eds. Timothy P. Mottet, Virginia P. Richmond, and James C. McCroskey (Boston: Pearson, 2006), 167–93.

if you have the time and the term is particularly hard to pin down for an audience, use as many as you can.

Difficult to Picture

Other concepts use familiar words but are difficult to understand because they are difficult to picture. Concepts or processes might be a challenge to imagine because they are abstract ideas or because the process or object is happening at a microscopic level that cannot easily be seen. There are two ways that something can be difficult to picture. First, it might be difficult to get an overall impression of the thing being explained, and second, it might be difficult to see the parts, processes, and interrelations of the phenomenon.

When you explain something that is difficult to picture, you should use a **quasi-scientific explanation** to help the audience better understand the phenomenon. A quasi-scientific explanation should include two key parts: (1) a graphic feature that helps the audience get an overall big picture of the phenomenon, such as a model, simplified drawing, cartoon, or diagram; and (2) verbal organizational cues that indicate the relationships among the parts or subprocesses of the phenomenon, including transitions, summaries, previews, and statements that clearly state the relationships. Some of the best quasi-scientific explanations include titles that suggest what the overall structure is, analogies that help the audience organize the information by comparing it to something familiar, and thesis statements or topic sentences that suggest a model that shares similar characteristics with the unfamiliar phenomenon.

quasi-scientific explanation helps the audience get an overall picture of the phenomenon and see relationships among the parts

For example, it can be difficult to picture how herd immunity helps prevent the spread of vaccine-preventable diseases, even when a few people cannot be vaccinated because they are newborns who are not yet old enough to receive the vaccine or because they have a medical condition that weakens the immune system and would make getting vaccinated dangerous. To help explain how vaccinating a large proportion of a population protects those who cannot be vaccinated, you might explain that humans fighting off diseases like the measles are in some ways similar to a herd of cattle trying to fight off coyotes that prey on young calves. In both instances there is power in numbers. Along with this analogy, you might choose to provide a diagram that shows how easily diseases can spread through a population once a critical mass of people choose not to be vaccinated.

Difficult to Believe

transformative explanations
explanations that help the audience transform their everyday ideas about how something works into a more accurate understanding of the phenomenon

Sometimes concepts use simple language and can be imagined easily but are difficult to believe because they are counterintuitive. In these cases, speakers should use **transformative explanations** to help the audience change their everyday ideas about how something works into an accurate understanding of the phenomenon.

Transformative Explanations Have Four Parts

1   Acknowledge people's everyday, or "lay," theory about the concept, perhaps by asking the audience to tell you about the concept.

2   Acknowledge why their understanding seems plausible on the surface.

3   Explain why their impression is incorrect, and show examples that demonstrate why it is not adequate for explaining the phenomenon.

4   Explain the theory, and illustrate why it is effective.

For example, when we think that we see things, we are actually seeing reflected light off the objects, not the objects that we are looking at. This is counterintuitive because we think that we are actually seeing the object that is in front of us. If you were to use a transformative explanation to help your audience understand how we see things, you might say something like this:

> "Most people think that when we see something, we are actually seeing the object that is in front of us. This makes a lot of sense because, in our experience, when we see something, it is really there. However, if this were true, we would be able to see everything that was in front of us all of the time, but if you have ever tripped over something while walking through a dark room in the middle of the night, you know that sometimes things are in front of you that you cannot see when there is no light. Instead, when we think we see something, we are actually seeing the light that is reflected off of the object that is in front of us."

This statement includes all the elements of a transformative explanation and illustrates how you can explain and correct a misunderstanding someone might have in a logical and civil manner.

STRATEGIES TO HELP YOUR AUDIENCE UNDERSTAND

In addition to the tips for explaining difficult content to your audience, there are several other strategies available to you as a speaker for helping your audience understand your topic and remembering the key points of your presentations. These six methods may seem simple, but they go a long way in helping ensure your audience understands and remembers the information you provided.

Use Repetition

If you only say something once, your audience is unlikely to remember it, but if you expose your audience to the same idea multiple times and in multiple ways, they are much more likely to remember the information. This is especially helpful with important, complicated material within your speech. The more you repeat something, the greater the chance the audience will pick up on it.

Give Rewards

Your audience will pay more attention to what you are saying if they perceive that they will be rewarded for doing so. Rewards can be immediate, such as giving candy to audience members who can answer questions correctly, or delayed, such as telling the audience how they will benefit from the knowledge that you are sharing. When you have a choice, though, the latter works better for using rewards because the reward is much longer lasting for the audience.

Show and Tell

Although show and tell is a game played mainly by elementary school students, it also can play a vital role in helping even adult audiences understand material. It essentially uses visual and verbal organizational cues to help your audience identify the most important concepts and understand how those concepts relate to each other.[4] Visual organization cues might include putting key words for each main point on a PowerPoint slide when you preview your main points, showing important definitions or quotations while you are talking about them, showing your audience diagrams or images that will

---

4. B. Scott Titsworth and Kenneth A. Kiewra, "Spoken Organizational Lecture Cues and Student Notetaking as Facilitators of Student Learning," *Contemporary Educational Psychology* 29, no. 4 (October 2004): 447–61.

help them to visualize how concepts are related, or giving your audience a handout that will help them follow along during your speech. Using matrices or other diagrams that summarize information and visually demonstrating how ideas are related can be especially helpful because the audience can more easily understand the connections between concepts.[5] Verbal organization cues include signposts, reviews, and previews that help draw the audience's attention to important concepts and help the audience understand how ideas are related. This is why the preview of main points in the introduction of your speech, transitions between main points, and the review of main points in the conclusion are so important.

Build on What Your Audience Already Knows

When explaining concepts that are unfamiliar to the audience, you can help them understand by connecting the new information to something that the audience already knows.[6] For instance, you might use an analogy or metaphor to show the similarities between something familiar and something new. One of the most effective ways of both explaining a difficult concept and identifying with an audience is to connect your topic or information to something with which they are already familiar. This helps them make the association themselves in terms they understand, making it more likely the information will be remembered.

Use Humor

Incorporating humor that is related to the topic of your speech can help you capture and keep your audience's attention. However, you will want to be careful to make sure that your humor enhances your audience's attention to your topic rather than distracting from it. In short, humor must help them focus on the content and not on you. You will also need to be careful that your humor can be easily understood by your entire audience through the use of idioms and terms you expect the audience knows. Just because a speech delivers information does not mean it needs to be boring and uninteresting.

---

5. Kenneth A. Kiewra, "How Classroom Teachers Can Help Students Learn and Teach Them How to Learn," *Theory Into Practice* 41, no. 2 (2002): 71–80.

6. Jerome Bruner, *The Process of Education* (Cambridge, MA: Harvard University Press, 1960).

Check for Understanding

Finally, you can help your audience learn by checking for understanding periodically. Ask your audience to answer questions or provide examples to see whether they understand the concepts that you have explained so far. If you find that your audience does not quite understand the ideas, adapt your speech by explaining the ideas in a slightly different way until your audience shows that they understand the concepts. To do this, you should try and prepare a few different ways to explain the same point, even if you do not end up needing all of them.

GOALS AND STRATEGIES FOR INFORMATIVE SPEECHES

Each of the four types of informative speeches attempts to achieve a specific set of goals with an audience. Each also can employ particular strategies to achieve those goals, including determining the best organizational pattern for your speech purposes and integrating other tools into the presentation. In this final section, we provide a few strategies to help you maximize your ability to achieve the goals of each type of informative speech.

Tips for Informative Speeches about Objects

Many times it is difficult to precisely describe an object, and the less familiar your audience is with the object, the more description you will need to provide. This is why it is important to find out in advance how much your audience already knows about your speech topic. Doing so allows you to determine whether you need to bring a model of the object as a visual aid for your speech so the audience can actually see what it is you are talking about.

In the health field, doctors often find models useful when speaking to patients because medical conditions and procedures can be very complicated for those not trained in biology and anatomy to fully grasp. Let's use a dental procedure as an example. In any dentist's office, you will likely find a model of a mouth, or at least a poster with a picture of the mouth on it. When dentists try to explain to patients what is happening with their teeth, where cavities are, or where and how they need to brush better, they often need to pull out the model to show the patient. This allows the patient to have a visual representation and understand the complicated information the dentist provided them.

Tips for Informative Speeches about Processes

As we previously noted, process speeches consistently use a chronological sequence. These speeches are generally easy to understand, if logically presented, and are easy for the speaker to keep on track as one thing follows another. When one thing logically follows another it becomes important to detail for the audience when and how one stage progresses to another. For example, if you are developing a speech about the process of applying for a job, your speech will have several stages that build upon one another. First there is the research process of finding a job for which you wish to apply, after which you must prepare an application letter. With the letter, you must also prepare and submit a resume. In this presentation, you need to make sure the audience understands how each step relates and connects to the next.

By explaining the connections between main points, you do more than list things or provide directions to the audience. In essence, you are explaining the complexities of the process. Informative speeches about processes are more than recipes and lists of stages. They are explanations of each step and the dos and don'ts that come with each stage of the process. Take the time to explain the process and each of its steps to ensure that the audience understands it all.

Tips for Informative Speeches about Events

In many ways, events are more complicated than processes or even objects because they contain numerous elements upon which a speech can focus. So the primary tip in developing a clear and effective explanation of an event is to choose your focus and explain that focus to the audience early in the speech. This lets them know that you are not covering everything about the event but rather a specific aspect of it.

It is important that you also lay out the details of the event to the audience. Identify important people involved in the event that will appear in your speech. When covering what happened during the event, be sure to let your audience know how those occurrences will be covered. If you plan to cover the event spatially rather than chronologically or even topically, make sure your audience knows this. Focus only on what you can adequately cover in the time you are allowed, and be sure your audience knows how you plan to discuss the event so they do not get confused.

Tips for Informative Speeches about Concepts

Concepts are abstract, so they hold particular challenges for speakers. Concept speeches need to take abstract ideas and relate them to the audience as clearly as possible. One of the most effective ways of doing this is through concrete and hypothetical examples. This is the same tool teachers use to explain new ideas to students. The apple falling on Newton's head, for example, is a tried and true way of explaining the abstract concept of gravity.

Before employing examples, however, make sure you clearly explain the concept. There will be times when your speech contains abstractions, but make sure those abstractions are followed with concrete examples that illustrate the concept at work. Whenever possible, draw these examples from things that will resonate with the particular audience to whom you are speaking.

Summary

Good informative speaking explains complex material to nonexperts in such a way that they can easily understand and learn the new material. As we discussed in this chapter, that new material can come in four different forms: objects, processes, events, and concepts. There are also several ways you can organize this information to effectively explain it to an audience, and here we covered five patterns of organization. Finally, we provided a few tips for developing effective informative speeches that explain objects, processes, events, and concepts to an audience.

Key Terms

eluciding explanation 204

explain 195

inform 195

quasi-scientific explanation 205

transformative explanations 206

Activities

1   Identify a topic that would be especially appropriate for each of the five patterns of organization for informative speeches. For each topic, write out the thesis and main points that you would use if you were writing a speech using that pattern of organization.

2   What is one concept in your informative speech that will be difficult for your audience to understand? Which of the three strategies for

explaining difficult concepts will you use in your informative speech? Write out what you will say when using this strategy in your speech.

3   Choose three of the strategies for helping your audience understand. What is a specific way in which you could use this strategy in your upcoming speech?

PERSUASIVE SPEECHES

Objectives

◊ Learn about credibility and its role in the persuasive process

◊ Differentiate between types of persuasive speeches and the various ways they can be organized

◊ Become familiar with ways to approach topics with different types of audiences

We use persuasion in our personal and professional lives, and we are also subjected to others' attempts to persuade us. At home we may try to convince someone to see a particular movie, eat at a specific restaurant, or watch a television show. At work we may negotiate salaries, try to motivate members of our team working on a project, or even get a boss to agree to let us leave work early. In today's world, no matter where we are or where we look, there are advertisements trying to convince us to buy a product or believe a certain thing. Interstate highways are littered with billboards, hallways are filled with posters, and the average one-hour television show contains almost twenty minutes of advertising! Persuasion is all around us, and to be better at persuading others, as well as become more critical consumers of information, we must understand how it works.

In this chapter, we will cover the principles of the persuasive process and how to prepare and organize a persuasive speech. We will go over the persuasive process, paying particular attention to the role credibility plays in convincing an audience. Then we will cover the four different types of persuasive speeches you may be called upon to deliver. Third, we will explain the various ways those speeches can be organized. Finally, we will provide some tips for adjusting to different types of audiences during your speech.

THE PERSUASIVE PROCESS

Persuasion is more complicated than it may appear on the surface. It takes time and occurs through a four-step process. Additionally, attempting to persuade someone does not guarantee success or an immediate response. Many times the effects of persuasion occur long after the persuasive message has been delivered, when the audience member encounters a situation that makes him or her think more about your persuasive appeals or has the opportunity to act upon that information. In this section, we will unpack the persuasive process and discuss its four stages in more detail.

Stage 1: Issue Awareness

issue awareness
first stage of the persuasion process in which you focus the audience's attention on the issue and show why the issue is important

The first step in persuasion is **issue awareness**. Audiences often have some knowledge of an issue before you speak to them about it, but how much they know will vary as will how strongly they hold positions on the issue. Sometimes audiences have no knowledge about a particular issue until it is presented to them by a speaker. This is common when it comes to certain environmental or health issues that face a community.

To be effective in making an audience aware of the issue about which you are speaking, you need to know how familiar they are with the topic. Can you reasonably assume they know about the issue? How much do they know? Are they likely to share your opinion or disagree with you? These are important questions to consider when preparing to persuade an audience to believe or do something. Regardless, focus the audience's attention on the issue, and make them aware of your feelings about why it is important to them. Only when an audience is aware that an issue exists can you move on to the next step of the persuasive process.

Stage 2: Comprehension

comprehension
stage of the persuasion process in which the audience understands the relevant components of the issue and the position that you want them to take

Once an audience is aware of a concern or issue, you need to make sure they comprehend both its relevant components and how you feel they should handle it. Thus the next step in the persuasive process is **comprehension**. Only when an audience comprehends the complexity of an issue and what the options are for responding to it can they make an informed decision about whether they will follow your advice.

Comprehension can be simple or complicated, depending on the familiarity the audience has with the topic. If they understand the issue, you need to spend time making sure they comprehend your position on it, but if they do not know much about the topic, then you must spend significant time educating them. When helping an audience comprehend a topic, do not give in to the temptation of telling only your side of the issue; instead, give them as complete a picture as possible. This ethical approach creates goodwill with the audience and gives them the freedom to make an informed decision.

However, just knowing that an issue exists or comprehending its components does not create persuasion; for that we move on to stage three.

Stage 3: Acceptance

The third step in the persuasive process, **acceptance**, occurs when the audience accepts that the issue is relevant to them. This does not mean audience members are going to agree with you or do what you desire, but they at least accept the accuracy of what you are saying and recognize how the issue pertains to their lives. This is important because if they do not accept the issue, then it will not be possible to persuade them. Just think, how likely is it that an audience will agree with, let alone consider, an issue that does not affect them in any meaningful way? Not very likely, thus making persuasion difficult at best, but most likely impossible.

Getting an audience to accept an issue's importance depends on whether you adequately explain the issue and how clearly you describe it. The audience must be able to comprehend an issue and see its connection to their own lives in order to develop a position or change a position they may already hold. However, an audience can comprehend an issue and accept its importance to their lives but still disagree with you. That means there must be one more step in the persuasive process.

acceptance
third step of the persuasion process in which the audience accepts that the issue is relevant to them

Stage 4: Integration

The final and most important stage of the persuasive process is **integration**. In this stage, the audience adopts the position that you want them to take. This occurs when audiences fully understand the issue, accept that it is relevant to their lives, and agree with your proposition regarding what to think or how to act. Your position becomes a part of the audience's personal philosophy and way of seeing the world. This change will vary among audience members, but ultimately, because you are seeking to change their understanding and feelings about something or someone, you bear significant ethical responsibilities.

integration
the fourth step of the persuasive process in which the audience adopts the position that you want them to take

The ability to achieve integration with persuasive speeches and messages depends upon several factors. The evidence, reasoning, and logic you present are obviously key to successfully influencing an audience, as is the audience's disposition toward the topic itself. The third component of persuasion is your credibility as a speaker. When an audience sees you as reputable, fair, and ethical, your ability to integrate your position into their own worldview will be enhanced. This aspect of persuasion is called credibility, and it comes in several forms, which we will detail next.

TYPES OF CREDIBILITY

credibility
the ability of a person to inspire belief or trust in others

Credibility, or the ability of a person to inspire belief or trust in others, is an incredibly fluid concept. The degree to which we are credible varies based on who we speak with, what we speak about, and the way we speak about something. We can increase or decrease our level of credibility with our words or actions, thus making it something we must pay close attention to when delivering remarks to others. In persuasive speaking, it is essential that the audience see you as a credible source of information or your task of convincing them to do or believe as you ask will be almost impossible. In this section, we will explore three basic types of credibility.

Initial Credibility

initial credibility
the credibility that you have with the audience before you begin your speech, based on your experience and the audience's prior knowledge about you

The first form of credibility we will cover is **initial credibility**, which refers to the credibility that you have with the audience before you begin your speech. All of us carry a certain level of credibility on a topic going into a speech, but it varies depending on the topic and the audience. For instance, when giving a presentation in a classroom to fellow students you likely will have little initial credibility because they are unfamiliar with you and your experience. This presents a hurdle you must overcome if you want the audience to listen to you and believe what you say.

Initial credibility is not always zero for every speaker. In fact, the more experience speakers have with a subject, or the more recognizable their names, the more credibility an audience will give them before they even speak. Consider attending a presentation on fantasy novels by writer George R. R. Martin. You may recognize him as the mind behind *Game of Thrones*. These books are quite popular and successful, thus enhancing his initial credibility to speak on the topic. In your public speaking class, you and your classmates might even have some initial credibility based on classroom interactions and other conversations in class. Nonetheless, strong initial credibility does not guarantee success or even that the audience will continue to see the speaker as credible.

Derived Credibility

After the speech begins, whatever you say or do immediately influences your level of credibility, thus changing the initial degree of credibility with which you began. The form of credibility that manifests itself during your presentation is called **derived credibility** because it is the trustworthiness and believability you garner during the speech. After the speech begins, your level of credibility can either increase or decrease depending upon a number of different factors.

derived credibility
the form of credibility that manifests itself during your presentation

Factors That May Affect Your Credibility

◊ Your perceived level of preparation

◊ Your delivery

◊ The organization of your points

◊ The quality of your evidence and information

◊ The way you speak to the audience, regardless of whether they agree with you

Derived credibility is very important because it helps you win over members of the audience who may be skeptical of your position or, in some cases, even opposed to it. It also helps strengthen the level of agreement among your supporters. Relying simply on initial credibility and not trying to maintain or improve your trustworthiness with an audience can lead to disastrous consequences because audiences see through it and interpret it as being disrespectful to them. For that reason, you should take care to develop and deliver the best speech possible.

Terminal Credibility

Once the speech concludes you will have a new level of credibility on the subject and with the audience, known as your **terminal credibility**. This level is the initial credibility you walked in with plus the credibility you derived during your remarks. Obviously, you hope you finish with more credibility than you began with due to your efforts within the speech. The level of trustworthiness you finish with is referred to as terminal credibility, and it also becomes your initial credibility the next time you speak to a similar audience about the same topic.

terminal credibility
the level of credibility that you have when your speech concludes, which is the sum of your initial credibility and derived credibility

It is important to note that if you finish a speech and are less credible with an audience it is a significant challenge to recover that lost trustworthiness and believability. This can significantly hinder any future attempts at persuasion with that audience and possibly others as well. Suffice it to say, no matter what you plan to persuade an audience about, being perceived as credible is essential to your success. In the next section, we will discuss the different types of persuasive speeches and presentations you might find yourself delivering at some point. As we cover them, think about ways you might enhance your credibility in each situation.

TYPES OF PERSUASIVE SPEECHES

We are surrounded by persuasive messages that try to get us to believe something, feel something, or do something. There is so much information available today that you can find information to support almost any claim. There are four forms of persuasive speech we will cover in this section. Some persuasive speeches make claims about fact, others argue values, some suggest policies, and the final group refutes the positions of others.

Questions of Fact

Facts are not really the stubborn things people think they are. In actuality, facts are very hard to prove— just ask a lawyer, judge, or jury. Trying to convince someone of a fact is simply an exercise in persuasion, not science. Typically, persuasive speeches of fact occur when the speaker argues that something did or did not happen. Whenever there is a question about the occurrence or existence of something, we see a persuasive message regarding a **question of fact**. Often, things we take for granted can be disputed. For instance, look at the lunar landing by Neil Armstrong and his crew. There are people who argue that this whole occurrence was faked, and they have data that supports their argument, thus calling this "fact" into question. Whether or not Lee Harvey Oswald acted alone in killing President Kennedy is another example of a question of fact. Perhaps more common might be the question over global warming.

question of fact
when a speaker seeks to persuade people about how to interpret facts

Facts are called into question more than we might realize. In court juries are asked to listen to two different interpretations of an event and to try to decide what the facts are. This is a very difficult task, especially when both sides know how to effectively research and wield information. So facts are not stubborn things; they are more often determinations of which interpretations are the most accurate. This leaves the door open to persuasion on questions of fact.

Questions of Value

Sometimes facts are not in dispute, but rather we wish to try and convince people to place value on a belief or object. This topic represents a second type of persuasive speech, one that deals with **questions of value**. People place value on almost everything. We value money, time, freedom, choice, family, friendship, and a whole host of other things, but when people try to get us to value something more than something else, or to value it more than we already do, they are providing an argument in response to a question of value.

question of value
a persuasive speech about the rightness or wrongness of an idea, action, or issue

Questions of value arise in a variety of different contexts. In sports, teams trade players, but in order to be persuaded to do so they need to be convinced that they are receiving value in return. In politics, pro-life and pro-choice supporters clash over differences of value. In business, companies must often answer questions of value when staff members receive contract offers from rival companies and they must ask themselves how much they value keeping that employee. As you can see, we place value on a great many things in life, and people try to convince us to value things in the same order and way they do, thus creating an opening for persuasive messages about the value of objects, people, and positions.

Questions of Policy

Another common area in which persuasion comes into play is in policy, or decisions on how to act in the future. While questions of fact deal most often with what has happened already and questions of values are how we feel now or in the moment, questions of policy refer to persuasive efforts about how we should act in the future. **Questions of policy** advocate a course of action. Again, these types of questions come up in many different settings, from home life to governmental affairs.

question of policy
when a speaker takes a position on whether an action should or should not be taken

Perhaps the most common place for persuasive speeches on questions of policy is in legislative bodies, such as Congress or student government. These types of speeches question what should be done, such as where money should be allocated, what groups should be recognized, or what positions a group should announce on issues. These policies affect future activities in most instances, not past occurrences or present values.

Refutation

refutation
response to potential opposition

In some circumstances we are called upon to respond to the arguments made by another and attempt to defend our own positions. This is called refutation. These speeches try to disprove another's argument while also promoting your own. The topics can be facts, values, or policies. In order to be successful in refuting remarks by others, you will need to understand their argument and then address each of the points they raised while explaining the flaws in their position. This type of speech requires significant research and carefully planned responses.

What determines the type of persuasive speech you deliver is what you wish to accomplish. Also realize that you will likely use facts, refute other arguments, advocate for something to be done, or give your opinion on what you think is the best in any speech. Again, the type of speech is determined by your speech's goals. Your speech's goals also influence how you choose to organize your speech, and when advocating a position there are different organizational patterns to choose from than there are when explaining information to an audience. In the next section, we will cover those patterns available for advocacy speeches.

PERSUASIVE SPEECH ORGANIZATIONAL PATTERNS

There are four common ways to organize a persuasive speech that help maximize your ability to connect with and persuade an audience. Determining which one of these is best for you depends upon your topic and your goals, but all provide a clear way to lay out an argument for an audience in an easy-to-follow manner.

Problem-Solution

One of the more common times we present an argument is when proposing a solution to a problem we might encounter. The simplest way to organize this type of argument is in a problem-solution format. This organizational pattern typically has only two main points, but they are very detailed and explicitly connected to each other. The first main point presents the problem by explaining the issue in great detail. At this point, it is also important to explain to the audience how the problem affects them. Following the presentation of the problem, you provide a solution to the issue and explain what it entails. For example, a local homeless shelter is running low on money to provide services to disadvantaged people (problem), and you propose that they seek funds from the local government and wealthy donors (solution). In laying out the solution you need to explain how it will fix the problem you established in the first point. It is important to note, however, that most problems have a root cause that, if left unfixed, will cause the issue to reoccur, and this leads us to the second organizational pattern for persuasive arguments.

STEM Spotlight

Engineers often find themselves giving persuasive speeches as part of the solution validation phase of a project. During this phase you will be asked to present your proposed solution to clients and/or managers so they can learn about your solution, compare it with alternatives, and ask questions to identify potential problems. Your job is to persuade others that your solution is the best one, and you will need to have effective persuasion and communication skills as well as a firm understanding of the engineering concepts involved in your solution. At this stage, however, it is also important to listen carefully to your audience, consider their feedback, and be willing to discuss ways to adapt your solution so that it better addresses the problem and fits the constraints of the specific situation in which it will be implemented.

Other contexts in which these skills apply: Event Planning, Project Management, and Advertising

Problem-Cause-Solution

The second organizational pattern we will discuss simply adds a step to the prior problem-solution pattern. After presenting the problem in the first main point, you discuss the root cause of the problem in the second main point before moving on to offer your solution. Additionally, the solution you propose is not a solution to the problem but a solution to the cause of the problem, so that it never reoccurs. Suppose you have several potholes on your street that damage cars as they hit them. You take this problem to the local government, but rather than asking them to fill the potholes you point out that the potholes are there because the street was improperly sealed. You organize your argument so that you propose filling the potholes and resealing the road; that way the potholes will not come back. This is an effective example of using problem-cause-solution organization in persuasive appeal.

Comparative Advantages

In many cases, multiple solutions are offered to solve problems faced by individuals and communities. In these cases it becomes advantageous to organize your speech around a comparison of your solution with those proposed by other parties. This type of organizational pattern is called comparative advantages, and it can be used to show how your solution is superior to others. This type of organizational pattern can be especially effective in business settings in which you are competing with a rival company for an account. You can compare that company's product or service with yours and explain how yours is superior, thus making you look knowledgeable and helping the audience see the benefits of what you are proposing.

Monroe's Motivated Sequence Steps
1. Attention
2. Need
3. Satisfaction
4. Visualization
5. Call to action

Monroe's Motivated Sequence

The fourth and final type of organizational pattern for a persuasive speech we will present is Monroe's Motivated Sequence. This pattern follows five steps, with each taking place in order within your presentation. Monroe's Motivated Sequence is most often found in advertising and business presentations, and it can often be easily identified within commercials.

The first step in the sequence is attention, during which you focus the audience on the issue you plan to address. This is done by tying the attention getter directly to your topic. The second step calls for you to establish a need, so the audience becomes aware of a problem or issue that needs to be addressed. This is a creative endeavor, as you must find a way to establish the need for the audience by illustrating your familiarity with their particular situation. The third step of the sequence is to present a way that satisfies the need. This solution fills the need you created in the audience. Simply presenting the solution does not guarantee they will adopt it, however, and so the fourth step of visualization uses colorful language and vivid imagery to encourage the audience to see themselves adopting your solution and fulfilling the need. The last step is the call to action and takes place during the conclusion of the speech, when you reiterate the desire for the audience to do as you propose.

Ultimately, you decide the organizational pattern by determining exactly what you want to accomplish in your speech. Persuasion is a mental process, and at times the audience will not react as you desire. That is why it is important for you to know what to do if you notice a negative reaction from the audience. In the final section, we will provide some suggestions on how to adapt to audience feedback during your presentation to help ensure that you stay on topic and retain the best possible chance at persuading your audience.

Business Basics

If you work in sales, you will give persuasive speeches frequently to try to persuade clients to purchase your products or services. Sometimes you will be asked for bids and will be competing directly with others, while at other times you will cold-call potential customers to convince them they need something they might not have considered.

If you are competing for an account:

◊ Organize your presentation using comparative advantages.

◊ Highlight the strengths of your product or service.

◊ Address all of the key concerns your client identified in his or her request for proposals.

If you are not in direct competition:

◊ Organize your presentation using Monroe's Motivated Sequence or problem-cause-solution.

◊ Tailor your presentation to your potential client. Do your research and make sure you can meet his or her needs before you ask for the appointment.

Above all, tell the truth, even if it means admitting weakness from time to time. If you tell your client that your product will do something that it cannot, you will lose your credibility and the chance for future sales.

Other contexts in which these skills apply: Management, Advertising, and Marketing

ADJUSTING TO THE AUDIENCE DURING THE SPEECH

Just as credibility changes during a speech, so too does the audience's response to your presentation. Sometimes this is good, as they indicate enthusiasm and agreement with your position, but other times they can exhibit a lack of interest and even hostility as you lay out your argument. Knowing how to adapt to this feedback is an essential part of successful persuasive speaking. In this section, we will provide you with some tips for adapting to audience feedback.

Adapting to a Favorable Audience

The ideal audience is one that looks upon you favorably. You may be able to adjust your delivery to garner even more support, so be sure to not do anything offensive that could jeopardize this potential. If you notice nods of agreement with your statements, or clapping and cheering, capitalize on this good feeling by increasing the volume and tone of your voice. Mirroring their enthusiasm can help engender even stronger support for your position.

It might seem like engendering more support with an already favorable audience is unnecessary, but nothing could be further from the truth. It is imperative to maintain, and even increase, interest and enthusiasm for you and your position. When an audience sees your excitement, they will share it and take the message even further than the setting in which they heard you speak, thus giving your position even more reach than your speech. All of this can be created by adapting to and taking advantage of the good feelings and positive atmosphere created by a supportive audience.

Adapting to a Neutral Audience

In many cases, you may be presenting to an audience that does not know you or what you are talking about, and we characterize these audiences as neutral. This audience has no position regarding you or your topic and thus could go either way, depending upon your speech. In this environment, you will again not want to be offensive, but will need to make a strong case, as you are asking them to choose among options. In these instances, you need to elaborate on the issue and connect it to your audience's lives, demonstrating why they should care about it. Only then can you move forward to creating a persuasive call to action.

During your speech, you need to be prepared for several different audience reactions. Your audience may appear confused, in which case you need to reframe what you are talking about to make it easier to understand. They may begin to demonstrate agreement, which you can then reference as you move forward with the speech. They also may appear uninterested, in which case you need to pause and find a way to bring them back. Neutral audiences can be the trickiest audiences you might address.

Adapting to a Hostile Audience

There may be times when you are called upon to speak to an audience with an unfavorable disposition toward you and/or your topic. In fact, they might be outright hostile. In some ways this is easier than a neutral audience because you at least know in advance where they stand, making it easier to craft a message that might hit home. Establish common ground quickly with these types of audiences. Beginning from a place of agreement or familiarity will lessen their hostility and at least open the possibility that they will listen to what you have to say. In fact, even during the speech, when you notice disagreement or hostility in the audience, returning to these common issues can help dull that discontent in the audience.

You may also need to alter your delivery if the audience is not responding to you, as discontent can manifest itself not only in overt comments but also in disinterest and lack of attention. In these cases, try to change your style of speech to become more engaging, enthusiastic, and relaxed. Perhaps walking around the room or through the audience when speaking will help recapture the interest and attention of audience members. You also might pause from your speech to tell a story or reflect on the topic in a less structured manner. You might even consider asking for comments or questions just to break up the presentation.

In the real world, it is likely that when you are attempting to persuade an audience you will have a mix of attitudes toward you and your topic, including favorable, unfavorable, and neutral attitudes. Adjusting to the reactions of the audience can aid you in successfully persuading them.

Summary

Persuasion is a complicated process that does not always happen as quickly as we would like. In fact, more often than not it takes time, evidence, and coherent arguments to convince an audience to go along with what you are advocating. In this chapter, we explained the four-step process of persuasion and the important role credibility plays in appealing to an audience. We also discussed how fluid credibility is and how it can change during a presentation. Next, we covered the four different types of persuasive speeches and discussed the various ways they can be organized to maximize their ability to connect with an audience. Finally, we provided some suggestions for how to adapt to the different types of audiences you might encounter when delivering a persuasive message. All in all, persuasion is a complicated process, and effectively creating a persuasive message takes time, evidence, and careful attention to the audience.

Key Terms

acceptance 215

comprehension 214

credibility 216

derived credibility 217

initial credibility 216

integration 215

issue awareness 214

question of fact 218

question of policy 219

question of value 219

refutation 220

terminal credibility 217

Activities

1   Give examples (not those included in the book) of a speech that would be arguing a question of fact, one that would be arguing a question of value, one that would be arguing a question of policy, and one that would be a refutation.

2   Identify a topic that would be especially appropriate for each of the four patterns of organization for persuasive speeches. For each topic, write out the thesis and main points that you would use if you were writing a speech using that pattern of organization.

3   For your upcoming persuasive speech, what are some of the reactions your audience members might have? How do you plan to adapt to your audience in these situations?

COMMEMORATIVE SPEECHES

Objectives

◊ Become familiar with the different types of commemorative speeches

◊ Understand how commemorative speeches differ from informative and persuasive speeches

◊ Learn some general guidelines for creating and delivering a commemorative address

You will hear a great many informative and persuasive speeches in your life-time, but some of the more memorable presentations you encounter will be of neither type. Instead, you will be more likely to remember the creative and colorful commemorative speeches than you will the informative speech about the state of your company's finances or the persuasive speech designed to get you to vote for a candidate. These commemorative speeches are the third general category of presentations, and they contain characteristics that make them quite distinct from informative and persuasive remarks.

In this chapter, we will first explain the different types of commemorative speeches, paying particular attention to the contexts in which they occur. We will then detail how these speeches differ from informative and persuasive speeches before concluding the chapter with some helpful suggestions for creating and delivering a good commemorative address. As you will see, these speeches contain room for creativity and can be some of the most enjoyable speeches to write and deliver.

TYPES OF COMMEMORATIVE SPEECHES

Many different occasions call for a celebratory speech. These speeches are called commemorative because they commemorate, or celebrate, a person, event, object, or even an idea. In this section, we will identify and discuss five different forms of commemorative address with which you might be familiar. The first, and saddest, is a eulogy, which occurs when someone passes away. The second form of commemorative address is a toast, which is reserved for happier occasions. The next two take place when someone presents or receives an award. Finally, we will detail a specific form of commemorative address you will hear in the not-too-distant future: a graduation address.

Eulogies

eulogy
a speech that pays tribute to the life of the deceased

The first type of commemorative address we will discuss is a **eulogy**. Eulogies are emotional speeches; however, that emotion need not be one of sadness. As we indicated in the definition above, commemorative speeches are celebratory, not depressing, and so eulogies should be a celebration of a person's life, not a moment to focus on his or her death.

If you are called upon to deliver a eulogy you will most likely have a few days to prepare your remarks. These types of speeches should focus on major events and accomplishments in the life of the deceased. Since these speeches are celebratory and happy, you might also consider telling a humorous story about the deceased person. It is imperative, however, that you do not appear to mock the person but rather emphasize a positive quality he or she exemplified during life. This story helps to establish a common bond between you, the audience, and the dearly departed person.

Although eulogies are intensely personal and emotional speeches, you should take care to talk about the person in such a way that the audience feels involved. You should refrain from telling "inside jokes" that people in the audience would not understand or appreciate. The speech is as much a moment of emotional release for them as it is for you. In fact, eulogies are best understood as communal celebrations of a life and not personal retrospectives about another individual. They should emphasize the qualities of the person by telling specific stories from his or her life that illustrate those aspects. You are, in essence, creating a way to remember another person.

Toasts

toast
speech given to celebrate an important occasion

In contrast to eulogies, one of the more entertaining and enjoyable commemorative speech events involves giving a **toast**. The most common occasion when toasts are used is a wedding. If you are the maid of honor or best man at a wedding, you will likely give a toast for the bride and groom. Like eulogies, wedding toasts are personal in nature and are celebrations of the union of two people. Of course, toasts occur at other times as well, such as at holidays and dinner parties, but the same general expectations apply. Usually you will know that you will be delivering a toast well in advance, so you will have plenty of time to prepare your remarks for the occasion.

There are certain characteristics and expectations common to all toasts. First, the person making the toast should talk about the person being toasted by connecting that person to the occasion and the audience. Often this is accomplished by telling a brief anecdote about the person you are toasting. In all toasts it is important to name the people being celebrated or honored and discuss the qualities that make them deserving of a toast. Remember that these events are celebratory in nature and should never be confused with roasts, during which the honoree is mocked. Toasts also are usually quite short, rarely going beyond two or three minutes.

Presenting an Award

Toasts are not the only way we commemorate the achievements of others; sometimes we present them with awards. Like toasts, presentations of awards are usually short because you, as the presenter, are not the focal point of the event. The important person is the one you are introducing. When presenting an award, there are certain goals you need to accomplish before handing over the microphone to the award recipient.

It is important to know if the winner of the award has been announced in advance or if you are the first to make the person aware of the award. If the award is announced in advance, then it is acceptable to talk about the individual by name, but if the awardee is not known to the audience then you should reserve the name until the very end of your remarks to maintain a sense of excitement and anticipation.

Regardless of whether you say the name of the honoree or conceal it to the end, when presenting an award you still need to do several things. First, talk about the award itself. If it is named after someone be sure to discuss who the individual was and why the award is named after him or her. Explain the qualities required to win the award and how the winner fits those characteristics. This connects the award recipient with the award itself, thus commemorating the recipient and the occasion. These remarks, however, differ from those you should prepare when receiving an award.

Receiving an Award

As we mentioned a moment ago when discussing speeches that present an award, sometimes honorees know they are getting an award, and sometimes they do not. In either instance, usually (though not always) there is an indication that you might receive an award and should be prepared to speak. Based on contemporary practice, you might think that this type of commemorative address is a simple laundry list of "thank yous," but you would be mistaken. There are, in fact, certain expectations in a good award acceptance speech, and they begin with a level of humility.

Of course, expressing gratitude for receiving the award is important, and mentioning a few people who made your winning possible is always a nice thing to do, but it is not the only thing you should do. In fact, in accepting an award you should also express knowledge about the award itself and convey an appreciation of the qualities it celebrates. Thus, award acceptance speeches should exhibit gratitude and also an understanding of the award and what it commemorates. Doing this connects you to the award in a way the audience appreciates and wants to celebrate.

Graduation Addresses

Commencement, or graduation, is an important milestone in anyone's life, and that is why graduation ceremonies come paired with several different speeches celebrating the importance of the moment. School principals, presidents, keynote speakers, and class valedictorians often deliver remarks at these ceremonies. Should you be in a position to give a commencement address, there are several things you should keep in mind.

First, these speeches should be between five and seven minutes because there are many other elements to a graduation and you do not want to delay the ceremony with an unnecessarily long presentation. Additionally, these speeches should celebrate the achievements of the entire graduating class, not just yourself, so you should refer to common experiences and not personal achievements while in school. These speeches are also more forward-looking than eulogies, or even toasts, and should contain some discussion of what will come for everyone after graduation. In this respect, commencement addresses are hopeful regarding the future. Finally, commencement addresses should thank those who made graduation possible.

Tips for Giving a Graduation Speech

◊   Your speech should be between five and seven minutes.

◊   Celebrate the entire graduating class, not just yourself.

◊   Look to the future and be hopeful.

◊   Thank the people who made graduation possible.

Whether it is a commencement address, eulogy, toast, or award ceremony, all commemorative speeches require that you tie the occasion to the audience. They also call for a positive tone; after all, commemorative speeches are celebrations of milestones or achievements. As they are celebratory in nature, such speeches are different from informative and persuasive speeches, and in the next section we will detail those differences.

CHARACTERISTICS OF COMMEMORATIVE SPEECHES

All speeches have certain common requirements. For example, they need to be organized, keep the audience in mind, and rely on a balance of emotion, logic, and credibility in order to be successful. There are certain elements that make speeches different. Informative speeches, for instance, are designed to convey information to an audience, while persuasive speeches attempt to move an audience to a particular belief or action. Commemorative speeches seek neither of these goals; instead, they wield information in order to celebrate an event, person, object, or idea. This section of the chapter will illustrate what makes commemorative speeches different from informative and persuasive speeches.

Language Differences

One of the most significant differences between commemorative speeches and other forms of speech is that they rely on more colorful and ornate language. In an informative speech you fulfill the role of teacher by helping an audience understand a complicated subject. In a commemorative speech you draw an audience's attention with emotional and colorful language, not just information. As you are well aware, there are many ways to say something, and the occasion and audience often dictate the best way to do it.

Look at a couple of examples:

> **Basic:** "Today we graduate."
> **Commemorative:** "Today, we celebrate four years of tireless effort that allows us to open the next chapter in our lives."

> **Basic:** "Today we celebrate Larry's retirement."
> **Commemorative:** "Today we recognize Larry for his thirty years of service, the countless students he taught, and the lives he changed."

Notice in each example how the language makes the event more meaningful by being more elaborate and descriptive. This is a hallmark of any commemorative speech, whether it is a toast, a eulogy, or an award acceptance.

Emotional Quality

In using ornate language you tap into the second unique quality of commemorative speaking: the audience's emotions. How could someone not be emotional at someone's death or the celebration of a commencement? These are important events in our lives. Language provides a way to express that meaning to ourselves and others, so a commemorative address is by its very nature emotional. The emotions you express, however, must also be shared by the audience, so it is important to keep their feelings about the event in the forefront of your mind when developing a speech.

The Importance of Context

All speeches must pay attention to audience and context, but the degree to which this is necessary is heightened for commemorative speeches. Connecting the occasion to the audience through the values being celebrated is the core element of any commemorative speech. Yes, knowing and adapting to an audience is necessary in informative and persuasive speeches, but in commemorative speaking the context, or occasion, is the focus of the speech, which is not something to which you adapt.

Less Rigid Organization

One thing you should note when constructing a commemorative speech is that there are no set organizational patterns as there are with an informative or persuasive speech. When celebrating a person or commemorating an event it does not make sense to have previews or set patterns for addressing a problem. In fact, the best way to arrange main points in a commemorative speech is topically. Make sure the topics connect to the values you are honoring in the individual or event. This topical arrangement provides commemorative addresses with a less rigid structure.

Just because they are less rigid, though, does not mean that commemorative speeches have no required elements. Commemorative addresses still entail getting the attention of the audience and signaling that the end of the speech is near, but they do not contain summaries and have little cited material. They also still necessitate an engaging delivery and depend more than other speeches on the speaker's tone and delivery to emotionally connect with the audience. Simply put, if you are celebrating something your delivery and demeanor should convey excitement to the audience.

As you can see, commemorative speeches have some similarities and some differences from informative and persuasive speeches. In this final section, we will provide guidelines to help you construct commemorative speeches.

GUIDELINES FOR COMMEMORATIVE SPEECHES

Due to their unique nature, commemorative speeches require careful attention, often in shorter periods of time than persuasive or informative speeches. After all, we are usually given plenty of advance notice when we are asked to help nonexperts learn about something or give persuasive speeches, especially in a business setting. Commemorative speeches come with some, but often not much, time to get your thoughts in order before presenting to an audience. To help you prepare, we will provide three guidelines for constructing commemorative speeches.

Practical Politics

When working in politics, you will be called on to give numerous speeches, and many of these will be ceremonial speeches. Here are a few examples of ceremonial speeches you might be asked to give:

- ◊ speeches to pay tribute to those who are honored on holidays (Memorial Day, Labor Day, Mother's Day, etc.)
- ◊ speeches to commemorate the opening of new buildings, monuments, memorials, parks, and other public spaces

◊ commencement addresses at high schools, colleges, and universities

◊ toasts at dinners and receptions that honor special guests

◊ speeches to present awards traditionally handed out by those in the office you hold

◊ eulogies for other public figures

◊ speeches conveying gratitude when receiving honors or awards from organizations

Other contexts where these skills apply: Ministry, Counseling, and Human Resources

Connect the Audience to the Event

It is crucial for a commemorative speech to use language to connect the audience to the event. Examples of ways to accomplish this include:

◊ Note the reason why everyone is there together.

◊ Note the significance of the event.

◊ Note how you connect to the event, and then how the audience does as well.

◊ Tell stories that exemplify the values being celebrated.

Each of these strategies helps the audience members understand why they are gathered at the event and situates the actual gathering as the most important element of the occasion.

Use Descriptive Language

Commemorative speaking turns the speaker into an artist who creates a visual image of an important event. The best way to do this is by using colorful, vivid, and ornate language. Commemorative speeches do not happen every day, and so you should not use everyday language when delivering them. Rather, take the time to detail what the occasion means, why it means what it does, and why people should celebrate. This takes time and creativity, so be sure to think through exactly what feeling you want to convey and use language that does exactly that.

Consider the Audience

Finally, you need to consider the expectations of the audience. If you are speaking at commencement, then graduation should be the center of your speech, as that is what the audience expects to hear about. Sometimes speakers use these events to push their personal agendas, addressing politics and other topics not relevant to the occasion, but that is not what the audience is there for. This is not to say that a speaker could not exhort the audience, especially the graduates, to be involved in their cause, but that should be held to a minimum. Instead, focus on the moment and the values embedded within it that are being celebrated.

Summary

In this chapter, we identified various elements that make commemorative speaking the third form of address. We detailed five different types of commemorative speeches that you may encounter and provided tips for how to approach developing each of them. We also elaborated on the differences and similarities between commemorative, persuasive, and informative speaking. Lastly, we provided some guidelines for developing and delivering commemorative speeches.

Key Terms

eulogy 228   toast 228

Activities

1   Find a video clip (TV, movie, or YouTube) that shows someone giving a toast and share the link to that clip. What does the speaker do well? How could the speaker have improved?

2   Watch one of the commencement speeches that are available in the NPR collection at apps.npr.org/commencement. How does the speaker work to connect the audience and occasion? How does the speaker enhance the emotional tone of the occasion?

3   Imagine a situation in which you are likely to give a commemorative speech in the future. What will the expectations of the audience be for your speech?

PRESENTATION AIDS

Objectives

◊ Familiarize yourself with traditional forms of presentation aids available for use during a speech

◊ Learn various digital and multimedia forms of presentation aids available for use during a speech

◊ Become familiar with basic guidelines for using presentation aids during a speech

In many respects speeches are no longer what they used to be. Sure, they still have the same general formats, structures, and purposes, but the manner in which people deliver them has changed substantially in recent years. Until recently, speakers would stand in front of an audience and detail their main points. If the speech was complicated, then the audience just had to pay really close attention. Today, however, speakers have ways to take complicated materials and make them more understandable. These presentation aids have fundamentally transformed professions in which speaking is an essential part of the job, such as teaching. Today's advanced digital and multimedia platforms provide great assistance to speakers, but they must be used properly.

In this chapter, we will address presentation aids, or as they are more commonly called, visual aids, and explain how to properly use them in your speech. We will first go over traditional types of aids before moving on to more advanced technological types. Finally, we will provide guidelines for implementing and using these aids within your speech so that they help, rather than hurt, your presentation.

TRADITIONAL AIDS

Presentation aids come in a variety of different forms, but each has its purpose. Today we focus more on PowerPoint, Prezi, Keynote, and other digital means for aiding a presentation; however, much of what appears in these platforms is merely a digital representation of basic traditional presentation aids. In this section, we will discuss five of these traditional aids that have been used for many years. We call them traditional presentation aids because they do not necessarily appear in electronic forms. For instance, for many years transparencies were used by both professors and students when providing information such as graphs of data. Transparencies may be moving toward extinction, but graphs are not. So here we will explain the traditional ways of visually depicting complicated information so that you may then incorporate them into a multimedia presentation.

Models

model
a three-dimensional representation of an actual object

The first type of traditional aid we will go over is a **model**, which is a three-dimensional representation of an actual object. To be effective, models need to be made to scale so that the audience gets an idea of what they are looking at and how it might function in its actual environment. Science teachers often use a scale model of human organs, such as the brain or heart. Museums also contain models of prehistoric settings, while students at science fairs create models of the solar system, with the sun in the center and the planets represented in their proper positions. These visual representations show how things are represented in space while allowing the audience to see them at a reasonable size. It would be very hard, for example, for a speaker to use a model of the heart at its actual size when speaking to an audience of fifty, so they create a model to scale to enable everyone to see it.

Charts

chart
visual depiction of summaries of numeric data

Models are not the only traditional form of presentation aid useful to speakers. A more common example is a chart, such as a frequency table. **Charts** allow you to visually depict summaries of numeric data for an audience. For example, if a manager is briefing his superiors on how productive different geographic regions have been in terms of sales, he might construct a chart that depicts sales for each region of the country and rank them from highest to lowest earnings. Charts help audiences quickly identify key points about data that would normally take a longer time to explain.

Graphs

graph
a type of chart that illustrates numeric data by using a visual diagram

One specific type of chart that speakers often rely on is a graph. **Graphs** help illustrate how numerical data relate to one another. Statistics are helpful if the audience can understand them, and graphs illustrate the impact and relationship of numerical information. Graphs also come in many forms, and you should choose the one that best illustrates your information to the audience in an uncomplicated way.

Let's briefly examine the five types of graphs that are most commonly used as presentation aids. First there are line graphs, which use lines drawn along two axes to show growth, loss, or flat developments over time (Figure 18.1).

Next there are bar graphs, which also show two axes, but the bars run either horizontally or vertically to represent total achievement. For example, the vertical axis can be years, while the horizontal axis represents profit for a business in millions of dollars. The bars extend up for each year to the total profit achieved in that year (Figure 18.2).

The third type of graph is a histogram, which is similar in appearance to a bar graph. A histogram is a visual representation of a frequency table in which the categories are placed on the horizontal axis, while vertical bars are used to represent the number (or frequency) of individuals who fit into that category. Histograms are usually used when data is continuous, so the categories on the horizontal axis represent an interval of scores that make up that category. For example, you might use a histogram to represent the grades that were earned on the first speech in class. Grade categories (A, B, C, etc.) would be shown on the horizontal axis, and the height of the vertical bar would represent the number of people who earned a specific grade (Figure 18.3).

Fourth, we have pie graphs, which are circles that are "sliced" apart to represent percentages of the total "pie" for particular groups or categories (Figure 18.4).

Finally, a scatterplot is a graph that shows the relationship between two continuous variables. Scatterplots are useful for helping your audience understand the relationship, or correlation, between two variables. For example, the scatterplot on the next page has an upward slope and shows a positive relationship between height and weight, meaning that the taller people are, the more they tend to weigh (Figure 18.5).

There are several types of graphs from which you may choose, and you should select the one that best represents your point.

line graph
a graph that uses lines drawn along two axes that show growth, loss, or flat developments over time

bar graph
a graph that shows two axes and bars going either horizontally or vertically to represent total achievement

histogram
a visual representation of a frequency table in which the categories are placed on the horizontal axis and vertical bars are used to represent the number (or frequency) of individuals that fit into that category

pie graph
circular graphs that are "sliced" apart to represent percentages of the total "pie" for particular groups or categories

scatterplot
a graph that shows the relationship between two continuous variables

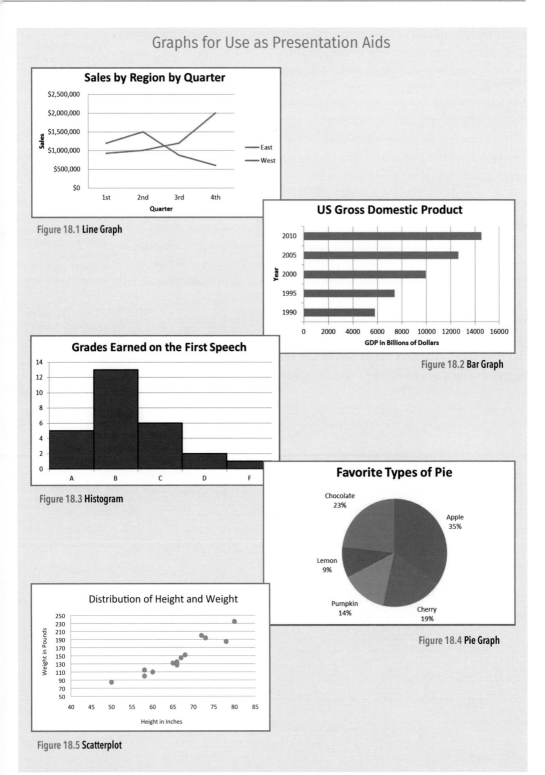

Graphs for Use as Presentation Aids

Figure 18.1 **Line Graph**

Figure 18.2 **Bar Graph**

Figure 18.3 **Histogram**

Figure 18.4 **Pie Graph**

Figure 18.5 **Scatterplot**

Objects

The fourth type of traditional presentation aid we will detail is an object. An object differs from a model in that it is the actual thing being discussed and not a representation of it constructed to scale. Objects are useful presentation aids for speakers who seek to demonstrate something to an audience. Think about the now-infamous infomercials for the cleaning product called a ShamWow. The speaker used the actual product in a demonstration for the audience while explaining how and why it operated. Objects should be used only when they are of a reasonable and accessible size, as you do not want to carry around large, bulky items. There are also some types of objects that you are not allowed to bring into a classroom, including weapons, alcohol, illegal substances, and live animals. In those instances you should simply use a model or a picture.

object
the thing being discussed, not a model or representation of that thing

Photographs

The fifth and last type of traditional presentation aid is a photograph. Today's digital cameras and cellular phones allow you instant access to an image. There is a vast assortment of photographs available on the internet. Photos allow the audience to experience the event, action, or person in a real-life context. They can also generate an emotional response from the audience, thus enhancing your appeal.

photograph
a picture of the object about which you are speaking

Traditional speaking aids have been around for a while, but with technological advances, speakers now have a variety of options available. In the next section, we will discuss how technology has enhanced our delivery options with presentation aids.

TECHNOLOGICAL AIDS

Technology has enhanced our ability to make presentations and changed the manner in which we can use traditional presentation aids. Now we can provide video and audio technology with our presentation, thus making it even more dynamic. It is important to remember, however, that these technological tools, although exciting and attractive, do not substitute for, and should not overshadow, your speech. In this section, we will discuss how video and audio can enhance a speech, as well as provide you with tips for constructing effective slideshow presentations using PowerPoint, Keynote, Prezi, or other similar programs.

Video

Video can be very effective in short bursts, but you must remember that you are giving a speech and that the video is an aid, not your entire speech. Frankly, the video should not be a large part of your presentation. Prerecorded videos, YouTube clips, or other such videos should be used to help an audience understand a point you are making, not just to fill the time. They also require that you explain where the video came from and how it is relevant to the point under discussion. Without the explanation the audience will feel that the video clip was used simply to add time, and they will not understand its connection to the speech topic.

There are numerous times when a brief video clip would help to enhance a speech. In a demonstration speech a presenter may use a video explaining how to use a particular tool or accomplish a specific task. In persuasive speaking, videos may be helpful to enhance testimonial evidence by allowing the audience to see the people as they endorse a product. Regardless of what you are trying to accomplish by showing the video, do not comment while the video is playing; let the audience focus their attention on the medium. If you need to explain something happening in the video, pause it to do so. This ensures that the audience stays focused on the message and not the presentation aid.

Business Basics

It is common for business professionals to deliver presentations and hold meetings via Web conference technology such as WebEx, Adobe Connect, or other videoconferencing software. In many businesses, especially sales organizations, this allows professionals to work from home part or all of the time, which cuts down on office and travel costs and allows them to interact with several clients in several locations in a single day. When using a conferencing tool such as WebEx you should follow the same guidelines you would if you were using PowerPoint for an in-person presentation. However, you will need to be deliberate about soliciting verbal feedback and using effective animations to draw attention to particular parts of your slides, especially in online presentations in which you are not using a webcam.

Other contexts in which these skills apply: Engineering, Accounting, and Education

Audio

In addition to video, audio can also be a good supplement to a speech, but, like video, it has some limitations. Audio clips allow an audience to hear expert and peer testimony straight from the source, rather than para-phrased or quoted by you. Audio can also help provide sound effects that illustrate key sounds in a speech that you cannot deliver on your own. For example, an engineer could explain how to identify when a machine is stalling due to a malfunctioning piece of equipment by providing the par-ticular sound it makes.

Audio is, however, not usually used on its own. In fact, you should always ask yourself if the audio clip you intend to play for the audience helps them understand something more clearly. If it does, then you are using it appropri-ately, but if it does not, then you should not incorporate it into your presen-tation. In any event, technologies such as audio and video can be combined with the more traditional presentation aids we discussed earlier.

Slideshow Presentations

In the last twenty years, presentation software has been readily available for students, professors, and professionals to use when delivering remarks. You can now choose from PowerPoint, Keynote, Prezi, and several other plat-forms to create a dynamic and colorful slideshow.

We first discuss a mistake that many novices make when creating slideshows: wordiness. Placing too many words on slides turns them into giant note cards that are then read to and by the audience. This design is unprofessional and defeats the purpose of visual aids by distracting the audience from your speech. Remember that these are presentation aids, not your entire presen-tation. Professors are often guilty of this approach. Think of teachers you might have had who put their entire lecture on PowerPoint slides. We would wager you paid more attention to writing down what was on the slide than listening to and understanding what the instructors were saying. Salespeople are also often guilty of putting too much information on slides for sales presentations.

Embedding Video and Audio

You may want to embed video or audio into your speech. Embedding a video allows you to save the video directly in your slideshow program so that you do not have to link to an external website, such as YouTube, to show the video clip. Most presentation software programs allow you to do this, but you should practice to make sure it works the way you want. This is especially important if you will be using a different computer during your presentation, because there are occasional compatibility problems among operating systems or software. Another option for displaying video is to link directly to the URL on an overhead slide. The problem with this approach is that the internet might be down, which would mean you would not be able to access the link. Whenever possible, it is a good idea to embed the video in the slide and include the URL in the notes field so that you have a backup option for showing the video.

Color Schemes

Figure 18.6 **PowerPoint "Create Theme Colors" window**

Slideshow presentation programs have a myriad of color selections from which you may choose (Figure 18.6). It is important to be aware, however, that not all color schemes go well together. Color can help your audience focus on a specific item on the slide, and it can also contribute to the mood or emotional dimensions of your speech. There are three significant areas for which you choose color applications on slides: background, borders, and lettering. It is important that the lettering be visible, so do not choose the same or a similar color for the background and borders. If you are using a dark background, use light-colored text, and vice versa.

One simple color scheme to use is black and white, but these colors do not generate much energy. Certain topics lend themselves to a particular color palette. For example a speech about breast cancer might use pink, while one about communism might use red. Whichever color pattern you use, realize that what you see on your computer monitor may not look the same as what you will see in a classroom on a giant overhead monitor. To avoid this potentially catastrophic problem, test your color palette in advance.

Animation

Many slideshow programs now allow for rudimentary forms of animation. Animation can be clever, but it can also be distracting and even cause headaches and nervousness in your audience. Having spinning pinwheels and stars fading in and out may be creative, but these types of animations can distract from your speech and are considered unprofessional in many contexts. If you use animation, make sure it is fleeting and does not run throughout your speech. For example, you might have a key word quickly fly into place or use animation to highlight a specific part of a diagram. After it has served its purpose, you should disengage the animation and focus upon the remaining portion of your speech. If used correctly, animation can help bring something to the audience's attention, but it can also distract from your speech.

Dos and Don'ts of Slideshow Usage

Constructing a slideshow can seem like you are writing a whole new presentation. Developing the slides can become a distraction when preparing to speak because it is a uniquely creative endeavor that taps into our desire to invent things. The following list provides a list of dos and don'ts for creating a slideshow.

Do

◊   Practice with your slides, and refer to your slides when discussing them.

◊   Show diagrams, charts, graphs, maps, photographs, and other visual elements that complement your message.

◊   Choose large (at least 28-point), nonserif fonts that are easy for your audience to read.

◊   Include blank slides in your presentation when you are not directly incorporating a slide.

◊   Choose visually appealing color schemes, and use a high level of contrast between your background and text.

◊   Use simple animations that make images and text appear at the moment you begin to talk about them in your speech.

◊   Have a backup plan in case the technology fails, and test your presentation before you begin your speech.

Don't

◊   Don't use your slides as note cards, as an outline, or depend on your slides too much.

◊   Don't fill your slides with excessive text, the outline of your speech, or entire paragraphs of writing.

◊   Don't use small, serif, or script fonts that are difficult for your audience to read.

◊   Don't use filler slides with distracting images, animations, or anything else that takes away from your message.

◊   Don't use colors that clash, have low contrast between the background and text, or are commonly confused by those who are color-blind.

◊   Don't use animations that introduce excessive movement, take too much time, or distract from your message.

◊   Don't rely on extended videos or audio clips to fill time in your speech.

As you can see, regardless of their format, presentation aids can assist you with your speech's success if used properly. In the final section, we will provide you with some basic guidelines to consider when preparing presentation aids. Realize that each speaking situation has its own opportunities and challenges, so what works in one speech does not automatically work in another.

GUIDELINES FOR USING PRESENTATION AIDS

There are several things you should think about when considering presentation aids. First, they should be used to help you accomplish the goals of your speech. They should help the audience understand complicated evidence, testimony, or arguments. They should not be used as a form of window dressing, nor should they be a distraction to you or the audience.

The type of presentation aid you use depends on what your topic is and what you want your audience to retain. Research has shown that presentation aids help the audience remember certain aspects of your speech but not the whole thing. Besides, you want the content of your speech, not the actual aids you used, to be the takeaway for an audience.

The next thing to consider is how to deliver a speech with presentation aids. When speaking, your focus should always be your audience; do not turn and talk to the aid. Speak to the audience as if the aid were not there, and if you need to mention it to the audience, then do so when discussing the points you wish to make. Remove each aid you use as soon as you are finished so that your audience is not distracted. One helpful way to do this with slideshows is to insert blank slides at points where you know the aid is not needed. This is much better than placing an unnecessary visual in view of the audience. Finally, practice your speech with the presentation aids. You need to appear comfortable handling them and transitioning between slides, and to do this requires practice. This also creates the impression that the aids are extensions of you and your content and not a distinctly separate element of the talk.

Summary

Presentation aids help speeches become memorable and dynamic, thus increasing the chances that your message will come across to an audience. They come in many forms, and the nature of your speech should dictate which aids are the most applicable to your presentation. In this chapter we reviewed the different types of visual aids, from the traditional forms to the contemporary digital slideshow. Regardless, the same general principle applies: presentation aids help the audience follow and understand, but they are not the speech itself.

Key Terms

bar graph 239

chart 238

graph 238

histogram 239

line graph 239

model 238

object 241

photograph 241

pie graph 239

scatterplot 239

Activities

1   What are three different types of presentation aids that you might want to use for your next speech? How will they help enhance your audience's understanding and interest?

2   Create a few PowerPoint slides that you might want to use in your next speech, or create template slides that you can use to add content later. Pay special attention to your color scheme and font choice to make sure that your slides are accessible for all of your audience members.

3   Watch Don McMillan's "Life After Death by PowerPoint" on YouTube at https://www.youtube.com/watch?v=MjcO2ExtHso. Which of the PowerPoint mistakes that he points out have you seen most often in others' presentations? What did you learn from his speech that you can use in crafting your own PowerPoint presentation?

LANGUAGE

Objectives

◊ Learn the characteristics of language

◊ Familiarize yourself with the structure of language

◊ Recognize different language devices used in speech

There are many things that separate humans from the rest of the animal kingdom, but none is more unique and powerful than language. This is not to say that birds, insects, reptiles, fish, and mammals do not communicate, but they cannot communicate abstract ideas. Human beings alone are uniquely capable of creating meaning in their surroundings through the use of a complex system of symbols we call language. Language is also the primary building block of any speech, whether it is informative, persuasive, or commemorative.

In this chapter, we will give some insight into language and how it influences people every day. First, we will discuss the particular characteristics of language and then cover how language is structured. Then, we will explore some language devices that creatively use words to help craft appealing messages. Finally, we will provide basic guidelines for how to use language in your speeches.

LANGUAGE CHARACTERISTICS

Not every noise people make constitutes language. In fact, there are several characteristics that define language. In this section, we will discuss four characteristics that define language and explain how language functions differently in spoken and written forms. Each of these components creates both inherent difficulties and opportunities when connecting with and influencing people around us.

Arbitrary

arbitrary
symbols used to represent things that are not intrinsically connected to those things

The first characteristic of language to note is that it is **arbitrary**. By arbitrary we mean that words, which are merely symbols, have no real relationship to what they represent. For example, the word "textbook" has no real relationship with the physical or electronic manifestation it represents; it only has the meaning and relationship that we assign to it in everyday usage. We assign meaning by using language to create labels for things, but those labels have no inherent tie to the objects they represent. This arbitrary nature of language helps explain how different cultures can have different words representing the same thing.

Ambiguous

ambiguous
language that does not have precise, exact meanings

In addition to being arbitrary, language is also **ambiguous**. The ambiguity of language refers to the fact that words do not have precise or exact meanings and can be used in a variety of different capacities. Take the word "viral," for instance. In one context viral could mean a virus, or illness, that someone may contract. In another it could mean an internet video that became immensely popular in a short period of time. Other words that exhibit this type of flexibility include "cool," "hot," "chill," and even "love." Language's ambiguous quality is what often leads to misunderstandings between people; one person uses a word to mean one thing, while the receiver interprets it in a different way.

abstract
words are not concrete or tangible items; they are only representations

Abstract

The third characteristic of language is that it is **abstract**. Language cannot be touched, no matter how hard you might try to touch it. It is intangible and thus abstract. Even more fascinating is that some words are more abstract than others when they refer to less specific things. For example, "animal" is more abstract than "dog," which is more abstract than "Golden Retriever." The more precise the language, the less chance for misunderstandings to occur. This shows how language can be more concrete or more abstract, depending on the labels you choose to use. Figure 19.1 shows a spectrum of abstraction, which illustrates how different words can be used to represent the exact same concept. You will notice that the words at the top of the spectrum of abstraction could elicit a lot of different images for what the word represents, and as you move down the spectrum of abstraction to more concrete terms, it becomes much easier to imagine exactly what the word is intended to represent.

Figure 19.1 **Spectrum of abstraction**

Hierarchical

As humans, we all seek to create order in the world around us, and the primary means by which we do this is through language. Language allows us to order things from top to bottom, more to less, or larger to smaller. This ordering process illustrates the fourth quality of language: it is **hierarchical**. This means that language creates structure and value through ordering things along a continuum. Think of how college is structured. You begin as a freshman, then move up to sophomore status, after which you grow into a junior, until finally you enter your senior year. This is framed as a progression upward, but there is no physical direction there except that which we provide through language. The structure creates new levels with higher value above the older ones, creating an artificial hierarchy. We do the same with main points in a speech by ordering them from least important or powerful to most important or powerful. In fact, outlining is itself an exercise in creating a hierarchy.

> **hierarchical**
> language that is structured according to more or less, higher or lower

Spoken Versus Written Language

Even though we use language in both oral and written forms, it functions differently in each. There are two key elements that differentiate language in these two contexts. The first is that spoken language is irreversible; once you say something you cannot "unsay" it. We can apologize or even try to refute our own statements, but the fact remains that we did say the words, and those words had an impact on anyone who was listening. On the other hand, when writing something on paper or even on a computer screen, you can erase it or destroy it before sending it to a recipient, thus making it as if it were never written in the first place.

The second difference between spoken and written language is that spoken language is less formal than written language; we do not speak the way we write. When speaking, we use more pedestrian or colloquial words, including slang. Additionally, we use contractions, whereas when writing an essay we do not use this shorthand method of message construction. Keep this in mind when writing a speech, because if you end up speaking the way you write, your language will come across as awkward to the audience.

Now that we have identified the key components of language and illustrated how it functions differently in oral and written media, we can get down to how language can be structured for maximum impact on an audience.

STRUCTURING LANGUAGE

Language, as you can tell from its characteristics, is a flexible thing that we can adjust, shift, and essentially play with to create impressions for our audience. Following are several different ways we can structure the language we use to create impressions that influence an audience. In this section, we will discuss four ways to structure words in a speech to create memorable lines and creative representations of our argument.

Repetition

repetition
repeating words and phrases

The first way to structure language is through **repetition**, which involves repeating words and phrases. One of the more well-known examples of repetition occurred in Dr. Martin Luther King, Jr.'s famous "I Have a Dream" speech, in which the title phrase is repeated over and over in one section. Any time you repeat a word or phrase it improves the chances that the audience will pay attention and remember what you said. Repetition is, therefore, a useful tool for highlighting key moments and ideas within a speech. Repetition also creates a certain rhythm to your delivery.

Alliteration

alliteration
repeating the same consonant or vowel sound at the beginning of subsequent words

Alliteration, or repeating the same consonant or vowel sound at the beginning of subsequent words, is another tool you can employ to enhance your speech. Here are some examples of alliteration at work:

> "Bitter batter befuddles the brain."

> "Time, talents, and treasure"

> "Peace, prosperity, and progress"

The use of the same consonant or vowel structure to start subsequent words makes the phrase much more appealing to the ear, but you must also make sure the words you use relate to each other in more ways than sound.

Parallelism

parallelism
similarly structuring related words, phrases, or clauses of speech

The third structure of language we will explain is **parallelism**, or similarly structuring related words, phrases, or clauses of speech. Parallelism places related concepts in a pattern that helps highlight the qualities they all have in common. Here are some examples:

"My hobbies are boating, hiking, and fishing."

"Who we are is who we were and everything we will become."

"Love is patient, love is kind. It does not envy, it does not boast, it is not proud."

In each example, the qualities and items listed relate to each other in the same way. In the first example, all three hobbies are described using present participle verbs (verbs that end in -ing). In the second example, "we" is repeatedly followed by a different tense of the verb "to be" ("are," "were," "will become"). In the third example, the first two phrases are identical except for the last word; similarly, the last three phrases end with a different word but are otherwise nearly identical. Parallelism adds a poetic element to your language, makes your message more memorable, and helps the audience pay close attention to the key elements of the message.

Antithesis

The last type of structure we will discuss is antithesis, which is when two ideas that sharply contrast with one another are put side by side in a parallel structure. This is a highly involved and creative way to illustrate a point by means of the careful construction of a sentence. One of the more famous quotations by a president is an example of antithesis. That was John F. Kennedy's famous declaration that citizens should "Ask not what your country can do for you—ask what you can do for your country." Here he takes two seemingly opposite ideas and contrasts them to make a point. Here are some other examples of antithesis:

antithesis
when two ideas that sharply contrast with one another are put side by side in a parallel structure

"As the jet soared higher in the air, the moods of the passengers sank."

"We can all learn together, or we can all fail individually."

Antithesis is very useful in pointing out how two ideas contrast with one another, and it is a very creative way to deliver a message to an audience. It forces them to think about the relationship between the parts of the statement in order to discern what it means.

These types of language structures are not the only creative capabilities of language. In fact, there are several other language devices worthy of note that you can use within your speeches.

LANGUAGE DEVICES

There are many different forms that language can take, and what words you choose to use will determine whether your speech is boring or memorable. These linguistic devices can be as creative as the grammatical structures we just covered or as simple as choosing the right word. In this section, we will focus on the latter and explore three linguistic devices that can help you create an interesting and appealing message.

Similes

simile
linguistic device that compares two things with the use of "like" or "as"

The first linguistic device we will discuss is the simile, which compares two things in a way that allows each to maintain its own respective properties while still making a connection between them. Similes are generally identified by the use of either "like" or "as." Here are some examples:

> "He sweats like a horse."

> "She is as happy as a lark."

> "Your smile is like a sunrise."

In similes both terms being compared are present in the statement. You know they are compared in certain respects, but not all, through the appearance of "like" and "as." Similes are useful, but they are not the only way to compare objects for an audience.

Metaphors

metaphor
linguistic device that allows for often implicit comparisons between two objects

Metaphors are another linguistic device that allows comparisons between two objects. The difference between metaphors and similes can best be explained by stating that all similes are metaphors, but not all metaphors are similes. (Yes, that last sentence was another example of antithesis.) Take the prior examples, for instance. They are metaphoric because they highlight qualities of each object in their explicit comparison. However, not all metaphors are so exact and explicit in their comparisons. In fact, most metaphors do not function that way. Let's briefly explore metaphors that do not qualify as similes.

◊ **Synecdoche.** The first type of metaphor we will explain is a

synecdoche
using one part of something to represent the whole thing

synecdoche, which is when we use one part of something to represent the whole thing. An example of synecdoche is the statement, "We watched a number of sails pass through the strait." The sail is not the entire boat or ship but rather a part of the ship being used to reference the entire ship. Synecdoches do not explicitly use "like" or "as," but rather, like most metaphors, make the implicit connection between the two objects.

◊ **Metonymy.** The next metaphor is metonymy, which involves using a tangible object to represent an otherwise intangible thing. Metonymies occur when you hear things like hard work being called "blood, sweat, and tears," or love being called someone's "heart." In both applications a tangible object becomes a metaphor for the intangible concept. This helps make a description more vivid and concrete.

metonymy
using a tangible object to represent an otherwise intangible thing

◊ **Archetypal.** Archetypal metaphors transcend culture, as they relate to common human experiences. Things such as seasons, disease, and light and dark are often used as archetypal metaphors. Think about how the forces of "light and darkness" are used to represent "good and evil," how some sports teams have players they refer to as "clubhouse cancers," or how senior citizens are sometimes characterized as in the "twilight of their days." Each of these metaphors uses common human experiences to describe another object, thus making them archetypal metaphors.

archetypal metaphor
metaphor that uses common human experiences to describe another object

◊ **Mixed.** The final type of metaphor is a mixed metaphor, in which you combine two unrelated metaphors. For example, we often hear sayings such as "wake up and smell the coffee" and "read the writing on the wall." A possible mixed metaphor combining these two might be "Wake up and smell the coffee on the wall." Mixed metaphors can add color to your speech, but be careful; because mixed metaphors weaken the imagery of each of the combined metaphors, they might confuse audience members who do not see the connection or who do not understand what you're trying to say.

mixed metaphor
metaphor that combines two unrelated metaphors

Narratives

Metaphors and similes use words and phrases to construct their meaning, but some other language devices use more than that to create impressions with an audience. One such extended language device is that of the narrative, or a story. Narrative theory suggests that all human beings are story-telling animals, and so everything we say is a story. We tell stories when we give speeches, and we use other stories as examples in our speeches. All stories should have a beginning, middle, and end, so you should never leave the audience without

narrative
a story

finishing a narrative you began. Narratives are powerful tools because, as the speaker, you control what happens in your story, and you can tell it in a way that maximizes its ability to connect with your argument and your audience. One especially effective way to use narrative in your speech is to use a bookend story. When using a bookend story, the speaker tells the first part of a story as an attention getter in the introduction of the speech and then finishes the story at the end of the conclusion.

bookend story
a narrative in which the speaker tells the first part of a story as an attention getter in the introduction of the speech and then finishes the story in the closer at the end of the conclusion

GUIDELINES FOR USING LANGUAGE

As we have illustrated in this chapter, language is a powerful tool for any speaker, and it can be deployed in a variety of different ways. Thanks to its ability to move an audience, there are several things you must keep in mind as you develop your speech.

profanity
language that is vulgar and irreverent

◊ **Carefully consider profanity.** Profanity refers to language that is vulgar and irreverent. Despite its common usage, you should think very carefully before making an intentional rhetorical decision about whether to use profanity. Curse words can be used to convey powerful emotions, which in some situations might deepen the impact of a particular moment in your speech, but in others can damage your credibility and leave an impression that you do not respect the audience or that you do not have the linguistic sophistication to choose more meaningful language.

hate speech
attacking a person or group of people based upon their gender, ethnicity, religion, sexual orientation, social actions, or any other category that indicates applications of a negative, unwarranted stereotype

◊ **Avoid hate speech.** Hate speech involves attacking a person or group of people based on their gender, ethnicity, religion, sexual orientation, social actions, or any other category that indicates applications of a negative, unwarranted stereotype. Sometimes people use this unethical behavior to incite violence against an individual or group. Be aware that your school very well may have a policy prohibiting hate speech. Whether or not such a policy exists on your campus, you should never use hate speech.

◊ **Do not overuse metaphors.** Metaphors can add color, be pleasing to the audience, and even help explain things to your audience, but their overuse can cause you to look like a bad poet and thus distract your audience and even hurt your credibility.

◊ **Use vivid language when telling a story.** Telling an interesting and vivid story can enhance your speech. Using vivid language paints a picture and makes it easier for the audience to comprehend your story and its relationship to your speech.

◊ **Use language with which you are familiar.** We have all heard people try to use words and phrases that sounded awkward or meant something the speaker did not believe they meant. Before choosing to use a word be sure you are comfortable with it, know its definition, and can pronounce it correctly. If you don't adhere to this recommendation, you will sound awkward and the audience will notice, thus taking the focus off your message and onto your misuse of language.

◊ **Use inclusive language.** It is certainly fine to use "I" language when needed, but if you can use "us" and "we," then this will help to generate goodwill with the audience by making them feel included in the speech. Moreover, you should make sure that your language includes all members of your audience. Many words and phrases that are commonly used imply unwarranted assumptions that particular jobs are only an appropriate choice for either men or women, or that all members of the audience have the same sexual orientation. If you are giving a speech about law enforcement and use the term "policeman," you are ignoring and excluding all of the women who also work as police officers. If you talk about women trying to find "Mr. Right" or men trying to find a girlfriend, you exclude and ignore everyone in the LGBTQ community. When giving a speech, use inclusive language whenever possible to help your entire audience connect with your topic and to show respect for all members of your audience. Table 19.1 gives examples of exclusive and inclusive terms.

Table 19.1

INCLUSIVE LANGUAGE	
TERMS THAT EXCLUDE	TERMS THAT INCLUDE
Policeman	Police officer
Mailman	Mail carrier
Stewardess	Flight attendant
Congressman	Representative, congressperson
Mankind	Humanity
Boyfriends, girlfriends	Significant others
Fireman	Firefighter

◊ **Use active voice.** Active voice is much more energetic than passive voice. You can easily identify passive voice by looking for forms of the verb "to be" immediately before an action verb. It takes care and effort to eliminate passive voice, but it is well worth it and creates a much more exciting speech. Here is an example of passive voice: "As his speed picked up while going downhill, the brakes were slammed on." Now note the difference when put into active voice: "He slammed on the brakes when he began to pick up speed while going downhill."

◊ **Avoid wordiness.** Wordiness occurs when you use too many words to make a point. You should be as concise as possible, ensuring that you do not leave out content. Wordiness can lead to rambling and can cause the audience to drift away. Wordiness also can hurt your delivery and cause you to get off track or even lose your place in the speech.

◊ **Adapt your language to your audience.** When choosing your words, keep your audience in mind. If you are speaking to an audience of experts, you can use words and jargon that are commonly known in that field, and using such language will help to show that you are a member of that group of experts. However, if you are speaking to an audience of nonexperts, you should use simpler language that the audience will understand easily.

Health Care Help

Adapt your language and the information that you share with your audience. If you are speaking with other medical professionals, you will be expected to use medical jargon, abbreviations, and acronyms. However, your patients will vary in their familiarity with medical jargon and their understanding of various medical conditions, so you will need to adjust your language accordingly. For example, you will probably want to use terms such as "heart attack" instead of "cardiac infarction" and "mild flu" instead of "influenza C."

Other contexts in which these skills apply: Management, Human Resources, and Advertising

Summary

Language is something that makes human beings unique in this world. The symbol system used to convey meaning and ideas to one another is a powerful tool for speaking. Language is both powerful and dangerous because it is arbitrary, ambiguous, abstract, and grounded in hierarchy. In this chapter, we discussed how using language in the oral tradition differs from the written form. In either context, however, the different structures and linguistic devices we explored in the chapter are useful for creatively and artfully constructing memorable messages for an audience. We also provided some quick and useful tips to consider when deciding how to say something to an audience in the best possible way.

Key Terms

abstract 250

alliteration 252

ambiguous 250

antithesis 253

arbitrary 250

archetypal metaphor 255

bookend story 256

hate speech 256

hierarchical 251

metaphor 254

metonymy 255

mixed metaphor 255

narrative 255

parallelism 252

profanity 256

repetition 252

simile 254

synecdoche 254

Activities

1   Explain the difference between abstract and concrete language. Choose a word and create a spectrum of abstraction for synonyms of that term.

2   Choose four of the structures of language that you learned about in this chapter. For each of the four structures, provide an example. (Choose examples that were not included in the book.)

3   Choose a speech that you think of as an important historic speech and share a link to the video or transcript of that speech. Identify at least three examples of metaphoric language or language structures the speaker uses.

DELIVERY

Objectives

◊ Understand the different modes of delivery

◊ Learn the verbal and nonverbal aspects of speech delivery

◊ Acquaint yourself with some tips for good speech delivery

When people think about the difference between a good speech and a bad speech, they focus almost exclusively on one aspect: delivery. Delivery is the most visual element of any speech, but it also conveys the least amount of concrete information. For that reason we spent significant time explaining ways to construct your argument before wading into instruction on delivery. Now, however, it is time to turn our attention toward delivery.

In this chapter, we will discuss four different modes of speech delivery, each of which is unique in its own right. Then we will cover verbal delivery, which involves anything related to the delivery of the speech's content via words to the audience, and physical delivery, which has to do with visual aspects of speech delivery. Finally, we will provide you with some tips for a successful delivery.

MODES OF DELIVERY

All speeches are not created, nor are they delivered, in the same way. There are four primary means through which a person may deliver a speech. Each one comes with a different set of challenges and benefits, and the choice of whether to use one or another is largely dependent upon the context in which you will speak. In this section, we will explore each of these four delivery types.

Memorized Speeches

The first form of speech delivery we will discuss is the one that engenders the most fear for novice speakers; it also happens to be the least commonly found speech in society today. **Memorized speech** delivery is when the speaker has no notes and has, instead, committed the entire speech to memory. This was

memorized speech when a speaker commits an entire speech to memory and delivers the speech with no notes a common practice in ancient Greece and Rome, but today it is not employed very often. In fact, it is so rare that we strongly urge you not to memorize your speech.

There are a couple of very good reasons for this recommendation. The first is that you might forget what you are supposed to say. With no notes to rely on, this would cause you to freeze and create a very uncomfortable situation for you and your audience. The second reason we advocate against memorizing your speech is that, unless you are trained in how to deliver it properly, a memorized speech will sound unnatural and awkward. Memorized speeches also force you to focus on content and do not allow for natural delivery, so you increase the chances of appearing stiff in front of your audience. Finally, memorized speeches leave no room for adapting to audience feedback, which we already emphasized as an important element of a successful speech.

Manuscript Speeches

manuscript speech
a speech that is written out word for word and in front of the speaker as he or she speaks

The second type of speech is a **manuscript speech**. Manuscript speeches are written out word for word in an essay format. This approach is actually more common today than memorized speeches. Politicians deliver manuscript speeches though a teleprompter, a machine that allows them to read the speech as it scrolls up the screen in front of them. Likewise, news anchors typically speak using a teleprompter. Manuscript speaking may sound simple at first, but it is harder than it sounds. Speakers usually have to be trained to sound natural when using a teleprompter or a written manuscript, and it usually takes a lot of practice to become comfortable doing so.

There are several advantages to manuscript speaking. Manuscript speaking allows you to plan exactly what you will say and exactly how long it will take, and there are some occasions in which precise language is especially important. For example, when the President of the United States delivers the State of the Union address, policy agenda is being set for the year ahead. Even though the speech is delivered to a joint session of Congress, it is also watched by people around the world and analyzed by the media for weeks afterward. In this case, a precisely planned message is important because even a few misspoken words could have dire consequences. Likewise, when giving the news, anchors must be certain that everything they say is correct and that all of their stories can be delivered in an exact amount of time, so using a manuscript is necessary.

However, there are some disadvantages to manuscript speaking. Like memorized speaking, manuscript speaking requires careful training and preparation. It is not as if you can simply write a draft and then read it to an audience. As you may remember from our discussion about language, there are significant differences in linguistic style between written and spoken messages, and manuscript speaking requires that you learn to write in a spoken style. Even when speaking off a manuscript, you should sound natural and conversational, and that is hard to do when reading what amounts to an essay. Manuscript delivery also reduces your ability to maintain eye contact with your audience and to use gestures and movement effectively, and this is an essential part of strong delivery.

Impromptu Speeches

The next style of delivery is an **impromptu speech**. Impromptu speaking can also be a scary experience, because this is when you are asked to speak to an audience with, at best, a few moments to prepare remarks. This often happens in the classroom when the professor calls on someone to talk about something from the readings or elaborate on a topic that emerged in class discussion. The lack of preparation time requires you to plan what you will say while you are speaking, which can be nerve-wracking for many people. On the plus side, however, you do not have to do any new research, as there is no time to properly conduct it, and you are more likely to make eye contact with your audience, because you do not have a manuscript that draws your attention.

impromptu speech
a presentation done with little or no preparation

Extemporaneous Speeches

The last mode of delivery involves elements of each of the others we have just covered. An **extemporaneous speech** is a practiced, polished speech that makes use of a speaking outline to properly deliver remarks to an audience. Extemporaneous delivery is the most natural sounding of all the delivery styles because it lacks the pressure of memory or the cadence of a written essay. Extemporaneous delivery also allows you to make eye contact with the audience and adapt to their feedback during your presentation. It is, by all measures, a combination of the best of each of the other delivery styles.

extemporaneous speech
a speech delivered with notes but without the entire speech in front of the speaker

No matter which delivery style you choose or are asked to use when delivering a presentation, it takes practice and experience to develop your own natural speaking rhythm. Rest assured that anyone can have competent delivery if they prepare, practice, and are familiar with their outline. To practice delivery, though, requires understanding the verbal and nonverbal elements of delivering a speech.

COMPONENTS OF DELIVERY

verbal delivery
elements of speaking that deal with voice

physical delivery
elements of speaking that deal with the body

Delivery can be divided best into two elements: verbal delivery, or elements of speaking that deal with voice, and physical delivery, or elements of speaking that deal with the body. In this section, we will address how each of these are two important dimensions of your delivery functions.

Verbal Delivery

Your voice is the conduit through which your spoken messages travel to an audience. Your voice, though, is not a simple thing but rather a series of interrelated elements. You must understand and pay attention to each of these elements as you practice and ultimately deliver your speech.

pronunciation
the accepted standard of how a word sounds when spoken

◊ **Pronunciation.** What a word should sound like when it is spoken is its pronunciation. When you mispronounce words, your credibility with the audience can be damaged, and the speech might sound like it was just recently developed and was not practiced.

articulation
physically producing the sound needed to convey a word

◊ **Articulation.** This is the process of physically producing the sound that makes a word. Common articulation errors occur when we run words together. Articulation errors are so common that they seem like they are actually how the words should sound. In fact, this happens because in casual conversation articulation errors are not seen as a big problem as long as everyone understands what was said. However, in formal conversation, such as in business settings and speeches, they should be avoided. Like mispronunciations, improper articulation will damage your credibility with the audience. Here are some common articulation errors:

"You all" becomes "y'all."

"I do not know" becomes "I dunno."

"You bet" becomes "you betcha."

◊ **Volume.** The third thing to consider is the volume of your voice. This concerns how loud your voice is. You should speak with enough volume so that the person farthest away from you can easily hear you without straining to discern what you are saying, but at the same time, you do not want to speak so loudly that the audience feels like you are yelling at them. If you think there are some people who cannot hear you, consider pausing your presentation and simply asking them if they can hear you. In many situations microphones are available that can help you augment the volume of your voice.

◊ **Pitch.** Pitch is how high or low your voice sounds, along with the rise and fall of your voice. Some people have deep voices, while others have higher voices. To determine your pitch and understand how you sound, consider recording your voice and listening to yourself.

◊ **Rhythm.** Rhythm is the pattern of movement, or cadence, of your voice. Most of us have a natural cadence to our voice and have a pattern in the way we speak. When we're nervous, though, we sometimes begin to speak in a repetitive pattern that gives our voice a sing-song quality, does not reflect the meaning of what we are saying, and sounds unnatural. When giving a speech, be careful to not let your voice fall into an unnatural, repetitive pattern that distracts the audience from your message.

◊ **Rate.** The next aspect is the rate, or speed, at which you speak. Some people, and some geographic regions, have different rates of speech than other people or geographic regions. Again, recording yourself and calculating the rate of speech is a great way to monitor your pace. Speaking too fast can make it hard for people to follow, and speaking too slowly can come across as condescending, so be careful to maintain a pace of between 125 and 150 words per minute.

◊ **Tone.** Tone refers to the variable level of your voice. Tone is important, as it helps convey emotions and interest. If you have low variance in tone, otherwise referred to as a monotone voice, your audience may quickly lose interest, as it appears as though you yourself are not interested in the topic or the audience. Conversely, getting too excited can also be a distraction.

◊ **Vocalized pauses.** Vocalized pauses occur when speakers feel the need to utter some sort of sound but do not have anything to say. Vocalized pauses are also sometimes referred to as filler words, throwaway words, or verbal tics. These sounds come in many forms, all of which you may recognize: "ah," "uh," "umm," and "y'know." They are not a problem if held to a minimum as they are quite natural, but too many will distract the audience, hurt your credibility, and likely increase your anxiety.

Your voice is a very important element of your delivery, but it is only half of the delivery equation. Your body is also an essential part of delivery, and we will next explore the facets of physical delivery.

Physical Delivery

Many people do not realize that the body also sends signals to the audience while you are speaking. There are five components of physical delivery that we will cover, and each plays an important role in effective delivery. Understand that these all have a purpose and a time to be emphasized during the speech, but only through practice and experience will you get a proper feel for your own physical delivery style.

◊ **Apparel.** The first thing we will discuss is your appearance. Consider the occasion when you speak, as more formal dress is required for weddings and funerals than for classroom speeches. You should, at a minimum, ensure that what you wear is neat, pressed, and not torn or stained. Your hair should be well groomed, and you should avoid wearing hats or caps that can cast a shadow on your face and make it difficult for the audience to see whether you are making eye contact or using facial expressions. There is a caveat to the rule on headgear, however, as certain religious traditions require certain forms of dress for adherents, and obviously these individuals must not be asked to violate their cultural or religious rules. Also remember that if you are giving a business presentation, you represent more than yourself; you also represent your employer and should do so with care and respect. If you do not know what kind of dress code the occasion calls for, remember that it is better to overdress than to underdress.

◊ **Posture.** Your posture refers to how your body is positioned when speaking to an audience. If you are standing, stand up straight, and place your feet about hip width apart in a relaxed and natural position. Roll your shoulders back a little bit as you stand up to speak to help open your airways and to make sure that you are not slouching. Though you want to be somewhat relaxed so that it doesn't look like you are squaring off with the audience, you also want to appear confident and in control. You also should not lean on the podium, although it is acceptable to place your hands on the podium as long you do not use it for support. Standing or sitting straight conveys confidence and respect, while a slack posture creates the impression that you are uninterested and uncomfortable with the situation.

◊ **Facial expressions.** Facial expressions are important from the first moment you stand behind the lectern to speak through the moment you finish. Your facial expression should reflect the emotions associated with what you are saying. In most situations, it is appropriate to smile before you begin a speech, which will help to create goodwill with the audience and help you appear happy to be there with them. However, you should consider the occasion. If you are about to deliver a eulogy, talk about a tragedy, or deliver bad news, a smile would be inappropriate. Be sure that your facial expressions mirror the tone of your speech and the occasion, as people will know your true feelings through how your face looks during the speech.

◊ **Eye contact.** As the saying goes, the eyes are the windows to the soul. Maintaining eye contact with the audience is essential for establishing a rapport with them, but it is also one of the most stressful aspects of delivery for novice speakers. Good eye contact does not require that you keep your eyes continuously trained on the audience but rather that the majority of your time is spent focusing on them. After all, you will need to consult your notes from time to time. One of the best ways to reduce the stress of looking out over a huge crowd is to change the way you see the process. Instead of staring at the entire audience, make eye contact with each individual member for a few moments at a time, thus treating the speech like multiple individual conversations instead of a lecture to a large group. Make sure that you include your entire audience and make eye contact with each person for at least a few seconds. Be careful not to stare at one person through your entire speech, as that is uncomfortable for everyone, but also be careful not to scan the audience so quickly that you do not connect with anyone.

◊ **Gestures.** Gestures are the movement of your hands and arms, and they can accentuate points that you wish to emphasize. If done improperly, they can also be distracting to your audience. Speakers often wonder what they should do with their hands when speaking, and thankfully, your hands can be useful during a presentation. Gestures should be used to emphasize important ideas and to help illustrate the relationships between ideas. These should be natural, not contrived, and in order to make this happen, you should practice incorporating them into your speech while standing in front of a mirror or in front of others.

Functions of Physical Delivery

The physical, or nonverbal, dimensions of delivery can serve many purposes during a presentation. Learning what these functions are and the most opportune times to use them during your speech helps you integrate physical and verbal elements of delivery with the content of your speech. This is the recipe for a dynamic and effective speech: good delivery that complements well-ordered points.

repeat
when physical actions restate verbal messages

◊ **Repeating.** Gestures and facial expressions can repeat the message you just stated. For example, you may call an audience member by name and then point at the person. This helps you make sure the audience understands the content of the message by using gestures to repeat that content in a different manner.

accent
nonverbal behaviors that augment a verbal message

◊ **Accenting.** Accenting gestures emphasize message content through action. You may accent a point by raising or pumping your fist in the air as in a spirit of triumph, or you may tap on the lectern as you make strong statements. These simple actions can let your audience know that this is an important moment in the speech.

complement
when the action demonstrates the message contained in the verbal content

◊ **Complementing.** Gestures and facial expressions can also complement, or mirror, content in a speech. Examples of complementing are shrugging your shoulders when you say, "I don't know" or smiling when you say something amusing. This helps the speech appear natural and not forced or planned, and makes you look comfortable in the situation with the audience.

substitute
physical actions that take the place of verbal messages

◊ **Substituting.** Nonverbal acts can substitute for verbal statements, which means that you give a nonverbal message that has no corollary in the speech itself. If you wave or smile at the start of the speech, but do not say "hello," then the waving and smiling substitute for the verbalized greeting.

regulate
nonverbal actions that help govern the course of a speech or interaction

◊ **Regulating**. Nonverbal behaviors that regulate act as controls for the flow of the communication situation. They indicate when other people should respond or when you have finished speaking. You may, for example, use a question to the audience at the start of your speech and expect a few responses before moving on. To indicate this you could lean back in your chair or raise your eyebrows and look at members of the audience. In situations in which you are a member of the audience, you may raise your hand, indicating you wish to ask a question. These behaviors regulate whose turn it is to speak.

All of these nonverbal behaviors can aid you in having a successful speech presentation. Ultimately, however, delivery and content must seamlessly merge into a coherent and natural whole for you to give a successful presentation. In this final section, we will offer some tips for successfully integrating delivery into your speech.

TIPS FOR GOOD DELIVERY

There are three tips we can offer you to help develop your skill at delivering a speech. Each one involves time and a change in the typical mindset regarding speaking, so do not consider these to be "magic bullets" but rather ways to help you as you gain more public speaking experience.

◊ **Practice your delivery.** Use whatever advance time you have to practice both the content of your speech and how you deliver it. You should practice at least three times a day, if not more, as the more you work at the speech the more natural it will feel. Also keep in mind that when you practice your speech you might go through it a little slower or faster than when you actually give the speech, so time yourself accordingly. In the next chapter we will discuss some specific practice strategies, but for now just understand that the more you practice speaking, the better your speech will become.

◊ **Discover your own speaking rhythm.** As you write and then practice your speech, remember that it should have a different rhythm than a written message. Everyone speaks at a different pace and with different pitch and tone. Speak in a way that feels natural and not forced, and as you find that rhythm, look to repeat it with each speech you develop. Write outlines and manuscripts that reflect that speaking rhythm.

◊ **Put delivery cues on your outline.** On your speaking outline you can draw signs like the ones you see used on highways that should help remind you when you should employ certain delivery techniques within your presentation. You can put in cues for physical as well as verbal delivery, but remember not to read those cues when giving the speech.

STEM Spotlight

When presenting a proposed research project or solution you can enhance your credibility or diminish the likelihood it will be accepted through your delivery. While strong delivery cannot make a bad proposal effective, poor delivery can make an effective solution look questionable. Make sure that you practice your delivery before you give your presentation. Dress in a way that enhances your credibility in the situation in which you are speaking, whether the situation calls for a lab coat, business casual, or a business suit. Watch your audience for nonverbal feedback and adjust your rate, gestures, and language as needed to make sure that your audience understands your ideas. The best plans in the world are useless if you cannot effectively communicate them to others!

Other contexts in which these skills apply: Interviewing, Management, and Sales

Summary

Delivery is a daunting task for novice speakers. In fact, many believe it to be the be-all and end-all of speaking. Good delivery, however, comes from practice and involves integrating verbal and nonverbal actions with the content of your message. There are verbal and nonverbal elements of delivery, and both are important to pay attention to when delivering remarks to an audience. In this chapter, we discussed the various elements of these two parts of delivery and provided you with tips for finding your own effective and natural delivery style.

Key Terms

accent 268

articulation 264

complement 268

extemporaneous speech 263

impromptu speech 263

manuscript speech 262

memorized speech 261

physical delivery 264

pronunciation 264

regulate 268

repeat 268

substitute 268

verbal delivery 264

Activities

1   Watch one of the commencement speeches that are available in the NPR collection at apps.npr.org/commencement. What type of delivery is the speaker using? Which aspects of verbal and physical delivery are effective? Which are ineffective?

2   Find a video clip (perhaps from a TV show or movie you have seen recently) that shows someone using nonverbal communication in a way that clearly fulfills one of the five functions of physical delivery. How is the nonverbal communication in that scene fulfilling one of the functions of physical delivery? How does it impact the interaction?

3   Think back to previous speeches you have given. What are your strengths and weaknesses in your own speech delivery? What is your plan for improving your delivery for your next speech?

PRACTICE

Objectives

◊ Recognize the different ways to practice your speech

◊ Acquaint yourself with the different stages of the practice process

◊ Learn some tips for creating useful practice sessions

Good content and an understanding of delivery are essential for any successful speech; however, the backbone of strong presentation skills lies in practicing your speech in advance. Public speaking is a skill and not a talent. Talents are individual aptitudes that people are born with; they cannot be learned. Skills are abilities individuals develop over time and are things any person can learn. Public speaking is one of those capabilities people can learn to do very well, but it takes time, dedication, and, most importantly, practice.

In this chapter, we will help you understand the importance of creating effective practice sessions. We will then discuss the stages of practice before finally presenting you with some tips for creating effective practice sessions.

QUALITY AND QUANTITY

All speakers need to practice, but some need more time than others. Those with speech anxiety issues need more practice time than those who are not as apprehensive. Due to this variance, you should focus more on the quality rather than the quantity of time you spend practicing. There is, after all, no prescribed number of times you should practice your speech to guarantee success. In this section, we will discuss some different types of practice sessions you can use when preparing to give an address. Understand, however, that you should try to make use of all of these and not rely solely on one.

Mirror, Mirror

The first type of practice session involves delivering your speech in front of a mirror. At first this may feel a bit awkward, but that will dissipate with time and experience. Note the expression on your face and how you use gestures and other aspects of physical delivery as you give the speech. Remember from our discussion of delivery in the preceding chapter that using your hands should look natural.

The mirror is also a good way to review your appearance. Even though there is no one watching you when you practice in front of a mirror, you should dress the way you will when you give your speech. The mirror practice session not only reflects you but should also be reflective of your speaking situation. Some people practice in front of a mirror quite a bit, while others do so less often. It is a good way to reduce anxiety and get comfortable with the speech.

Friends and Family, Gather 'Round

If you are comfortable speaking in front of the mirror and have a speech that you feel is ready for public consumption but not quite where it needs to be for the actual presentation, consider asking friends and family to listen to you practice your speech. Make sure when you do this that you tell the practice audience what you are doing and what type of feedback, if any, you hope to receive from them. This focused direction allows you to maximize your returns from this type of practice session.

Practicing in front of an audience helps you with anxiety and speech development and also helps you get a more accurate idea of how long it will take to deliver your speech. When friends, family, and colleagues listen to you at this point, they will be generally supportive, and thus they will be a good test audience that creates a reduced level of anxiety for you as a speaker. Additionally, when you provide them with specific items on which you want feedback, they can help you polish your message and delivery. Listen to their feedback, and make adjustments if you agree with their assessments. If you disagree, talk about it with them, and determine whether the changes need to be made. Ultimately, you are not required to act upon their feedback, but at least you have managed to get a sample audience's perspective on your presentation and should know what to expect when "showtime" arrives.

Lights, Camera, Practice!

A final practice session worth noting can actually be done with or without an audience. As you get more and more comfortable with your speech, consider video recording a practice session of it and then watching the video for things you could improve or adjust. Seeing yourself speak is a powerful, if somewhat initially awkward, tool for improving your organization and delivery. The key to effectively using a video to make adjustments is to focus on both delivery and content. Many people look at a video and only examine their physical delivery, but that misses some of the most important parts of the speech.

It also may be helpful to review the video from the mindset of someone who might be in the audience. Ask yourself if you covered the points that the audience would consider important. This can be especially helpful in advance of a sales presentation, because you will know who the audience is and can watch the speech to see if your message hits home the way you want it to. Practice, however, does not solely involve giving a finished speech. There are several stages of practice, and in the next section we will explore those stages in detail.

STAGES OF PRACTICE

Developing a speech should happen concurrently with practicing it. You can, and should, practice portions of the speech as you create and draft them to make sure they flow and fit the way you design them to. As you finish more of the speech, more and more things need to be practiced, so paying attention to the stage of development you are in will help you polish pieces of the speech as they are created.

Early Stages: Organization

After you start to put your research into a speech format, you should begin to consider practicing elements of the presentation. In these early stages of practice you should focus on organization and adjusting the outline of the speech. Keep in mind that what you have written and organized at this point is a draft and is not set in stone. There may be better ways to organize this information, and once you say it aloud it may not sound as good as when you wrote it. When you have gathered all of your information, lay it out, assess it, practice, and see which method of organization works best to help you accomplish your goals and make an impact on the audience. Then practice each section you create out loud to see how it sounds.

Middle Stages: Feedback

In the second stage of practice, you should begin to get feedback. This should be feedback on both the outline or manuscript and your delivery. In both cases, you will need to bounce elements of your speech off a willing and helpful audience. This is why you might be given time for a peer workshop during class, but if not, you should set aside time to work with others to obtain this feedback.

Questions for Useful Audience Feedback

◊   Have I adequately established the significance of this topic? Does my speech make you care more about this topic?

◊   Were the main points clear and logically organized?

◊   Were there parts of the speech that were confusing or hard to understand?

◊   Did I cite enough sources? Did the sources that I used add to my credibility during this speech?

◊   Did I leave anything out?

◊   Are there areas in which I need to elaborate more?

◊   What can I do to improve my delivery?

Each of these focused questions will help you get valuable feedback for developing your speech.

Final Stages: Refining Your Speech

The last stage of practice is when you refine and polish your speech. This usually takes place very close to the time of the actual presentation, and so it is more about shaping and cleaning things up than it is about major organizational adjustments. This is also when you practice extemporaneous delivery, ensuring that you are not reading your speech. While doing this you should focus on things such as eye contact, making natural gestures, and using facial expressions. By this time you should be comfortable with just glancing at your outline.

In terms of assessing the balance of the speech, there are several general guidelines to which you should adhere. The body, where most of your information resides, should constitute about 70–80 percent of the total speech. The introduction and conclusion should each be about 10–15 percent of the total speech time. Each main point in the body of the speech should take about the same amount of time to get through. If you deviate too much from this allocation your speech will come across as unbalanced, so during the final stages of practice you can and should make sure you are close to this type of time allocation within your speech.

GOOD PRACTICE SESSIONS

There are several common-sense things you can do to help create successful practice sessions. In this section, we will provide you with five suggestions for helping you create strong practice sessions as you work on your speeches.

Tips for Creating Strong Practice Sessions

◊ **Practice out loud.** Sometimes novice speakers believe they get just as much help from reading a speech to themselves as they would from orally practicing the speech. Nothing could be further from the truth. Practice means doing the activity you are expected to perform without the pressure of evaluation. Reading a draft to yourself does not help you with delivery, nor does it help you hear the words as they will sound. To this end, every time you practice you should do so out loud.

◊ **Provide questions to the practice audience.** When you get to a point that you want feedback from an audience, help them help you by providing them with a few brief questions that focus on areas in which you want them to give you feedback. If the speech is for a class, consider giving them a critique sheet to fill out. This ensures the practice audience will address your areas of concern. This will maximize these practice sessions and ensure you get more feedback than "I liked it" or "It could've been better."

◊ **Practice with a stopwatch.** In many speaking situations, you will be given a set amount of time to deliver your remarks. This puts added emphasis on practice sessions because you need to time yourself to make sure you stay within the allotted time for your remarks. Practicing with a stopwatch or a timer will help you mark how long your speech takes to deliver. This can then be used to adjust the lengths of areas of the speech if necessary. If you don't use a timer, then you run the risk of rambling on well beyond your time or, worse, not going long enough and looking underprepared.

◊ **Keep it simple.** It is possible to over-prepare, and when you do this for an extemporaneous speech it comes across as memorized. This makes you sound over-rehearsed, even wooden. Remember that, generally speaking, the best speeches are simple speeches. Even complicated material can be presented in an understandable manner.

◊ **Keep the audience in the forefront of your mind.** When you practice, the focus is always on yourself, because you are trying to create and deliver an effective speech. It thus becomes easy to forget that the goal is not to have the spotlight on you but rather for you to achieve the specific purpose of informing, persuading, or helping an audience to celebrate. Whoever the audience is for your speech, keep them in mind, and try to practice with an eye toward how you believe they will respond to parts of your speech as you deliver them. Don't forget who you are trying to reach, even when you practice.

Summary

Practice does not always make perfect, but it does help you achieve success when you speak to an audience. Practice is, essentially, a low-pressure way to gain speaking experience so that when the time comes you are prepared to do well. It is not about how much you practice but how well you use your practice time, so we provided several different ways that you can practice your speech. We also detailed different stages of practice during the speech development process. Remember, the more experience with speaking you get, the better you will become.

Activities

1   What is your plan for practicing as you prepare for your next speech? Which practice strategies will you use, and how many times will you practice your speech using each of these strategies?

2   Ask a friend to record you as you practice your speech, and then watch the video of your speech. What surprised you most when you watched yourself practice your speech? How can you apply what you have learned to improving your speech before you deliver it in front of a full audience?

3   During which stage of practice should you create your speaking outline on a note card, if you plan to use one? Why shouldn't you create your speaking outline and note card sooner?

GROUP PRESENTATIONS

Objectives

◊ Explain different formats for delivering group presentations

◊ Describe the different roles people take on in groups

◊ Detail the qualities of an effective team member

In many professions, you will find yourself working in teams, and those teams will often be asked to deliver their findings or project results to an audience. When this happens you will present as part of a group, not as an individual. These types of presentations may be informative, as in a corporate board report, or they may be persuasive, such as sales teams trying to persuade a client to purchase a particular product. Regardless of the type or topic of the presentation, there are certain elements of a group presentation that differ from individual performances.

In this final chapter, we will explain the requirements and expectations of group presentations. First, we will cover the two types of formats for group presentations. Second, we will explore different roles for individuals in groups. Finally, we will provide some guidelines for being a good group member.

GROUP PRESENTATION FORMATS

A common mistake that novice group speakers make is not seeing the presentation as one speech. Instead they see a group presentation as a loose connection between multiple individual performances. For instance, if there are five speakers in the group they often make the mistake of seeing the group presentation as five distinct speeches rather than one whole performance. This error is often made early in the development of a presentation and comes from not clearly establishing the most appropriate format for the presentation. To better equip you in making this determination early, and thus avoiding the error of a loose connection between participants, we will explain the two effective formats for group presentations: the bookend approach and the panel approach.

bookend group presentation
a group presentation in which the first speaker is also the last speaker, providing both the introduction and conclusion for the group

In the bookend group presentation approach, the first speaker is also the last speaker. This speaker's responsibility is to introduce the topic and provide an overview of which group members will explain each component and why they will do so. The "why" helps explain each individual's credibility regarding their topic. For example, suppose Kris, Jarrod, Liz, and Brian are giving a presentation proposing a parking shuttle system to and from campus. They are going to use the problem-cause-solution organizational pattern for the body of the presentation. Kris will introduce the topic and the qualifications of each group member and then conclude by introducing Jarrod, who will speak next. Jarrod will detail the problem, and when he is finished he will introduce Liz, noting that she will discuss the cause of the problem. When she finishes discussing the cause, Liz will transition to Brian by explaining that he will provide a solution that addresses the cause of the problem. After Brian presents the solution, Kris will deliver a conclusion that summarizes the group's talk.

There are several benefits to the bookend approach for a group presentation. The bookend approach gives a nice sense of closure by having the same person begin and end the presentation. It also gives the performance continuity by having each speaker connect his or her topic with the next. Additionally, the bookend approach allows for a degree of individuality in performances by giving each person a specific focus to develop on his or her own and then connect to the other parts developed by the group. It is important, however, that the individual aspects of each presenter do not overshadow the need to have a fluid presentation. Be sure to have clear transitions between speakers, and have all speakers work together as they develop the individual components of the presentation. Keep in mind that in a group presentation every speaker is still required to provide evidence, cite sources, and use logic, just as they would in an individual speech.

panel group presentation
a group presentation in which individual speakers present their ideas on a single topic or a subset of a topic

moderator
a person that acts as the coordinator of the discussion flow and ensures a civil, organized, and complete delivery of information to the audience

The panel group presentation approach is another common approach for giving a group presentation, and it is structured differently from the bookend model. Panel presentations occur in both formal and informal settings and are most appropriate when audience interaction is expected or encouraged. Panel presentations are individual performances, but all cover the same topic in different ways. Each member of a panel may present his or her ideas on a single topic, or each may have a specific subset of a topic. Panel speakers may agree or disagree with one another and sometimes even challenge other speakers on their content or positions. To handle transitions between speakers, panels need to have a person play the role of moderator.

Moderators are unique participants in a group presentation using the panel approach. First, they should be objective and should not present their own opinions, ideas, or thoughts on the topic or speaker presentations. Second, they introduce the entire panel at the start, establish the order of speakers, and transition between speakers when each individual completes his or her remarks. It is important that panelists and the moderator talk before the panel convenes so that there is no miscommunication when the performance is delivered to the actual audience. Moderators also serve the important role of handling interactions between speakers and the audience. They indicate when individuals may ask questions and let the speakers know when they reach the end of their allotted time to talk. Ultimately, their task is to maintain an orderly presentation and keep the interaction on topic. It should be obvious that the panel approach does not have as much structure as the bookend approach, but it has the advantage of being more interactive and covering more material than the bookend model.

GROUP ROLES

In covering the two forms of group or team presentations we explained the two speaking roles used in each approach: moderator and speaker. Good team presentations begin well before they are convened to address the audience. Members of a team need to be aware of the different roles and responsibilities that occur in the development process. In this section, we will cover the three broad types of roles that people fill in small groups when developing a team presentation.

Task Roles

task roles
the parts people play that move a group toward a goal and are performed by all members of the group at one time or another in the development process

Task roles refer to the parts people play that move a group toward a goal, and these are performed by all members of the group at one time or another in the development process. When developing a presentation, a group needs to accomplish several important tasks, and although everyone may not be involved in each task, every person will help in some way with some tasks. For people to accomplish important tasks to the best of their ability, it is important for the group to identify the strengths and expertise of all members before proceeding. This allows the group to assign members to develop the parts of the presentation with which they are most qualified to help. Table 22.1 gives some examples of group task roles.

Table 22.1

GROUP TASK ROLES	
EXAMPLES OF GROUP TASK ROLES	
Meeting facilitator	organizes the information and tasks during the meeting, keeps group members on track during meetings, makes sure that everyone gets to contribute during meetings
Logistics coordinator	schedules meeting times and locations, sends out reminder emails
Notetaker	takes notes during meetings, sends minutes to group after meetings, keeps records that the group can refer to when needed
Compiler	takes all of the components prepared by individual group members and compiles those components into an initial draft of the group presentation

There are multiple tasks a group needs to accomplish when preparing a presentation. The first two are identifying the information they plan to present and then assigning people to gather relevant research and information. Once the data has been collected, the presentation needs to be outlined and organized. This should not be done individually unless the format will be in a panel, and so several members of the group should review, edit, and revise the presentation outline. When this is done, the speaking roles should be assigned, and practice should commence. Each of these stages involves tasks for people to perform, from research to revision, but task roles are not the only roles necessary for a successful group presentation.

Maintenance Roles

In the United States, task roles receive the highest degree of emphasis, but relational dimensions of the group are also important, and maintaining functioning relationships between group members is essential. Without good working relationships between group members, tasks may not be completed well, or at all, because time will be spent dealing with disputes and conflicts between members instead of achieving the group's goal of developing a presentation. To succeed, a group needs to take a collaborative approach, not create a combative or competitive environment in which people constantly angle to do what they want regardless of the needs of the group.

Maintenance of good relationships involves having people who help the group stay loose and supportive. This can sometimes involve joking, attending social events together, or participating in other activities that help group members bond and get to know each other's personalities. If all a group does is focus on the task, then stress will mount and potentially become an obstacle to developing a successful presentation. On the other hand, too much joking and emphasis on relationships also can contribute to an atmosphere in which constructive criticism is never delivered, and the presentation suffers just as much as when no emphasis is placed on **maintenance roles**. The responsibility to balance the needs of the group falls to the leader.

maintenance roles responsibility of establishing and keeping a positive and loose environment with well-functioning relationships between group members so the group can complete its tasks

LEADERSHIP STYLES

Each group has a leader, the person who keeps the group focused, motivated, and on task. Sometimes the leader is formally selected by the group, and at other times, a leader emerges naturally as that individual begins taking on leadership roles or is regarded by others in the group as the leader. However, there are several different approaches that someone might take as the leader of the group. Scholar Daniel Goleman[1] has identified six different leadership styles, each of which can be effective in some situations, but none of which is effective all of the time (Figure 22.1 Goleman's six leadership styles).

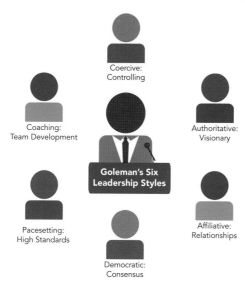

Figure 22.1 **Goleman's six leadership styles**

---

1. Daniel Goleman, "Leadership That Gets Results," *Harvard Business Review*, March/April 2000, 79–90.

Coercive Leadership Style

coercive leader
the type of leader who tells others what to do and expects it to be done

Coercive leaders, also sometimes referred to as autocratic or commanding leaders, take a top-down approach to decision making in which the leader tells others what to do and expects it to be done. This leadership style often stifles team creativity and participation because it involves pushing members to do what the leader wants instead of motivating group members to succeed. Over time, this leadership style can erode group cohesion and limit the group's ability to perform. Leaders who utilize this leadership style are often driven to achieve high results and have a strong desire for control. While the coercive leadership style is usually seen as a negative approach to leading groups, it can be useful during genuine emergencies when discussion is not feasible or when a leader is brought into an underperforming company to try to turn it around.

Authoritative Leadership Style

authoritative leader
the type of leader who provides a team with a vision and mobilizes people to work toward that vision

Authoritative leaders, also known as visionary leaders, provide a vision for their team and mobilize people to work toward that vision. This style is similar to the coercive style in that the leader is providing the direction, but instead of trying to control others and enforce a particular approach, the leader is confident, empathetic, enthusiastic, and motivating to team members. This leadership style can be beneficial when the leader has a higher level of expertise than other team members and when team members respect and want participation and input from the leader, or when a team is lacking motivation and needs a new vision. However, this leadership style can be detrimental when group members have high levels of experience and expertise because it can be interpreted as condescending or overbearing in those types of situations.

Affiliative Leadership Style

affiliative leader
the type of leader who is flexible, encouraging, and focuses on building relationships and trust among team members

Affiliative leaders are flexible, encouraging, and focus on building relationships and trust among team members. Affiliative leaders try to maximize harmony and create a positive environment, which is a leadership style that is especially useful when a group needs to heal rifts or overcome an especially stressful situation. However, the drawback to the affiliative leadership style is that affiliative leaders often avoid confrontation and sometimes fail to give constructive feedback, which can result in a lack of direction or tolerance of mediocrity.

Democratic Leadership Style

Democratic leaders work to solicit ideas and get buy-in from team members and often make decisions through collaboration and trying to achieve consensus within the group. Democratic leaders listen to their team members, communicate openly, are flexible, and can usually keep morale high while helping everyone maintain realistic expectations of what is possible. The democratic leadership style is useful when the leader is not sure what the best solution is, when team members have high levels of expertise, and when there is plenty of time to make decisions. However, the democratic style can be time-consuming because it typically requires many meetings, can be problematic when team members do not have enough information or expertise to help make a good decision, and does not work in times of crisis when there is a limited amount of time for decision-making.

democratic leader
the type of leader who solicits ideas from team members and makes decisions through collaboration

Pacesetting Leadership Style

Pacesetting leaders are driven, set high standards and expectations for performance for all team members, and set an example by achieving those high standards. These leaders demand excellence and try to achieve quick results. This leadership style can be effective when working with an already motivated and competent team that does not need much direction, especially when trying to reach a specific goal. However, pacesetters have a tendency to micromanage and often lack emotional intelligence, and morale can quickly decline on their teams if team members do not have a good sense of how their individual efforts fit into the bigger picture, need guidance to develop their own skills, or become overwhelmed by the drive to constantly do more at a faster pace.

pacesetting leader
the type of leader who is driven, sets high standards and expectations for performance, and sets an example by achieving those high standards

Coaching Leadership Style

Coaching leaders focus on helping individual team members develop and grow through training and constant feedback. Coaching leaders help team members identify strengths and weaknesses, help team members work toward their own long-term goals, and requires an ongoing investment of time to work with each team member individually. This leadership style can be valuable when building long-term relationships and growth and can help result in a positive climate if team members want to be coached. However, this leadership style can be time-consuming and can be detrimental if team members do not want to receive constructive criticism or if the leader does not have the appropriate knowledge and skills to coach team members.

coaching leader
the type of leader who focuses on helping individual team members develop and grow through training and constant feedback

While many people have a specific leadership style that might feel more comfortable or natural to them than the others, the reality is that none of these leadership styles is effective all of the time. Each leadership style has benefits and drawbacks, and it is important for leaders to understand which leadership style will work best in different situations. This also means that the strongest leaders are typically people who can use several leadership styles and can easily identify which style they should use in specific circumstances.

BEING A GOOD TEAM MEMBER

Being a good team member has several characteristics. The first of these involves the ability to listen to several messages at the same time. To be an effective member of any group, you need to be able to listen to the leader of that group and offer feedback and ideas whenever appropriate. Additionally, you have a responsibility to listen to other group members when they offer ideas and comments related to the task or group as a whole. Finally, you need to listen to the audience at the presentation to make sure you can help the group adapt to feedback during and after the performance. Remember that listening means paying attention to these other people, because only if you do so will they do the same for you when it is your turn to offer ideas.

Listening can be hard, because it often means suppressing our desire to comment in favor of hearing someone else out. Therefore, remember that one of the strengths of any group is that there is a multiplicity of ideas and opinions, and only through hearing them out completely can you identify the best way to accomplish the task and still maintain positive relationships between members. Be patient with others, even if you disagree with them, and give their thoughts fair and unbiased attention. Realize that just because someone might not want to do something in the same way you would doesn't mean that it is not a viable approach; there are usually several ways to accomplish something. A good idea for facilitating and developing good listening skills is to take detailed and accurate notes to which you may refer at a later time. Even if the group has an assigned notetaker, take notes anyway for your own reference.

Just as you have the group obligation to listen attentively and in an unbiased manner to the ideas and opinions of others, group members also have the obligation to extend that same courtesy to you. Group sessions usually have brainstorming sessions, so if you have an idea, present it to the rest of the group members. Good groups function on the principle of civility, which means all have a responsibility both to pay attention to each other and to assert their own ideas about the task at hand. See Table 22.2 for examples of productive and disruptive behaviors.

Table 22.2

PRODUCTIVE VERSUS DISRUPTIVE BEHAVIORS	
PRODUCTIVE BEHAVIORS	DISRUPTIVE BEHAVIORS
• Listen carefully to others	• Attack others or their ideas
• Ask for clarification when needed	• Bring up unrelated topics
• Make connections between others' ideas	• Arrive late or miss meetings
• Provide constructive feedback	• Dominate the conversation during meetings
• Arrive at meetings on time	• Fail to complete your components of the project
• Distribute agendas and meeting minutes	• Be inflexible and unavailable
• Identify and utilize individual strengths	• Speak rudely to others

A second characteristic of high-performing groups is the ability to identify the skill sets of each member and assign tasks that take advantage of those skills. People come to groups with differing talents and abilities, which is often what makes groups stronger than individuals. Some people are good analysts, some are better at researching, some better at organizing presentations, some at keeping records, and others at actually delivering the remarks. Determine your best set of skills and offer to work on tasks that fit your talents. Beware, however, that asking for the assignment does not mean that you will get it, so don't be afraid to go out of your comfort zone and try something new. After all, you may discover that you have strengths you did not know you had!

A third characteristic of a good group member involves helping facilitate efficient and productive meetings. As group members work on their tasks, it is important to stay in contact with each other. These meetings can occur via conference calls, in person, or even through Skype, but each group member should be aware of what is going on elsewhere in the group. This allows people to offer assistance if necessary and also to get feedback on their part of the project to help make the presentation more seamless. That is why frequent meetings are often necessary; each group member needs to know what the others are doing to avoid redundancy and wasted effort as well as to ensure that the material is consistent.

These meetings are run best when there is an agenda provided to group members in advance. This allows everyone to bring information relevant to what will be discussed and to know roughly how long the meeting will take. Agendas serve important task functions and are often the responsibility of a group leader to both produce and disseminate among the group members.

Another obligation for group members is to meet deadlines. Group tasks often rely and depend upon one another, so when one is delayed, all are delayed. It is both unprofessional and unethical to have others waiting on you. This behavior is also rude and can cause tension and feelings of resentment and distrust, ultimately damaging the harmony of the entire group. If you do fall behind and do not believe you will make a deadline, be sure to let your group know immediately so they can see if they can assist you in completing the task on time.

All group members are also expected to be present for all meetings. Anyone can have a conflict that requires their absence, but this should be avoided if possible. Missing meetings is rude and can result in negative feelings, as someone else may have to do your job in addition to his or her own.

Attendance is also essential when the group plans to practice the presentation, and being a good group member means being there for the practice sessions, even if you do not have a speaking role. Groups must practice together to ensure a smooth delivery, because if any one speaker does something different or unexpected, the whole presentation will become disjointed. Remember that a group presentation is not a set of individual speeches but rather one speech with several speakers. Speakers should polish their individual portions of the address before meeting with other group members but also be open to changes and adjustments when the group practices together. A group presentation is more than just the sum of its parts.

During the practice sessions, group members should critique one another's performance, assessing all aspects of content and delivery, and provide helpful feedback to make the presentation more successful. If possible, implement the feedback immediately. Also realize that if you provide feedback others may disagree, and ultimately it is up to each speaker what to cover. Feedback can be very useful if given in the right manner. Never criticize the person but, rather, note how the project or presentation can be improved.

Group presentations require more effort because of the need for multiple people with divergent skills, abilities, ideas, and opinions to work together. Many hands, when it comes to group presentations, do not make light work.

In many instances when you might deliver a group presentation it will be followed by a question and answer, or Q&A, session in which the audience becomes involved. We will cover this part of the presentation in the next section of the chapter.

GROUP DISCUSSION AND Q&A SESSIONS

After all the information has been presented to the audience, they may be given the opportunity to offer feedback and ask questions. This practice is most common in the panel format of group presentations, but it is not unrealistic for it to happen in bookend group presentations as well. This part of the presentation can be stressful for members of the group, so, to help reduce your anxiety, think about it as a conversation rather than an interrogation. Here are some other tips for handling Q&A sessions.

First, you should always allow audience members sufficient time to ask their questions or offer their comments. In doing so you should never interrupt them when they are making their point, as this will only irritate them. If the person's points are not easily discerned and his or her statements seem unclear, ask for clarification. Whatever you do or say, remain polite. Even if an audience member becomes agitated, you should "keep your cool," as you have the obligation to the rest of the audience and to your group to do so. Just because an audience member is emotional does not mean that you have to behave in the same manner.

It is also a good idea to take notes when a person asks a question or makes a comment, especially if the comments are somewhat long. You may learn some things from the audience and might want to consider those points in a later presentation. Taking notes also signifies that you value the feedback that you get from the audience and that you paid careful attention to them when they spoke.

It is also important to be comfortable with the fact that you do not know everything and may even be stumped by a question from the audience. This is not a bad thing, as delivering a presentation is not a quiz show, and you will not be eliminated for not knowing the answer. In fact, it is far worse to lie or make up an answer than to state the honest truth. The audience does not expect you to always know everything. There is nothing wrong with saying, "I do not know the answer to that question, but I will find out and get back with you. Make sure I have your contact information before we leave here." Audiences usually respect this answer.

Summary

In this chapter, we have discussed several aspects of group presentations. We went over the two different formats and the main tasks and roles that emerge in groups, paying particular attention to both leadership and how to be a good team member. Group projects and presentations can be rewarding, and you may discover skills of which you were unaware, but they are not easy. In fact, group presentations often take a lot more work and effort than individual presentations because of the constant interaction between different people.

Key Terms

affiliative leader 284

authoritative leader 284

bookend group presentation 280

coaching leader 285

coercive leader 284

democratic leader 285

maintenance roles 283

moderator 280

pacesetting leader 285

panel group presentation 280

task roles 281

Activities

1   Identify the two group tasks that you do most often when you are in groups. Explain how you fulfill each of those tasks, and identify whether they are fulfilling task roles or relational roles.

2   Which leadership style do you use most often when you are working with groups? What are the advantages and disadvantages of using this leadership style? Is there another leadership style that you would like to be able to use more effectively?

3   What can you do to be a better team member for your next group project?

A BRIEF HISTORY OF COMMUNICATION

When we say "communication" we can mean a variety of things. The most obvious is that communication is something we do with each other. It is also a discipline of study that examines the way we interact with each other. "Communication" is a noun that can refer to a written or oral statement sent to someone else. No matter how you define it, though, communication is something human beings have always done with each other, and it is often one of the first things we do after entering this world. This fact illustrates the long history of communication as a practice and an item of study. In this appendix, we will briefly explore the rich tradition of communication as a discipline that studies and explains the way we relate with one another; we do so in an effort to show you that the information in this handbook was generated not from some thoughtful tips we created, but from a long tradition of developing principles and theories for the best way to send messages to other people.

THE GREEKS AND ROMANS

Many of the foundational ideas that inform good communication skills were developed over 2,000 years ago by Greek and Roman rhetoricians. You might find these thinkers familiar from other areas of study, such as philosophy, history, political science, and even biology, but their imprint on communication is just as important as it is to those disciplines. In this section, we will highlight a handful of prominent figures from this era and briefly describe their contributions to what we know about message construction. We will begin with the classical Greek thinkers known as sophists.

Greeks

The sophists were essentially travelling teachers who roamed the Greek city-states in search of work as tutors. They were prominent in the city of Athens, where, although they were not citizens, they were important members of society. Two sophists worthy of note were Gorgias and Protagoras. Gorgias taught his students that delivery was the most important element of any speech, because with a dynamic delivery the speaker could "bewitch" the audience and convince them to do or believe anything. Protagoras, on the other hand, focused less on delivery and more on using content to win an argument. He trained his students to study both sides of an argument and then construct the best possible argument for the position they sought to take, even if it was the weaker side. His critics often derided him for teaching people how to make the worse argument sound better but not actually be better. Sophists such as Gorgias and Protagoras had ideas that influence communication today, but not every Greek liked what they had to say.

In fact, the most famous Greek thinker we will cover had little respect for the sophists. He believed that they simply taught people to manipulate audiences rather than educate or appeal to them in an ethical manner. Aristotle, a student of Plato's and tutor to Alexander the Great, developed perhaps the most comprehensive analysis of persuasion during his time. He also contributed many different ideas to fields such as political science, philosophy, biology, and zoology. On communication and persuasion, though, he identified several important components of effective messages. First, Aristotle proposed that all good persuasion contained what he called *ethos* (credibility of the speaker), *pathos* (the emotional connection to the message), and *logos* (the logical elements of the appeal). He also said that ethical persuasion had a style that valued clarity, correctness, and propriety. Aristotle's ideas on persuasion are still taught today and are the foundation for ethical and effective persuasive appeals.

One final Greek bears mentioning, and he was more understanding of the sophists than Aristotle. Isocrates, who was an Athenian citizen, taught his students that one of the impossibilities of life was to know everything about a subject, but that did not mean they could not be knowledgeable about a topic. In fact, he believed that to be a good speaker someone should be well educated on a variety of topics, because only by understanding the many different facets of life could someone both adequately comprehend and effectively construct good ideas and messages for the public. Isocrates actually had a significant influence on Roman philosophers, whom we will address next.

Romans

Historians typically divide Roman civilization into two periods, the Roman Republic and the Roman Empire. The span of both Roman eras is quite large, and their influence on society today is even larger. For our purposes, however, we will focus on two individuals, one whose life straddled both periods of Roman life and the other who lived during the reign of the Roman Emperor Vespasian. In both instances we see further definition and understanding develop about communication and public speaking.

Although he was a contemporary figure of Julius Caesar, Cicero was no friend of his. In fact, Cicero spent a significant portion of the latter part of his Senate career attacking those who sought to take power from the Roman people. Ultimately, Cicero's objections and sharp oratory cost him his life when Marc Antony had him executed and his hands and head nailed to the door of the Roman Senate as a warning to others who would speak against the rule of Antony and Octavian. Despite his gory demise, Cicero's attacks on his power-hungry contemporaries also served as guides for good public speaking. For instance, he established the five canons of rhetoric as invention, arrangement, style, delivery, and memory. These canons remain the foundation for understanding the development of speeches.

After Cicero's execution, Rome plunged into an era when training in speech making was reduced to teaching people how to speak at ceremonies. That is, until the reign of the Emperor Vespasian, who tried to reinvigorate Roman education by establishing grants for teachers and other artistic efforts. One of those who received a grant was Quintilian, who provided us with a twelve-book volume explaining a variety of aspects of speech. One aspect, initially identified by Cicero and which Quintilian gave substantive treatment to, was stasis theory. Stasis theory helps understand the arguments offered on a given subject. Essentially, stasis is the issue under debate, which does not change, but the way it is argued can and does change. People will argue about the definition of the issue, whether it was done or not, whether it was right or wrong, and ultimately, if all else fails, they will argue over the competence of the judge in the debate.

The Greeks and Romans we mentioned approached communication and persuasion from different perspectives, but you can see how their ideas helped shape what we teach about effective presentations in this book. However, these foundational figures are not the only ones who have shaped our understanding of communication, speech, and the power of language.

CONTEMPORARY SCHOLARS

Over the last one hundred years or so, scholars have tried to update, apply, and rethink what the classical philosophers discovered about communication practices. They have examined the very nature of language in greater detail, updated the application of speaking principles to illustrate how they work with media and even social media, and have also worked to identify categories or genres of speech. In some instances, their efforts resulted in greater debate and more questions than answers, but in every case, what they discuss helps us better understand the *why* behind the *how* of communication.

Marie Hochmuth Nichols

Marie Hochmuth Nichols was one of the leading scholars in the communication discipline during the twentieth century. She was the first woman to serve as president of the Speech Communication Association and served as editor of the most prestigious journal in the discipline. Most importantly, though, she advocated for scholars of communication to focus less on being like the sciences, where models and paradigms are developed to explain the way the world works, and more on understanding the deep power of symbols and speech to move people to action. She believed in staying true to the tradition of communication by examining how what people say influences others.

So prominent was Hochmuth Nichols that the National Communication Association named one of its highest awards after her. The award is given to authors of significant and well-developed essays on examples of public address.

Kenneth Burke

Kenneth Burke was another influential communication scholar in the last century. Interestingly, he never received a college degree, but still managed to serve on the faculty at several universities and publish more than twenty books on communication and language. In one piece, written in 1939, he conducted an extensive analysis of speeches by Adolf Hitler in which he identified how Hitler rose to power by scapegoating an entire race of people. He concluded that the man would be a grave danger to the rest of the world simply by examining his speeches from the 1930s.

Burke also developed a method for analyzing a speech to determine the motive of the speaker. This process, called the Dramatistic Pentad, calls for a researcher to use the text of a speech to identify who the speaker establishes as the actor, what the actor does, where it is done, why it is done, and how it is done. In deriving this information from a text, a researcher can better understand how a speech was persuasive and what the speaker really intended with the message.

Burke's Pentad

In rhetoric, Burke's Dramatistic Pentad is the set of five problem-solving probes (developed by Kenneth Burke) that answer the following questions:

1. What was done (act)?

2. When and where was it done (scene)?

3. Who did it (agent)?

4. How was it done (agency)?

5. Why was it done (purpose)?

These are just a handful of contributions to our understanding of speeches and language made by Kenneth Burke, a man who dropped out of not one, but two universities.

Others of Note

One of the most famous phrases about communication and media in the twentieth century was coined by a Canadian, Marshall McLuhan, who said, "The medium is the message." The medium is the channel through which a message travels, and McLuhan stated here that how we state a message means just as much as what we say.

Kathleen Hall Jamieson and Karlyn Kohrs Campbell use presidential addresses to categorize specific genres of speech. They identified that presidents repeatedly deliver similar types of speeches that respond to similar situations, and so the speeches themselves must have common characteristics. This application of principles developed by the Greeks and Romans demonstrates how contemporary scholars work to build new understandings of communication while using preexisting knowledge.

Finally, one of the signature debates of the communication discipline—where does meaning come from—is best demonstrated in the academic debate surrounding the rhetorical situation. Lloyd Bitzer first defined the rhetorical situation as a specific moment in which we are invited to speak. Each rhetorical situation has a specific audience and places constraints on what we can and cannot say in a given moment. If a person chooses not to speak, then the moment is lost to them. Because speech is determined by the audience and context, Bitzer argued that meaning is something we discover. Richard Vatz disagreed with Bitzer's last point and argued that meaning in such rhetorical situations is constructed by the speaker, not something inherent in the moment. For Vatz, speaking is a creative enterprise, not an exercise in discovery.

Summary

In this handbook, we have provided you with tools, tips, and tricks for becoming a better speaker, but all of that information and guidance is informed by a long and rich tradition of studying the way people interact with each other. That tradition stretches back to classical Greece and Rome but has also been developed and enhanced by some of the greatest minds of the last century. We urge you to think of communication as something you can become better at not just by doing but also by studying.

KEY TERMS

TERM	A	PAGE
abstract	words are not concrete or tangible items; they are only representations	250
accent	nonverbal behaviors that augment a verbal message	268
acceptance	third step of the persuasion process in which the audience accepts that the issue is relevant to them	215
active listening	when we pay a high degree of attention to a message; we process, store, and potentially evaluate the content of the message to come to conclusions or understanding about what was said	39
ad hominem	fallacy committed by attacking the opposing person's character instead of his or her argument	189
ad verecundiam	appealing to the arguer's authority as the thing that makes his or her argument correct or accurate	189
affiliative leader	the type of leader who is flexible, encouraging, and focuses on building relationships and trust among team members	284
alliteration	repeating the same consonant or vowel sound at the beginning of subsequent words	252
ambiguous	language that does not have precise, exact meanings	250
antithesis	when two ideas that sharply contrast with one another are put side by side in a parallel structure	253
arbitrary	symbols used to represent things that are not intrinsically connected to those things	250
archetypal metaphor	metaphor that uses common human experiences to describe another object	255
articulation	physically producing the sound needed to convey a word	264
artistic proofs	constructed by the speaker for the occasion; concerns *ethos, pathos*, and *logos*	147
authoritative leader	the type of leader who provides a team with a vision and mobilizes people to work toward that vision	284
TERM	B	PAGE
bar graph	a graph that shows two axes and bars going either horizontally or vertically to represent total achievement	239
begging the question	assuming certain facts that have not been proven	192
bias	an unfair preference or distortion of information	97

bookend group presentation	a group presentation in which the first speaker is also the last speaker, providing both the introduction and conclusion for the group	280
bookend story	a narrative in which the speaker tells the first part of a story as an attention getter in the introduction of the speech and then finishes the story in the closer at the end of the conclusion	256
Boolean operator	using words such as "AND," "NOT," and "OR" when typing in search terms to focus the results	103
brainstorm	to create a list of possible topics and keep adding to this list as you think of new ideas	84
brief example	an example that makes a very quick point and can be effective at any point in a speech	133

TERM	C	PAGE
categorical syllogism	a syllogism in which the argument is based on membership in a group	184
channel	the medium through which an encoded message is transmitted from a source to a receiver	3
chart	visual depiction of summaries of numeric data	238
civility	the use of tact when dealing with others; a genuine and reciprocal expression of respect for ourselves and others through actions and statements	47
clincher	the final statement of your speech	180
co-cultures	a variety of smaller, specific cultures that intersect in our lives	68
coaching leader	the type of leader who focuses on helping individual team members develop and grow through training and constant feedback	285
coercive leader	the type of leader who tells others what to do and expects it to be done	284
communication apprehension	the fear or anxiety associated with real or anticipated communication with another or others	14
complement	when the action demonstrates the message contained in the verbal content	268
comprehension	stage of the persuasion process in which the audience understands the relevant components of the issue and the position that you want them to take	214
concept map	also known as a mind map; visual representation of the potential areas that you could cover in your speech	85
conditional syllogism	a syllogism in which the major premise contains a hypothetical condition and its outcome	185
coordination	all information at the same level has the same significance	159
courtesy	showing consideration of and attention to others	46
credibility	the ability of a person to inspire belief or trust in others	216

critical listening	when we evaluate a message and assess whether or not we agree with what is said; requires the most cognitive effort of any listening purpose	39
culture	the collective programming of the mind distinguishing the members of one group or category of people from another	67

TERM	D	PAGE
dais	a raised platform similar to but larger than a podium, often on which multiple speakers can stand	146
decoding	the process of drawing meaning from the symbols that were used to encode a message	3
deductive reasoning	an argument that reasons from known premises to an inevitable conclusion	184
democratic leader	the type of leader who solicits ideas from team members and makes decisions through collaboration	285
demographics	categories of definable characteristics of groups of people, such as age, race, religion, socioeconomic status, education level, and sexual orientation	121
derived credibility	the form of credibility that manifests itself during your presentation	217
dialogue	speaking in a way that encourages others to listen and listening in a way that encourages others to speak	78
disjunctive syllogism	a syllogism in which the major premise includes two or more mutually exclusive alternatives	184
division	principle that if a point is divided into subpoints, there must be two or more subpoints	159

TERM	E	PAGE
either-or fallacy	assuming there are only two alternatives when in actuality there are more than two	191
elucidating explanation	helps your audience understand the definition term by distinguishing the essential characteristics that are always present from the associated characteristics that are only sometimes present in the objects, concepts, or processes that are examples of the term that you are defining	204
encoding	taking an abstract notion and providing it meaning	3
environment	the context in which the communication process takes place	5
ethics	morals and the specific moral choices to be made by a person	27
ethnicity	a group of people who identify with each other based on a common experience, which might include geographic or national origin, ancestry, history, cultural and social norms, religion, race, language, ideology, food, dress, or other factors	70

ethnocentric	believing your group's perspective is the only correct one and thus judging others based on their conformity to your way of doing things	79
ethos	the credibility of the speaker	147
eulogy	a speech that pays tribute to the life of the deceased	228
expert testimony	testimony from someone who has conducted extensive research on the topic, has significant experience with the topic, or holds a position that lends credibility to his or her ideas on the subject matter	137
explain	deepen the audience's understanding of that phenomenon	195
extemporaneous speech	a speech delivered with notes but without the entire speech in front of the speaker	263
extended example	an example that takes time; the importance lies in the details	133
TERM	**F**	**PAGE**
fallacy	an error in reasoning	189
false cause	fallacy assuming that one event causes another unrelated event to occur	192
feedback	the receiver's response to a message that is sent to the sender	5
figurative analogy	when the two cases being compared are from completely different classifications	187
TERM	**G**	**PAGE**
gender	a social construction that includes all of the beliefs, attitudes, actions, and roles associated with being masculine or feminine	71
general purpose statement	a brief statement representing what you aim to do with the speech; there are three types	81
global plagiarism	taking an entire piece of work and saying that it is your own	32
good manners	behaviors that societies deem as appropriate and positive ways of interacting with others	45
graph	a type of chart that illustrates numeric data by using a visual diagram	238
TERM	**H**	**PAGE**
hasty generalization	drawing conclusions about broad principles or categories based upon a small sample of evidence	191
hate speech	attacking a person or group of people based upon their gender, ethnicity, religion, sexual orientation, social actions, or any other category that indicates applications of a negative, unwarranted stereotype	256
hearing	the physiological process of capturing sound conducted by ears to the brain	38
hierarchical	language that is structured according to more or less, higher or lower	251

high-context cultures	culture where meaning is derived from the nonverbal expressions, environment, and situation in which the communication is taking place, and less emphasis is placed on the words	70
histogram	a visual representation of a frequency table in which the categories are placed on the horizontal axis and vertical bars are used to represent the number (or frequency) of individuals that fit into that category	239
hypothetical example	an example that is fictional	132

TERM	I	PAGE
ideology	a set of ideas, beliefs, and ideals that form our worldview and provide a basis for action	74
impromptu speech	a presentation done with little or no preparation	263
inartistic proofs	all the evidence, data, and documents that exist outside of the speaker and the audience but nevertheless can aid in persuasion	148
incremental plagiarism	using part of someone else's work and not citing it as a source	32
inductive reasoning	an argument that comes to a probable, instead of an absolute, conclusion	185
inform	make the audience aware of a phenomenon	195
information literacy	the ability to recognize when information is needed and to locate, evaluate, and effectively use that information	94
initial credibility	the credibility that you have with the audience before you begin your speech, based on your experience and the audience's prior knowledge about you	216
integration	the fourth step of the persuasive process in which the audience adopts the position that you want them to take	215
interactive model of communication	communication theory that views communication as a two-way process that includes feedback and the environment	5
internal preview	serves as an outline of what is to come next in a speech and is often combined with transition statements	179
internal summary	a statement that summarizes what you have already covered and precedes transitions	178
invention	the creation of a topic and how it will be addressed	81
issue awareness	first stage of the persuasion process, in which you focus the audience's attention on the issue and show why the issue is important	214

TERM	L	PAGE
lectern	the stand behind which people speak and on which they place their notes	146
linear model of communication	theory that views communication as a one-way process in which a source conveys an encoded message through a channel to a receiver, who then decodes that message	2

line graph	a graph that uses lines drawn along two axes that show growth, loss, or flat developments over time	239
listening	the process of receiving and interpreting spoken and/or nonverbal messages	38
listening for appreciation	listening for enjoyment; it is not high in cognitive commitment	38
listening for comprehension	listening to understand and learn something new; requires a significant degree of mental effort	38
listening to show support	listening to someone in order to make them feel valued and to show that we care about what they have to say	38
literal analogy	when the two cases being compared are classified the same way	187
logos	the logical dimension of the appeal	147
low-context cultures	culture where meaning is derived mostly from the language used in an interaction, and very little emphasis is placed on the nonverbal communication, environment, and situation	69

TERM	M	PAGE
maintenance roles	responsibility of establishing and keeping a positive and loose environment with well-functioning relationships between group members so the group can complete its tasks	283
manuscript speech	a speech that is written out word for word and in front of the speaker as he or she speaks	262
margin of error	a measurement of the potential sampling error in polling; it provides a likelihood, not a certainty, that the result of the poll will be within a certain range	136
mean	the average in a distribution of numbers	134
measures of central tendency	statistics that indicate where the middle of a distribution lies, including the mean, median, and mode	134
median	the middle number in a distribution of numbers	134
memorized speech	when a speaker commits an entire speech to memory and delivers the speech with no notes	261
message	the content or idea that the source tries to convey to the audience	3
metaphor	linguistic device that allows for often implicit comparisons between two objects	254
metonymy	using a tangible object to represent an otherwise intangible thing	255
mixed metaphor	metaphor that combines two unrelated metaphors	255
mode	the score that appears most often in a distribution of numbers	135
model	a three-dimensional representation of an actual object	238
moderator	a person who acts as the coordinator of the discussion flow and ensures a civil, organized, and complete delivery of information to the audience	280

TERM	N	PAGE
narrative	a story	255
necessary cause	arguments in which a cause must be present for an effect to happen	186
noise	anything that can change the message after the source encodes and sends it	4
non sequitur	making an unjustified move from one idea to another	190
TERM	O	PAGE
object	the thing being discussed, not a model or representation of that thing	241
TERM	P	PAGE
pacesetting leader	the type of leader who is driven, sets high standards and expectations for performance, and sets an example by achieving those high standards	285
panel group presentation	a group presentation in which individual speakers present their ideas on a single topic or a subset of a topic	280
parallelism	similarly structuring related words, phrases, or clauses of speech	252
passive listening	occurs when we do not engage the topic in any noticeable way and just try to absorb what is said	39
patchworking	taking original source material and changing a few words in it, but not enough to consider it a paraphrase, all the while not citing the original source material	32
patchwork plagiarism	taking ideas from more than one piece of work and putting them together into a new piece of work, and then presenting them as original work without giving due credit to the sources	32
pathos	the emotional dimensions of the appeal, which can influence an audience's disposition toward the topic, speaker, or occasion	147
peer testimony	testimony from someone who is in the same peer group as the audience but who is not necessarily an expert on the topic	137
phobia	a persistent, irrational fear of a specific object, activity, or situation that leads to a compelling desire to avoid	13
physical delivery	elements of speaking that deal with the body	264
physical location	the immediate environment in which the speaker will be speaking	143
photograph	a picture of the object about which you are speaking	241
pie graph	circular graphs that are "sliced" apart to represent percentages of the total "pie" for particular groups or categories	239
plagiarism	taking the intellectual achievements of another person and presenting them as one's own	31
podium	a raised platform on which the speaker stands	146
polite	showing consideration for others in accordance with social decorum	44

profanity	language that is vulgar and irreverent	256
pronunciation	the accepted standard of how a word sounds when spoken	264
TERM	**Q**	**PAGE**
quasi-scientific explanation	helps the audience get an overall picture of the phenomenon and see relationships among the parts	205
question of fact	when a speaker seeks to persuade people about how to interpret facts	218
question of policy	when a speaker takes a position on whether an action should or should not be taken	219
question of value	a persuasive speech about the rightness or wrongness of an idea, action, or issue	219
TERM	**R**	**PAGE**
race	a set of physical characteristics shared by a group of people, such as skin color, body type, facial structure, and hair color	70
real example	an example that is factual	132
reasoning by analogy	comparing two similar cases to argue that what is true in one case is also true in the other	187
reasoning by cause	arguments that claim one event or factor produces an effect	186
reasoning by example	the process of inferring general conclusions and making general claims from specific cases	187
reasoning by sign	occurs when the presence of one thing indicates the presence of another	188
receiver	the person or audience that a message is being transmitted to	3
red herring	introducing irrelevant ideas to focus attention away from the real issue	192
refutation	response to potential opposition	220
regulate	nonverbal actions that help govern the course of a speech or interaction	268
repeat	when physical actions restate verbal messages	268
repetition	repeating words and phrases	252
respect	an acknowledgment of the inherent humanity and dignity of other people	46
TERM	**S**	**PAGE**
scatterplot	a graph that shows the relationship between two continuous variables	239
self-fulfilling prophecy	a process in which your expectations about yourself, another person, or an entity eventually lead to you, the other person, or the entity behaving in ways that confirm your expectations	15
sex	one's biological classification as male, female, or intersex (having both male and female physical characteristics) based on one's reproductive organs and chromosomes	71

sexual orientation	refers to the sex and gender to whom a person is romantically and sexually attracted	72
signposts	key words that signal to the audience that you are moving from one part of the speech to another	179
simile	linguistic device that compares two things through the use of "like" or "as"	254
slippery slope	asserting that once a course of action is taken, other unavoidable events will inevitably occur	189
socioeconomic status	a person's relative position in society, usually measured as a combination of their education, income, and occupation	76
source	the person responsible for inventing the idea on which they intend to speak and crafting that idea to an audience	3
speaking tool	device that assists speakers, such as a microphone, podium, lectern, or lighting	145
specific purpose statement	a narrower version of the general purpose statement that identifies what you will talk about, what you will say about it, and what you hope the audience will take away from the speech	87
standard deviation	a measure of variability that indicates how spread apart the numbers are in a distribution	135
statistics	numbers that summarize and organize sets of numbers to make them easier to understand or visualize	133
straw man	fallacy committed when the speaker misrepresents the opponent's position by oversimplifying that position, taking comments out of context, or representing an entire group's position with bad arguments from one person in that group	190
subordination	process of creating a hierarchy of ideas in which the most general ideas appear first, followed by more specific ideas	158
substitute	physical actions that take the place of verbal messages	268
sufficient cause	a cause that can produce the effect in question	186
syllogism	a logical argument consisting of at least two claims that build upon each other to reach a conclusion	184
synecdoche	using one part of something to represent the whole thing	254
systematic desensitization	the process whereby a person is slowly introduced to a fear such that each time he or she overcomes the fear the intensity is decreased	24
TERM	T	PAGE
task roles	the parts people play that move a group toward a goal and are performed by all members of the group at one time or another in the development process	281
terminal credibility	the level of credibility that you have when your speech concludes, which is the sum of your initial credibility and derived credibility	217

testimony	using the words of other people as evidence	137
thesis	a carefully worded one-sentence encapsulation of exactly what you will cover in your speech	175
toast	speech given to celebrate an important occasion	228
transactional model of communication	theory that views communication as a constant process in which all parties simultaneously play the roles of sender and receiver	6
transformative explanations	explanations that help the audience transform their everyday ideas about how something works into a more accurate understanding of the phenomenon	206
transition	connective statement that signals you are finished with one point and moving on to another	177
TERM	V	PAGE
verbal delivery	elements of speaking that deal with voice	264

INDEX